D1394738

A Cinder Glows

To Cathie,
With Love & Best Wishes.
Mary Morton Hardie.
July 1993.

A Cinder Glows

The story of a Remarkable life

Mary Hardie

Eric Dobby Publishing

Published by Eric Dobby Publishing, 12 Warnford Road, Orpington, Kent BR6 6W.

A catalogue record for this book is available from the British Library.

ISBN 1-85882-000-6

Typeset in 10pt on 12pt Palatino by Origination, Luton and printed by BPCC Wheatons Ltd, Exeter.

Contents

Some won't believe, they did not then.
If they had, this never would or could have been
written.

The Telegram

'Mama, mama come quick, it's that boy, the "tegrum" boy, he is coming here, Mama!' Turning quickly, my face brushed a bowl of velvety primroses freshly picked from the hedgerow that morning. Gertie had taken a bunch to school. Not to be outdone, I had gathered some for Mama.

I almost fell as I scrambled off the high, green velour-covered chair which stood at the window. I had been watching my sister, Gertie and her school-friends running to school, waving to me, wishing with all my heart I was old enough to join them at the village school, whose tall glass windows glinted not far away, in the grey stone walls.

Now, I ran to Mama, tugging at her hand, we hurried to the door, just as the boy rattled the heavy iron knocker. He called out, 'Telegram for Mrs Morton. He took a yellow envelope from the leather pouch attached to his belt and held it out. Mama, being a tailoress, always had scissors hanging from her waistband. She lifted the small ones, and cut open the envelope, the boy standing expectantly, waiting on a reply. Mama stared at the letter she had taken out of the envelope and shook her head. He mounted his red-painted cycle and pedalled off, quite bursting with importance, smart in his tight blue jacket, with high round collar, and red stripe down the side of his blue trousers and round the band of his funny round hat, which fastened under his chin.

The few women at the gates of the cottages froze, hands lifted to mouth or chest. There were many of these boys running round town, taking messages to the families of men in the Services. There were few telephones, letters took too long, so the 'telegram' boys were kept busy.

The year was 1916, the Great War was now in its second year. As children, we were only vaguely aware of the dreadful news which filtered through from the 'Front' lines. Women would gather in small groups, speaking of someone who had lost a husband, son or brother, always subdued and tearful, asking when it would all end!

Recently there had been news of a big 'push' in France. Thousands of men had been killed, wounded and taken prisoner by the German Army. In our warm, pretty cottage, it all seemed far away. My sister Gina had a little cat, her name was Kiki. She had been given it when it was tiny. Mama had said, 'Here is a pretty little kitty for you to play with.' Gina was just two years old, and called out, 'Kiki, Kiki.' She could not speak clearly yet. Small, with silken, golden curls, gleaming in the bright sun of that May morning, huge blue eyes in a sweet face, Mama called her 'my little angel'!

My name was Mary, I was only 4 years old at this time. I was born on the 5th May, 1912. Gina was 2 years younger, and my sister Gertie just 18 months older than me.

But now, a silence descended, sending little thrill of alarm through me. Mama walked very slowly to the rocking chair, her face paper-white, great violet eyes like blots of ink. I whispered, 'Mama, Mama.' She did not at first seem to see me, then said in a strange voice, 'Get Kirsty.'

I pulled at the door-latch and ran as fast as I could to the next cottage where Kirsty lived with a houseful of children and babies, a happy, laughing rosy-cheeked Irish girl, married to a big, strong steel-worker, 'Himself' she always called him. Kirsty was already on her way, a baby in her arms, two toddlers hanging on to her ample skirts. 'Mother of God have mercy, what news? Bad by the looks of it! Holy Mother!' She ran into the house, put the toddlers' hands in mine saying, 'Mind the children, Mary!' I dragged at them as I wanted to be with Mama.

When Mama saw Kirsty she gave a hoarse cry, and burst into tears, sobbing so deeply and painfully that Gina and I cried too. Kirsty laid her 'babby' on the thick rag-rug in front of the fire, then enveloped Mama in her arms, with many 'Dear Mother of Gods and Holy Maries'. Other women neighbours slipped in asking, 'What news?' They sensed it was bad. Often telegrams were sent to wives to let them now their men were coming home on leave. Then everyone laughed and joked, but not this time! Expectantly they crowded round, Kirsty lifted the yellow paper and read out, in her rich Irish voice these words: 'WE REGRET TO INFORM YOU THAT SERGEANT GEORGE MORTON HAS BEEN REPORTED MISSING, BELIEVED KILLED IN ARRAS, FRANCE, ON OR ABOUT 20 FEBRUARY 1916. FURTHER INFORMATION WILL BE FORWARDED BY LETTER'

There were gasps and sighs from the women. Mama broke into fresh sobbing, saying, 'What's to happen to us, why him?'

A small, neat figure now entered. I flew to her side. It was Granny Morton, my father's mother. She, too, had received a telegram, and had come immediately. Kirsty, streaming tears, hugged her too. 'Your son, Lord have mercy!'

Granny, disengaging herself, lifted the baby, gave her to Kirsty, and gently shooed them out, saying, 'Leave us with our sorrow.'

Soon we were alone, Granny put the kettle on, and rummaged in her big, roomy black bag, producing a small bottle of brandy, and gave some to Mama in a cup. Mama had stopped sobbing, but looked dazed, and was shaking so much she could scarcely hold the cup. Then suddenly she remembered that Granny was her husband's mother. 'Oh Gran, here I am carrying on, how can you be so calm?'

Granny said 'It's not definite, he could be alive, we must hope we will see him again.'

Mama lay down in the box bed in the kitchen.

Granny spoke to Gina and me, saying 'Mama will sleep for a while, don't make a noise.'

I climbed up to my favourite seat at the window. Small latticed panes opened easily, and I listened to the birds, saw the daffodils and tulips in the tiny front garden of the house. The house was quite large, with windows each side of the door, where you entered a stone-flagged corridor, we called this the 'lobby'. Half-way along, a door opened on each side, one to the kitchen, the other to the sitting room, or 'best' room. A small bedroom led off the kitchen, which had two box beds. A wash-house and lavatory at the far end of the lobby, through a back door, led to a large garden. A low wall encircled this garden, sufficiently high to keep out the cows and sheep in the adjoining fields, but we children could clamber over it quite easily. We looked out on the road which ran from Wishaw to Overtown. Our house was named Burnhall House, and the few cottages round it comprised the village of Waterloo. Here Gina and I were born. They told me the night I was born the chimney had gone on fire, was it an omen?

Granny now made a meal, and Gertie came running in from school, stopped when she saw Granny, and plied her with questions. She was disappointed she had not been at home when the telegram boy came, that would have been so exciting! Granny gave Mama some soup, then tidied everything up, and dressed us in our best Sunday capes, telling us we were going in the tramcar to Wishaw to see Granny Stirrat (our mama's mother). We did not want to go there.

Granny Stirrat lived in the school-house with her daughter, Jane, whose husband was the headmaster of Wishaw High School. This was situated on the main street. Granny Stirrat always seemed to be sitting in the large window, watching the tramcars passing, and the many people shopping in the street. She wore very high lace collars, and a square of lace adorned her snow-white hair. Her black shawl was changed to a pale grey and lavender striped one on Sundays. Aunt Jane taught the very young children but had no children of her own.

The school-house was prim, highly polished, extremely tidy, and full of heavy Victorian furniture which seemed to leave no room for anyone but themselves. When Daddy was at home we went to church every Sunday. Our parents had been married in that church (just a few yards from the school-house). After the service we visited Granny Stirrat, Aunt Jane and Uncle Edward. They were a very serious-looking couple, we never saw then laugh or smile. We had to wipe our feet very carefully before we entered, then, deposited on chairs in the kitchen, given a glass of water between us, a very small bun each, told to stay still and touch nothing. A tray was carried through to the front room, we could hear them talking in low voices. When we had finished our buns, we were called into the front room, told to say 'Good morning' to all of them. Granny Stirrat seemed to gaze at us in complete disapproval.

Five minutes later we were across the road, waiting for the tram to take us to Granny Morton's house. The three of them gave us a very small wave, unsmiling and cold. Uncle Edward had a huge handlebar moustache and a very long nose. Daddy was always making remarks about him which made us laugh. He only visited them for Mama's sake, she felt it was their duty. The Stirrats did not seem to like Daddy either. Among the family wedding photographs arranged on the high mantelpiece, we noticed Daddy's was kept behind the others, though Mama was the prettiest bride of them all, in a large hat, a tiny-waisted dress with many frills all round the hem. Daddy had a big smile on his face, his hair plastered down, parted as straight as a tram line down the centre!

When the tram came, we jumped on, talking and laughing, Daddy carrying Gina. We loved going to Granny Morton's. She lived in a row of houses in Ladywell Road, near Motherwell Cross. She had seven children, nearly all married now, but they all came on Sunday with their children. They would arrive from church, like ourselves. Granny would have the girdle on the swee (an iron hook that lowered the girdle and turned it, so that the heat of the fire could reach all round the girdle). Oh, the smell of her treacle scones, pervading the whole house. Home-made jam and fresh butter spread thickly on the hot scones, mugs of tea and cocoa were enjoyed by all; the scones disappearing as quickly as they came off the girdle, Granny sitting by the fire, turning the scones, made an unforgettable picture in my memory.

On nice days, Daddy and his brothers, John and Andrew, would take us down the Roman Road, with its little-arched stone bridge, it really had been built by Roman soldiers, Daddy said. Into the Clyde Park, where in summer there were rowing boats and people picnicking. We had great fun, trailing our hands in the water and chasing swans and ducks. On the way home, we looked for Granny Stirrat from the tramcar window, she was always there. In winter the blinds were down, but we could see light shining between the slats.

Now it was with some alarm and foreboding we stepped off the tram, crossed over to the school-house and Granny rang the bell. We had to wait some time. The school was in, we saw Aunt Jane's face at a class window, with a look of alarm at this most unusual visit. They had a cleaning woman in the morning, but she had gone home. Granny Stirrat was very fat and stiff, not like our Granny Morton, who often said she should get off her fat backside!

At last, the door slowly opened. Granny had knocked twice, thinking the bell was not working. Granny Stirrat stared at us.

Granny said, 'Have you heard the news about George?'

The old lady said, 'What are you doing here at this time of day? That child (pointing to Gertie) should be at school.'

Granny Morton asked if we could come inside, but receiving no invitation, said 'George has been reported missing, believed killed; Mary is taking it badly.'

'H'm, serves him right, he did not need to join up, should be looking after his wife and children. Tell Mary to visit me herself in future.'

Granny Morton, lifting up Gina, turned away, saying 'May God forgive you, Mrs Stirrat!'

We were disappointed that we were not going to Motherwell, but Granny said we had to look after Mama. When we got home, Mama was in her usual place, cutting material on the table. She looked very pale, but composed, telling Granny there was more need now to make money, how long would it take the War Pensions Department to send her allowance? She was angry with her mother Mrs Stirrat for not letting us into the house, decided she would not go to church on Sundays but just go to Wishaw on Saturdays. This way she could combine her visits to the shops and the Grannies. She never took us to see her mother again. Now we went to the local Sunday School with the children we knew at school, and that was great fun.

I leant later that Father had joined up at the start of the war. The glamour of the uniform, and the dullness of his job and married life all transpired to send him poste-haste to the recruiting office. The Stirrats were appalled! Mary was expecting his third child, who was in fact born shortly before he was called up. He could have found work in the huge steel mills, many a man took refuge there to escape compulsory call-up. Father was a first-hand in the Dalziel Co-operative Society, which was big business in those days. He had entered the society as a boy, and worked his way up through the Grocery Department. As women could fill his position, he argued that he would be called up, anyway, very few jobs were exempt. Miners, steel-workers and others making ammunition, guns and tanks were about the only 'safe' jobs. The Stirrats called him a 'bounder', they thought their youngest and prettiest daughter had thrown away her chances of a better marriage; he was not what they wanted for her at all, and said they were not surprised when he joined up, just to avoid his family responsibilities'.

Now we loved our Saturday visits to Granny Morton's, where mama would leave us to shop and maybe visit the Stirrats. Uncle Johnny would toss little Gina up in the air, golden curls tumbling over her face, Granny making hot scones. Now we had a much longer time and often were taken to the Clyde Park, and out in a rowing boat, watching warily the big white swans, shooing the ducks, and drawing our hands through the water, making tiny ripples. Mama had made us pretty frilly aprons, which we always brought with us. Granny would say grace before we ate, always ending with 'May God help our soldiers and bring them safely home.' Uncle Johnny would play the fiddle, another uncle the harmonium. Some sang popular songs like 'Keep the Home Fires Burning' or 'Goodbye Dolly Gray'. Granny always begged them to play 'Danny Boy', and would sit pensively listening while the others joined in. The tune brought back memories of her childhood spent in Ireland. When I asked Mama why, she said 'Granny will tell you some day.' One Saturday when Mama was shopping, Gina sleeping, and the house quiet, we pleaded with her to tell us of her childhood. So we sat, Gertie and me, completely engrossed as she unfolded her story.

Granny's Story

Granny was the only daughter of a horse breeder in County Down in Ireland. Her name was Gertrude Jane, but known as Jenny. One day a young Scotsman came to buy a horse. Jenny was feeding a young colt which was trying to get out. The top half of the stable door was closed and Jenny backed out of the bottom half. She heard this gruff Scottish voice saying 'If that is not the neatest little backside of a filly I ever did see!' Jenny was furious, scarlet with indignation. She spun round and slapped him hard, before running into the house. He came again the next day, apologised, and she fell in love with the 'Hairy' Scotsman. He had a great mass of brown curly hair and a bushy beard! His father owned a brick and tile factory in the area. George bought horses to pull the heavy drays. Married, they set up house in the family home. As he was an only son, he would inherit eventually, his parents moving to a small cottage nearby.

All went well for a while, then suddenly disaster struck. Potato blight ruined the small farmers; men were idle, and there was great poverty in Ireland that year. Hungry, desperate men, armed with anything they could lay hands on, ransacked the countryside, looking for food for their hungry families. At first, the better-off farmers started to run soup kitchens. Women and children lined up with jugs and pots, but in a few weeks not a vegetable was left growing in field or garden. Farmers barricaded their cattle and sheep, hens and pigs, no outhouse was left standing. The angry men took anything and everything; straw and wood for their fires, leaving nothing but stone walls. George's parents took refuge with a daughter in Belfast. That same night their cottage was ransacked, then set on fire. Horses disappeared, these were to be sold at the horse market in Belfast for money which would buy food in the black market.

George closed the factory, paid off the workmen, promising to open again when the 'troubles' were over. The angry men set fire to the factory, after looting it, marched to the 'big' house and threatened to burn it down too, if he would not give them a retaining wage. George told them he would do what he could, asked them to give him a few days. He still had two farm trucks, and after the men went home he and Jenny filled them hurriedly with a few cases and boxes. Jenny was now expecting her first child, and was very frightened.

George was even afraid to board up the windows, lest the men became suspicious. At 1.00 a.m. they each drove a truck to Belfast. Jenny cried as she looked back at the lovely house, but George said they would be back soon. Arriving at the docks in Belfast, they had to wait for two days, so many people had the same idea. George sold the trucks for next to nothing, and poor Jenny had to sit guarding her boxes nearly all the time. She was also very sea-sick on the boat and by the time they reached Glasgow she was quite ill. George had quite a few relatives around Glasgow. He deposited Jenny in a small hotel, saw her safely in bed, her boxes almost filling the tiny room, and travelled to Motherwell. There were one or two places they could have temporarily, but George knew it would be years, if ever, before they could return to Ireland. At Carstairs, Lanarkshire, he discovered two maiden aunts who were willing to let half of their large country house to them for as long as necessary.

Next day, he took Jenny and the boxes to Carstairs, and leaving her in the kindly hands of his aunts, he travelled back to Belfast. He had only been gone a few days, but although the house had not been burnt down, it was as empty as the sky above! He searched everywhere for something to take to his beloved Jenny. Wood from doors, windows and cupboards, all gone, every stick of furniture, even floorboards. Carpets and curtains, china and pictures, all gone; nothing remained of the family home, but the bare walls.

Turning sadly away, he saw something shining in the mess of broken bricks and, looking closer, he found a small silver cross, the first present he had given Jenny. Returning to Belfast he visited his parents, who were badly shocked at his news. They pressed their life-savings into his hand, and offered to send money or goods whenever he asked. In the market at Belfast he was able to buy some good, cheap horses. In a few weeks he had set up a new factory in Law, not far from Carstairs. This prospered, and by the time Jenny's baby was born, they had bought a cottage of their own.

Jenny had seven children, and they were prosperous and happy when an even greater tragedy struck again. Great bags of jute, bales used in the making of sacks, were imported from abroad to the factory. One load brought a disease. Granny named it Black Death. Some of the workmen died, the factory was closed down for fumigation and the jute was burnt. Jenny's youngest daughter, just seven years old, contracted the disease, then George himself. Both died within a week and were buried together. Jenny had the house fumigated, rented a small house in Motherwell, and sold nearly everything, factory and cottage.

Her family had nearly all reached the age when they would have to work for their living. Jenny was determined to give them all a trade, as was customary in those days. The first and eldest daughter was Mary (Morton). She became a journalist and was the first lady reporter on the staff of the *Glasgow Herald*. Maggie came next, and was apprenticed to a milliner. Jessie became a school-teacher. George (my father) entered the Dalziel Co-operative Society. Andrew became a joiner, and John a butcher. (Their names will crop up at different times as I write.) Jenny lived in the house in Motherwell all the rest of her life, all were married except Uncle Johnny, her youngest son. Their children were my cousins, who played with us when we visited Granny at weekends. Before I finish writing of Jenny's life, she used to make us laugh, saying when her husband wanted to tease her, he would say the 'first he ever saw of her was her neat little backside!'

Now we must return to where I left off, but first, another bit about Jenny (Granny). She said the great love of her life was horses, she had been riding since she could sit on one, and she greatly regretted losing them. She never did go back to Ireland, which seemed very sad to us. Listening to her story had transported us to another world. Looking at her now, small and neat, her dark eyes shadowed with pain, we wondered how she had had the strength to cope with all these disasters, even now, with her son 'missing' she was still gentle, smiling and always busy. Her treasured silver cross that George had recovered for her was always at her throat;

she had other jewellery of more value, but that was her most precious possession.

But even now, the routine of our life was changing, the government decreed all tailors should make uniforms for the servicemen. One day a van drew up at our door, and a big roll of khaki cloth was carried in. A tall delicate-looking man with fair hair told Mama that she was to cut out and sew collars and cuffs, that she would be paid on what she completed, after inspection. Every Saturday morning he came, bringing his heavy rolls of cloth, sometimes blue as well as khaki.

Now Mama worked long hours, Kirsty was paid to do our washing and clean up the house. We still went to Granny's on Saturday afternoon. Mama shopped for thread, linings and shoes for us. We did not stay so long as Mama said she wanted to get on with the new 'batch'. Granny said she was working too hard, and not getting enough fresh air, to which Mama replied 'It helps me to forget about George.'

A year passed, now Mama was happy again, laughing and singing as she used to before the telegram. We hardly remembered the man in the photograph beside Mama. One day she put the photograph in a drawer, 'Too many memories', she said to Granny, who did not seem very pleased. Hughie Aird was the fair-haired man's name, he was so nice to Mama always kissing and cuddling her. He brought tit-bits which were hard to come by during wartime; oranges, chocolates or sweets. We were all very happy.

Hugh Aird Moves In

One day Mama said Hughie was coming to stay. He brought a big heavy industrial sewing machine, and a few boxes, putting them all into the small bedroom, which led from the kitchen. Mama had had no more news about Daddy, nothing at all. Granny had tried to find out where prisoners-of-war had been taken, but all came to nothing. Hughie and Mama sewed so much now that Kirsty took Gina to play with her brood of children and pets. Gertie and I were both at school. How we looked forward to Saturday mornings! That was when Mama got paid for her sewing and did all her shopping at the carts.

Not many women went shopping to Wishaw or Motherwell in our village. They either had little money for tram fares, too many babies to leave or take, or, owing the cart men so much for the week's groceries, they had little money left and had to live on credit from Saturday to Saturday. Mama paid them all but the milk-man. He left a two-pint can hanging on our door handle very early in the morning. It had a very long handle, a hinged lid, and was made of metal, zinc, I think. Milk was a penny a pint. He came round to be paid on Friday night, bringing eggs, butter and cheese.

Gertie and I were often sent out to collect the messages. We knew the horses and men by name. The milk-man's horse was named Meg. She was very patient, looking round for a sugar lump which Mama gave us to give to her. We giggled and squealed in mock terror when she put her big head over the gate, sending us running into the house. Then came Jim, the baker. He had a covered cart to keep the dust off the bread and cakes. There was no wrapped bread, a loaf (plain white) with a thick brown crust consisted of two halves joined together, costing threepence half-penny ($3\frac{1}{2}$d). A half-loaf cost $1\frac{1}{4}$d. The baker kept a box of $\frac{1}{4}$d chocolate bars, most customers giving him the two pence and they would receive a loaf and a chocolate bar. Mama always bought a penny-worth (ie four chocolate bars), one for each of us and one for herself. A bag of 'teabread' containing seven buns cost threepence. We loved to watch Mama put them on a plate, pink icing on two buns, currants on one, sugar on another, a pancake, a plain soda scone and a treacle one. Jim's horse could be bad-tempered, and would stamp one foot on the ground, she would gnash her big teeth at us (safely behind the gate), then Mama would give her a sugar lump too. Jim would growl, 'Steady Bess' and they would move down to Kirsty's house.

We watched in awe when Kirsty came back from the cart, the older children carrying armfuls of bread, teabread by the dozen, choc-biscuits and bars. Mr O'Brien had a good wage packet, he was a smelter in the furnaces of Colville's Steel Works in Motherwell. They had many mouths to feed, and Kirsty never seemed to tire of cutting endless slices of bread for them all! Jack, the butcher, had a big, black horse named Tammy. Then the fishman came. We loved his little grey donkey, which pulled a very small cart with a few boxes of fish. We stroked and patted her, fed her a sugar lump, her name was Patsy. The fishman was very old, always grumbling, we felt sorry for little Patsy. Next came the grocer. A lot of women gathered round his cart. He had everything you could think of, and a fund of local news and gossip.

He had heard Daddy was missing, and for a long time asked Mama for news. his horse looked tired and dejected, he kept saying she was ready for the knacker's yard, but he hadn't the heart to put her down. Mama said later, he was too mean to buy another horse and poor Billy would probably fall dead in the street some day. We would gaze at Billy and secretly hope he would fall down dead at our gate, and he would not have to work so hard when he went to heaven!

The coalman's horse knew every house that took coal, and if the person was out, would refuse to budge, no matter how the whip cracked. Bert, the coalman, had to keep a sack full of hay and straw which he would drop off at the door, pretending he had made a delivery. That he returned with it did not seem to bother Hercules, who would then walk sedately to the next customer. A bag of coal cost 11d (eleven pence) per cwt, or 15/- (fifteen shillings) for a ton. Briquettes, made from pressed coal dust, which burned slowly for hours overnight, were 6d a dozen.

Last, but not least, came Prince, a pure-white pony, who pulled the farmer's cart of fruit, potatoes and vegetables. We would feed him, and he would let us stroke his white nose, and admire his long white eyelashes and mane. There were a few more pedlars and carters, but they did not come regularly. One man sharpened scissors, scythes and bread knives on a wheel, and sparks would fly up in the air. Pedlars would produce stockings, lace, elastic, thread, tape, shoe-laces and pretty ribbons from a very battered old case.

Hughie had now stayed with us for over a year; we were all very happy together, though Granny did not come very often, just once at Christmas with some small presents. We were too young to realise the implications of another man living in her son's house, and with her son's wife. She would often send for us to spend the day with her. Hughie would drop us off at her door, and come back for us at night, when Mama would often be in the van, having been to the 'pictures' (cinema). She did not get out very often.

Armistice

On 11 November 1918 there was a great deal of shouting in the streets. People ran from door to door, crying, 'The war is over, Armistice has been declared!' Bonfires sparked into life on top of Tinto and the surrounding hills. Tables were pulled into the streets, 'Bring all you can.' Kegs of beer were carried by the men, who all stopped working. Shops and factories closed when they heard the news. People danced, and cried and sang, but Mama seemed upset, and would not join in the celebrations.

Hughie took us to see the fireworks, the first I had ever seen. We were utterly spellbound. Dancing went on in the streets all night, next day was declared a holiday and we did not go to school. We were delighted to get a visit from Granny, they talked very seriously about how the soldiers would be coming home soon, prisoners would be released. What if George were still alive? And what about the 'child'? Granny said she hoped and prayed her son was alive and well above everything else.

One day Gertie said to mama, 'You are so fat, mama, just like Kirsty O'Brien when she has her babies. Will you have a baby too?'

Mama drew us close to her, kissed us lightly, and said, 'Yes, my dears, you may be going to have a baby brother, it's our secret, don't tell anyone yet.' To our excited inquiries she answered that it would be two months yet, at the end of January. The three of us were thrilled to think we would have a baby brother or sister of our very own, and even more so when Hughie produced a wicker cot from his van the next day. Mama tied blue ribbons on it, and sewed blankets, nightdresses, carrycotes (a gown or binder for new babies, tied with tapes), vests and nappies. Hughie also bought a blue rattle, with a bell on it. We rattled it so much, mama put it away in the cot, and this was kept in the bedroom.

Diphtheria Epidemic

A week after Armistice an epidemic of diphtheria emptied our school, which was closed down for a time to be fumigated. Nearly every house had a sick child, and Kirsty had two who were very ill. I had a sore throat, the doctor said 'Diphtheria, and should be in hospital' as Mama was in no condition to nurse me, and the other girls could catch the infection. Alas, every hospital was full, Stonehouse, Roadmeetings, Motherwell, Law, Strathclyde and even further. Soldiers were coming in great numbers with dysentery, malnutrition, malaria or suffering from the effects of war wounds and gas-poisoning.

Kirsty could not help, she had her own sick children. Hugh went to Granny for advice. She put a clean blanket in his hands, and said, 'Bring Mary to me.' I was wrapped up, put in the van beside Hughie, and he carried me to Granny's house, laying me on the sofa. Granny liked Hughie, but not the fact that he was living with her son's wife, he was a very thoughtful, kind person. She said, 'Tell Mary we will pull her through.'

When I left Mama, she pressed my hand saying, 'Fight it, Mary. Fight'.

I sweated and shivered, my throat getting more painful, soon I was gasping for breath. Granny put me in Uncle Johnny's arms, and while he held my struggling, panicking shoulders, she put a long, white feather down my throat, dipping it first in whisky. It seemed to me to never end, the choking and gasping for breath was so painful. Each time the feather tickled my throat, the raw whisky made it burn, I would throw up. Granny said, 'That's what we want.' I was bringing up dark-grey pieces of phlegm almost as tough as skin. I desperately wanted to just lie back and sleep, but soon I was gasping for breath. I wanted to give up the struggle, but from somewhere I could hear Mama say, 'Fight, fight.'

Eventually I drifted into sleep, the crisis was past. I had to stay in bed till the doctor saw me. I must have slept for hours, when I did awake, I found poor Granny asleep beside me, utterly exhausted. Hughie came later, told me Mama was glad I was getting better. He brought my school book, slate and pencil, I was to work at my lessons, which the teacher had marked for me. It was three weeks before I came home. Although I had a nice time at Granny's, I missed the family at home. No one came to visit Granny at all, they were all afraid their children would catch diphtheria. Kirsty had lost her two youngest children, little Bill and Danny; she said they had gone to Jesus, they would be better off there than going to war! There were many sad scenes, men without arms or legs, blinded and scarred, many more wore white armbands with a redcross on to show they were wounded soldiers or sailors.

The cloth which Hughie now brought home had changed from service colours to navy blue. He and Mama were very busy making civilian suits for the returning soldiers.

In January I went back to school, still very pale and thin. Christmas Day, we had a party, a real one, with crackers, mince pies, a huge dumpling that Hughie set on fire (to my great consternation), with shortbread, black bun and ginger ale. Mama had made each of us a velvet dress, with lace collars. Gina's was cornflower blue to match her eyes, Gertie's a rich deep blue and mine was scarlet! In our stockings we found chocolate, handkerchiefs and oranges. Gertie had Ludo in hers and we played with Hughie and mama. How happy we were, especially that we had their attention; for there was no sewing done on Christmas Day. Kirsty and Paddy O'Brien came in later, it was strange to see Kirsty without her 'babies'. They talked long into the night of families whose lives had been wrecked by war one way or another.

The Soldier's Return

On 3 January 1919 Kirsty banged on the door. It was only 6.00 a.m. Hughie opened it. The noise wakened me, and I saw Kirsty standing there, trembling and crying. She carried a newspaper in her shaking hand, crying to Mama, 'Holy Mother of God, have mercy on us.'

She went on and on till Hughie, now pale-faced, shook her by the shoulders, saying, 'Calm down, Kirsty, what is it? Tell me.'

Kirsty just pointed to the paper saying, 'Himself was on night shift, and brought in the paper to me, look at it.'

The headlines stated that another hospital shop had docked at Southampton with 300 prisoners-of-war. Their names were printed in long columns in alphabetical order. Hughie ran his finger down, stopped, then read out in a hoarse voice: MORTON, GEORGE. SERGEANT OF THE 1st BATTALION ROYAL SCOTS REGIMENT.

Mama stared at him, then slipped sideways in her chair, half-fainting. He gave her a little water, and when she spoke, she whispered, 'What shall we do?' over and over again.

Hughie, the quiet gentle man, became a man of action. He told Kirsty to get Mama dressed, fed and ready to leave, packing everything that belonged to the two of them. He was going to see his boss, he could not work again till Monday (this happened on a Friday). He would hand in all the finished work, take the van, and contact his sister in Glasgow. Before leaving he bent down to Mama, 'Listen, Mary, we can't stay here. Pull yourself together for our baby's sake, if you have it now, God help us.' She murmured something about the 'girls'. He just said, 'Enough, get ready, I will be back with a lorry.'

Kirsty made tea and toast, helped us to dress, and told us to help Mama pack her boxes, saying we were going to stay at Granny's, as our Daddy was coming home from the war. While this pleased us, we wanted to know when we would see our new baby. Hughie arrived, driving a heavy lorry, and Paddy O'Brien with him. They lifted Hughie's heavy machine first. 'Himself' looked strong enough to lift it easily. Then Mama's machine, all the irons and steaming cloths which hung above the fire on a brass rod. Curtains, rugs, bedclothes and boxes, and to our dismay, the wicker cot with its wonderful contents! Soon all was packed under a large tarpaulin as it was an open lorry.

It was only January, sleety rain blotted out some parts of the lorry. Patches of slush and ice met us as we ran out to see Mama climb in to the front of it. Kirsty had hugged Mama close, with many 'Holy Mother of God, have mercy for our sins'. We had kissed and held on to her, her eyes were filled with tears. She was near collapse. Hughie put his arms round her, saying, 'Hold on, and let's get on our way.' Some of the neighbours had gathered, shaking heads and wiping their eyes. Hughie said something about wishing it had been dark, 'but we have a long way to go, and we can't stay another minute!'

The engine roared, Mama cried out 'I'll come back for you, be good to Granny.'

Kirsty said to us, 'Come along, it's time to pack up your clothes now', but we lingered outside on the road, watching the dark mass of the lorry as it disappeared into the now drifting snow. However, we were not unduly worried, quite certain that mama would come back for us when she had her new baby, and we always looked forward to staying with Granny. All our belongings were packed in two boxes, Kirsty kept the fire burning, as Granny would be cold when she came for us. Poor Granny, she had waited till Mama and Hughie had gone, she had wanted no part in the breaking-up of the house. Hughie had stopped at her door to tell her the (to her) 'good news' and his plans for leaving.

We looked round at the strange emptiness of our dear familiar home, little realising we were about to leave it for ever. Granny and Uncle Johnny came in a cab, talked for a while to Kirsty. They were so unlike their usual cheery selves and Granny said, 'How can we tell George? He will be expecting to see his wife and children at the station!' Kirsty shook her head, speechless for once. Uncle John was in a hurry. He had come to collect us, and Granny, in his lunch hour. Soon we were off, waving happily to Kirsty.

Granny had written a note to our teachers, explaining why we were absent. Later we heard that 'Beeny', who was in my class, had announced that Mary's Mama had gone to have a baby, and her Daddy was coming home after being in prison for years! This statement must have raised some eyebrows, a lot of talk and scandal among the neighbours. I wished I had been there to hear it! Kirsty was to keep the key and send a message if another telegram came, which they seemed to expect.

Entering Granny's warm kitchen, Gina dropped Kiki on a chair. Granny's cat spat and hissed at her, but Granny said they would get along all right. Later that day a telegram was delivered. Kirsty had redirected it to Granny's house as arranged. This one read, 'ARRIVING 3.30 P.M. CENTRAL STATION. SATURDAY 4th JAN. GEORGE.' Granny was both excited and frightened, 'Who could tell him? What a home-coming!' she would say over and over again.

She summoned all her family that evening. His two brothers and three sisters were to meet George at the Central Station in Glasgow. They were to stall his questions and talk of a 'surprise' in store for him. When they all arrived at Granny's he would meet his children (us) and Granny would take him into the front room and tell him herself. She thought he would feel humiliated if the whole family were watching. Wife or no wife, all agreed on a 'Welcome Home' celebration. The town hall was booked for that evening with orders from Granny to make George as drunk as they could, it would be next day before the truth hit him! Next Granny took us round all the neighbours, dispatched invitations, inviting all to the 'Welcome Home' party. A big banner was hung across the window, flags were stuck on all the windows in the street. At 4.00 p.m. Granny washed and dressed us in our new velvet dresses, beads and ribbons, with new white stockings and black patent shoes. Our hair was well brushed, my long plaits tied with red ribbon to match my dress.

Uncle John had left some time ago, he had arranged to meet the other brothers and sisters at the station. All should arrive at Granny's house about 5.30 p.m. The party was to start at 7.00 p.m. Daddy would be hungry, and Granny hoped he would have got over the initial shock!

Welcome Home

We stood at the door as a taxi drew up, waving our little flags. The neighbours came running, shouting and cheering. To me the figure who now approached us looked very spectacular! Wearing a huge top-coat over a colourful uniform of tartan trousers, white belt and spats, gold buttons on a khaki tight-fitting jacket with chevrons on the sleeves, a forage cap with large silver buckle, black, white and red checked ribbons which hung down the back of his neck. Granny chased us indoors and Daddy came marching in, his face wreathed in smiles.

He hugged his mother, we noticed he had a white armband with the red cross on it. he turned to look at us, seeming very surprised. His bright-blue eyes took in everything. He commented on his lovely Gina, her golden curls, said Gertie was a real beauty, and how we had all grown. He gazed at me till I felt quite uncomfortable, remarked how pale and thin I looked, but Granny told him I had just recovered from diphtheria. I was lucky to be there at all.

Then, with a great flourish, he threw off his top-coat and said, 'Where is she hiding?' and ran into the front room. Granny quickly followed, closed the room door, there was no sound. All the family left at this point, only Uncle Johnny was left with us, listening intently should Granny need him.

When they both came into the kitchen, Daddy's face looked grim, he said, 'It's happened to a lot of men, I never thought it would happen to me. Why couldn't she have waited?'

Granny asked why he could not get a message through, 'the long silence made her think you had been killed!'

He asked so many questions, showed us his right hand, which

was only a stump with two fingers. He told us he had scars from head to foot all down his right side. He had led his company of men to take a farmhouse in Arras. It was occupied by German soldiers, who threw everything they had at the British soldiers. A bomb exploded among the men on Daddy's right hand, all were killed and he was knocked unconscious. When he came to, he was lying in blood from his own and other bodies. He moved his head, the enemy soldiers threw him out of the cart, they had already put him in with the dead. He thought his last hour had come, but soon after a German field ambulance picked him up and he was taken to a French hospital. Six weeks later, his wounds not quite healed, he was considered fit to travel, he and other patients were packed into cattle trucks and taken to Germany. He did now know where he was, no one could speak English. He joined the other prisoners at a labour camp. As his injured hand prevented him from holding a heavy pick and shovel properly, he was put to kitchen work.

Granny cut him short, saying she would make him some tea, he said he had not had a decent cup of tea since he left home, and how he had dreamed of her hot scones, where were they? Although he kept looking at us, we did not approach him. He tried to lift Gina on his knee, but she was painfully shy and would not speak to him. He made no attempt to touch us, but reached into his kit-bags for some 'wee' gifts. There was a lovely silk shawl for Granny, little carved wooden boxes for us, but the highlight was a lovely carved wooden musical box which played a Swiss tune. He had bought this for his 'bonny Mary'. He only played it once, wrapped it up and said something about 'that stupid woman!'

Now we got ready to leave for the Town Hall. Father objected at first, saying he could not face so many close friends and neighbours. Granny coaxed him saying he would be a hero tonight, no-one enjoyed a party more than him, he could not disappoint everyone there by not coming, sitting brooding at home was not going to change anything. He was alive and well, and was that not the best reason in the world for celebrating? The taxi coming to the door stopped all further argument. We all piled in, and when we stopped, Granny said, 'You go first, George.' The reason for this was soon apparent. Two pipers in full Highland dress started to play a lilting tune. They turned and walked up the few steps, preceding Daddy, who, shoulders straight and head high, walked behind them. Granny and we three girls followed. How wonderful it was, just like a church wedding, but they had no pipers! As Daddy and pipers entered the hall, everyone there stood up, singing, 'For he's a jolly good fellow'. At the top table the minister and his wife were waiting to welcome him, and sit him in the centre seat. Granny and us sat on his other side, then the immediate family. There must have been about a hundred guests altogether. The tables were loaded with food, as though making up for the years of deprivation. Small Union Jack flags adorned the walls; red, white and blue streamers hung from the ceiling.

Now, Daddy stood up to reply to the minister, saying the dream of his captivity had been his home-coming, and how he had imagined the taste of a good Scot's pie. After a toast of champagne to fallen comrades and their families, we started on the delicious steak pie, served by waitresses from the Co-operative where Daddy had been employed. (In fact they had organised, provided and paid for everything but the drink.) Roast potatoes, vegetables, followed by slices of hot dumpling, trifle or apple tarts, rhubarb tarts, currant cakes, shortbread, and most delicious of all, delectable cream cakes, for which the west of Scotland has no equal!

The minister and his wife now spoke, saying they would have to leave. When they were gone, the tables were cleared and out came the beer and whisky. The pipers left for another engagement, and a dance-band took up the music. At first it was a slow waltz, and we just watched, but then came the more familiar dances, the first being 'Grand Old Duke of York'. Daddy took Gertie up first, then me. As we passed through the arch of arms, he kissed me so hard I could feel his teeth bruising my lips. There seemed a fierceness about him, but soon I was dancing round the room with everyone and getting in the way of the grown-ups. Little Gina clung to Granny, quite overawed by the noise, the wild hoochs, the swirling skirts, and the flying feet of the eightsome reel had the sitting ones stamping and clapping in unison!

What a night, everyone fiercely determined to make the most of it, helping Daddy to forget. He was besieged by girls and women, danced till he pleaded for mercy, and, sitting down, had his arms round some pretty girl. A neighbour remarked to granny, George was so handsome that he could have any girl he wanted; but the one he did want was not there.

Now some men were very drunk, but the music and dancing grew louder and faster. Gina had fallen asleep, her head cradled on my lap. Gertie, breathless with excitement, wanted to know when we were going home, not wanting to leave. Granny said, 'Like Cinderella, we will be home by midnight.' This so fired my imagination that I half expected to see Cinderella and the Prince appearing at the door. But it was not a pumpkin driven by white mice, but a taxi which took us home, leaving Daddy very drunk, to be brought home later by his brothers. We slept so soundly in Granny's bed, we did not hear him come in.

Next day, being Sunday, we slept late, and were surprised to hear Daddy and Granny arguing. He was going to apply for a divorce immediately, and demand custody of the children. Granny said, 'You can't look after them if you are away, and I am too old, and Mary did love her weans.'

'Love them,' he stormed, 'walked off and left them, that's what she did! She will never get them, never!' He would make arrangements for us, where she would not find us. He had only a few days' leave, then had to report to a military hospital. After that he would be trained for the Civil Service.

He sold the house in Waterloo, also the furniture, saying he wanted nothing that would remind him of the 'slut'. Next day he told us we were going to an orphanage, run by nuns for the children of ex-servicemen, promising he would have a lovely home for us to go to when he started work, where or when he did not know yet.

Thursday morning, Granny dressed us in our best clothes, hugged us tightly, promised to look after Kiki and said she would visit us soon. We were confused and unhappy, Gina hung round Granny's neck, but Daddy got angry, and without more ado, marched us off to the station, pulling Gina by the hand, Gertie and I carrying a case each. It was the first time we had seen a train at close quarters. This great snorting, smelly monster, belching black smoke and steam frightened us. Gina buried her head on daddy's shoulder, he had had to pick her up or she would have run screaming from the platform. We jumped into the dark interior of this awful 'monster' white-faced and trembling. After a while we emerged from our fear, and watched in wonder as we were borne through the countryside.

At the Forth Bridge, Daddy gave Gina a penny to throw out of the window, he said it would bring good luck.

The Orphanage

Arriving at Queensferry, we walked up a long hill, to a large square stone building. Above the door it said 'St Joseph's Hospice'. I noticed that there were no curtains on the tall, narrow, arched windows and said, 'It looks like a church', to which Daddy replied, 'It is a kind of church, a nunnery to be exact'. The heavy doors opened, and a young girl, dressed as a nun, showed us into a small room marked 'Office'. Daddy pushed us all in front of him. Sitting at the desk was a very old-looking nun, in a huge white hat, wearing grey robes. She took our names, and ages, then rang a bell.

The young nun entered, lifted our cases, and smiling to us, said, 'I will show you where you will be sleeping.'

I turned to daddy in panic crying 'Don't leave us here, Daddy, take us home.'

He frowned at me, and said, 'Off you go now, you should be very grateful to get into such a nice home, and you will have other children to play with.'

He did not even say goodbye, just shook his head and said, 'What *that* woman has to answer for!'

We followed the nun along a very shiny long corridor, and up a wide uncarpeted stair to a landing. Here several doors opened out to dormitories. Ours had ten narrow beds, each with its own patchwork cover, a small bed-side table with a drawer, a cloth bag for our hairbrush and comb, and another for our dirty washing, hung at each corner at the bottom of the bed. A row of pegs near the door had numbers above them. We were given our numbers there and then. The young nun said her name was Sister Louise, the old nun in the office was Sister Marie. She was very important. The other nuns were Sister Ruth and Sister Martha.

Now we had to undress and put on the clothes which lay on the three beds. Each pile consisted of soft white cotton vests and blouses, grey tunics and jerseys, black stockings, navy-blue knickers and black elastic garters. Our own clothes were taken away, and Sister Louise said we would wear them on the day we left the orphanage! Dressed exactly alike, we walked downstairs with Sister Louise to meet the other children.

We could hear them talking and laughing as we entered a very large room. Three long tables were set with blue and white bowls, a spoon and a plate. Girls of different ages were sitting on the benches, they all turned to stare at us, which made us feel very embarrassed. Gina held my hand so tightly, her nails were digging into my palm. Sister Louise motioned us to sit down, directly in front of a smaller table. Sister Marie looked at us, she alone sat at the small table, now she picked up a bell, rang it and there was silence.

Beckoning the three of us to come forward, she said, 'Children, I want you to meet our new family, this is [pointing to each in turn] Gertrude Morton, Mary Morton and Georgina Morton. You will show them what to do, and where to go.' Sitting down, we were served soup out of a large tureen by girls of about 14 – 16 years old. They ladled the soup into our blue and white bowls. A piece of bread was placed on the small plate. Before we could start, the bell rang again. Grace was said by Sister Marie in her shaky voice; it seemed very long.

Gertie and I were really hungry, having had nothing since leaving Granny's house that morning. The broth was the most delicious soup I had ever tasted. Gina would not eat, she was overtired and bewildered. Just four days since Kirsty had made her momentous entry, and we had lost our mama, Granny, home, and Kiki. Gina sobbed herself to sleep that night; she was to be allowed to sleep with us till she settled down. She woke once in the night, screaming, 'Mama, Mama.' Gertie jumped into her bed and held her tightly. Sister Louise came in, carrying a lamp and made Gina drink something from a glass, and sent Gertie to her own bed. She sat beside Gina till I fell asleep, so she would probably sit there till Gina, too, fell asleep.

Next morning, some girls came to our room asking questions, and telling us about themselves. Jean's father had been killed in the war, her mother had died shortly after and there was no one who could look after the family of five, three girls and two boys. She did not know where her brothers were, but she pointed out her two sisters, saying one was Betty, and the other Peggie. They were sleeping in our room, as the Sisters liked to keep families together. New girls kept coming in all the time, till all the ten beds were occupied.

A red-headed girl had the bed next to me. Both her parents had died of TB (tuberculosis), her name was Fiona McDonald, and she was alone in the world now. Chrissie and another girl, also named Betty were English, their parents were divorced, and neither parent could nor would have them.

Last, but not liked, was Samantha Smith. She was noisy, cheeky and loved to torment the younger children, she also stole and swore. She had run away from home so often that her parents had been forced to place her in the orphanage, hoping a few months there would improve her behaviour. She would be assigned the usual kitchen duties, but she refused to work, disrupting the routine so much that she was sent home, leaving one bed empty.

As Fiona McDonald was an orphan, she was to be trained as a nun, and at present she helped to look after the youngest children. St Joseph's was a training school for nuns in peacetime, later she would attend classes in other convents. Sister Louise had been an orphan since she was three years old, and had lived in St Josephs's for sixteen years. Sister Marie had been like a mother to her, and she never wanted to leave her. That lady had to run the orphanage on a very small budget, most of the money came from charity or donations. Some, with a parent (which we were), paid towards our board but these were the exceptions.

We soon learned about economy. The very young children unravelled wool from second-hand clothes. Older children were taught to knit the wool into squares. These were sewn together, and the senior girls sewed the squares together to make bed-covers. Every bed had one, the surplus were sent on to hospitals. They could not get enough of them at that time. Temporary hospitals were filling up daily with the returned wounded, diseased and crippled servicemen. The older girls were taught to sew by machine. Flour bags were handed in by the dozen from bakers in the town. These were beaten to remove the flour, washed, boiled white and unpicked, making sheets of soft, warm cotton, which were extremely hard-wearing.

The nuns and older girls sewed every day, making sheets, pillowslips, mattress-covers, nightdresses, blouses, vests, aprons, even dish towels and dusters! The familiar sound of the sewing machines reminded us of home, and we would talk sadly of Mama and Hughie, wondering if the baby had arrived yet and when Mama would be able to come for us. We utterly believed she would, hadn't she said so!

We began to enjoy the company of the other children. The highlight of every day was the *'shining time'* after the last meal. The tables were pushed to one side, bigger girls swept the floor, put wax on a mop, rubbing the mop over the floor. We were all given knitted slippers, which tied over our canvas shoes, making a pad. With much shouting and laughing we skated over the floor that had been waxed, and not until it was shining in every corner, were we allowed to stop. Then the tables, including Sister Marie's, were pushed to the other side, and we would slip, skate and fall about to our hearts' content, and the Sisters' approval. This served two purposes; to provide us with exercise, and keep the floor shining like glass!

Sometimes we polished the long corridor, having races up and down. The bedrooms were only polished once weekly, the staircase by hand, which nobody liked.

Idleness was a great sin, we had lessons every day, taught the three r's (reading, writing and arithmetic). We were supplied with slates, slate pencils and a rag (to wipe our slates). We were divided into small groups, but all sat in the same room, each Sister to a group.

A month passed when we were told our Granny had come to pay us a visit. How excited we were! Gina was trembling so much she could scarcely eat or speak. We were taken to the office, and there was Granny, in her dear, familiar Sunday best! How we hugged her, and she us. Even Sister Marie was moved and left us alone with Granny.

Breathlessly we asked her about Mama, had she had our baby brother, when was she coming for us? Granny said, 'Yes, Mama had a baby boy, its name was Hughie too. She could not come for us, but Daddy would in a few months.'

We cried, 'We want Mama, take us home *now*, Granny.' Poor Granny was in tears too, and assured us she would look after Kiki, and tell Mama we were waiting for *her* (she *had* promised).She gave us some sweets and was gone. We were led tearfully away by Sister Louise. Granny never visited us at the orphanage again. What we did not know was that Daddy had sued for divorce on the grounds of his wife's adultery.

The Divorce

The court case created headlines in the local and daily newspapers. Even Granny remonstrated at the way Father acted. He could not hurt Mama or her family enough! Demanding full custody of the children, such a woman was unfit even to have 'access' to them. None of *her* family would be allowed to see them. Knowing how prudish the Stirrat family were, he could not say enough to shame them. Their daughter was a Jezebel, the family all hypocrites! He was the martyr, the injured husband, the suffering hero.

Pictures showed him returning from the hospital ship, and the headlines in the newspaper read

WOUNDED PRISONER OF WAR RETURNS TO FIND HIS HOME
EMPTY, HIS CHILDREN ABANDONED

PREGNANT WIFE FLEES WITH LOVER

WIFE ACCUSED OF NEGLECTING CHILDREN

PUTS SICK CHILD, ALMOST DYING OF DIPHTHERIA OUT OF
HOUSE

TOO BUSY MAKING MONEY WITH LOVER TO ATTEND TO
CHILDREN

WIFE NOW BANNED FROM HER OWN MOTHER AND FAMILY

When Mama stood up in court, saying she loved her children and wanted them, she was booed by the crowd. Pleading that she had heard nothing from or about her husband for nearly three years, she thought he had been killed. The judge gave Daddy complete custody, and no access for Mama. She pleaded for one child but that was booed out, Daddy leading the sneers and cat-calls. He had caught the sympathy of the public.

Mother never looked at him, though he kept staring at her. She looked so pretty and piteous (Granny said) that even the judge pitied her saying, 'This war has a lot to answer for, there are almost as many tragedies at home as there are on the battlefields.'

I was fourteen years old when Granny showed me the cuttings about the divorce case. I was horrified and angry at the false and wicked interpretations of Mama's actions. It was just not like that! Mama loved us and wanted us, why did you not tell them so! Granny said she had to stand by her son, he had suffered so much already. She could do nothing to make him change his mind or accusations. He knew Mama loved us, and by cutting her off completely from us, he was hoping to make *her* suffer. So it was *not* love or consideration for us that made him press for custody. We 'belonged' to him and that was final! Mama had had her baby a few days after she left us, and had been very ill. That was her one and only appearance at Hamilton Sheriff Court to plead for our custody.

She married Hughie Aird soon after the divorce, and they moved to Ireland. She never saw her family (the Stirrats) again. Her mother disowned her for bringing shame on the good name of the family, and would not have her name mentioned. We did not see any of the Stirrats again. Passing the school-house in later years, I used to picture Granny Stirrat in her window seat.

We had now been in the orphanage for six months, were quite happy, well looked after, and had almost given up hope of going home. We had settled into the routine; the Sisters were firm, but very kind and gentle. Little squabbles were gently talked over, and quickly forgotten. On Sunday we marched to chapel, wearing wooden clogs, sounding like a company of horses trotting fast. Other children, with their parents, would stop, stare and even snigger! Some of us were not averse to putting out our tongues and making faces at them. One member of the congregation said, in our hearing, we were the tragic left-overs of the bloody war! Most people smiled. We wore heavy knitted grey shawls over our dresses. We liked to see these other children in their brightly coloured clothes. We were literally starved of colour. Everything in the orphanage was grey or white, even the patchwork bed-covers were mostly knitted with grey or khaki army wool. It was now July, 1919. There were many soldiers walking about, some wearing light-blue hospital-ship clothes, with the usual Red Cross band. The men who wore these had not yet been 'kitted' out in civilian clothes. When they had been rescued from prison camps and cells, they were infested with lice.

On the French coast the British Army set up 'clearing' houses. Every man was stripped naked, his clothing burnt, and he had to have as many as three baths before he was completely deloused. He was issued with a pale-blue cotton suit (more like pyjamas), before they were allowed to step on board a hospital ship. In a few weeks he had a new uniform or a civilian suit. As these men were desperate to get home quickly, no time was lost after they had landed in Britain; hence the appearance of so many men in light blue.

One morning the three of us were taken to Sister Marie's office. We wondered why, hoping that Granny had come back to visit us. Telling us to sit down, she proceeded to read from a letter in her hand. The letter was from Daddy, it said he was now in a position to take us out of the orphanage, and had bought a house in Rothesay. He had just been married, was on his honeymoon, but would be calling to collect us next Saturday. We chattered all day, wondering and guessing what the new house would be like, not really aware of 'getting married and being on honeymoon', this meant nothing to us all.

Daddy had not visited us once in the orphanage. He had told Sister Marie (by letter) that Granny had been very distressed after her one and only visit. We were very happy and excited to wear again the clothes that Mama had made for us. We were now taller and fatter than when we had first arrived. Sister Louise put down the hems and moved the buttons on our velvet dresses. It gave us a lovely feeling to be in the dresses again. Our shoes were too small, so we had to wear the canvas shoes the orphanage provided. Sister Louise said no doubt we would get new shoes when we reached home.

All the orphanage clothes would be used for other children, how happy we were to wear our own pretty dresses. Gina tip-toed round and round, trying to see herself in the polished surfaces. I only wanted to be part of the outside world again, where there was light and colour.

Beatrice

The bell rang, Sister Louise opened the heavy door, as she did the first day we had arrived. There, just outside stood Daddy, in the brilliant sunlight of a hot July day. He waited for us to come out, smiling broadly, dressed in a pale-grey suit, white spats, a slim walking-stick, and a rose in his buttonhole. Behind him a cab was stopped, and stepping carefully down from it, holding Daddy's hand, was the most beautiful vision I had ever seen outside a picture book! This lady was dressed in cream lace, with frills down to her ankles, pink velvet ribbons adorned her small waist and a huge cream hat. There were pink roses on the hat. She carried a lace bag, and had a cream parasol in the other hand. Her red-gold hair hung in little curls round her forehead, the rest gathered in a bun lying low on her neck.

I could only stare open-mouthed, then Daddy said, 'Meet your new Mother!'

Without thinking, utterly taken-aback, I said 'That's not my Mother!'

Daddy said, 'Say hello to Mother.'

But whether in fantasy I had somehow expected Mama to be here, waiting for us, I could not accept this was my mother. I cried out, 'That's not my mother, where is Mama, she was coming for us!'

Now all had moved into the cab but Daddy and me. His face was red with anger, he said again, 'Say hello to your Mother.'

I stamped my foot, in rage and disappointment, repeating, 'That's not my Mother!' Daddy drew his good hand across my face as hard as he could. I froze with shock, no-one had ever hit me so hard. he gave me a push into the cab, jumped in and we were off. He talked to Gertie and Gina, he called the lady Beatrice.

When we reached the station we boarded a train for Edinburgh. Now I could look more closely at Beatrice. Her face was pink and white, her lips very red. A black beauty spot on her cheek and long eyelashes reminded me of an actress I had seen on a poster. She caught me looking at her, turning her large brown eyes on me, and stared into mine. Her eyes were almost black, and sent a shiver of alarm through me.

Arriving at Edinburgh, Daddy ushered us into a shop (Patrick Thomson's). Gertie and I were fitted out with school uniform, the badge and colours of Rothesay Academy. Gina was dressed right away in a sailor suit and hat; she looked really lovely. We were led to a shoe department and Gina had little sailor boots to match her outfit. We tried on strong black 'brogues', Daddy said they had to last for a few years, they felt very heavy.

After the shopping, we had a meal in the restaurant. Beatrice had chicken salad, we were allowed one cake each and a glass of milk. We gazed at the sumptuous (to us) velvet hangings and chairs. Carpets so thick you did not hear people walking on the floor. Even the powder room was all gilt and red-carpeted, except in the white-tiled lavatory, which had real toilet paper. Beatrice had come in with us, she only spoke once, telling us to hurry. She spent all the time in front of the mirror, putting on fresh powder and lipstick.

She had a strange high nasal voice, we were to learn she was American, a dancer and showgirl. Coming over to Britain to entertain the troops with a concert party, she met up with Daddy in Glasgow after the divorce. Six weeks later they were married, he besotted by her apparent beauty, and anxious to make a home for himself and his family. He made no secret of the fact he wanted a son, which made Beatrice drop her eye lashes and look coy, smiling and saying, 'Oh, George, not in front of everyone!' She was about twenty five years old, and just beginning to lose her figure. A slightly double chin and very tightly laced corsets were signs. Granny said later, she knew her dancing days were just about over, and had grabbed George for a meal ticket.

On to Glasgow, where we boarded the steamer at Broomielaw to sail to Rothesay. At the pier we felt dwarfed as we stood beside the great sides of the blue and gold ship. The *Glen Sannox*, painted in large letters near the front in gold. Two huge funnels belched smoke and steam, just like the trains. There seemed to be masses of people, and we were told to stay close to Daddy. Beatrice had hold of Gina's hand, many people smiled at the lovely woman with the golden-haired child in her new sailor dress. Father looked very proud and attentive, in his smart suit, with the rose in his buttonhole. He was to be remembered all his life for the rose in his jacket. I can picture him yet, charming the ladies, taking the rose from his lapel and handing it to one of them, with a compliment such as 'One sweet rose to another,' or 'The petals on this flower are not as fair as you.'

A gangway clattered down, and we joined the passengers. At the top we could see the water away down below, but still too near for comfort, to me anyway. On deck the floor moved under our feet. Daddy escorted Beatrice carefully downstairs into the interior of the ship. We followed, carrying the heavy parcels of our new uniforms. He bought her some magazines, deposited our luggage beside her, then took the three of us to see the engines. We were fascinated by the power of the great gleaming pistons, the reverberation of the great paddles as they threw up water in shining cascades, propelling the boat forward. The smell of oil nauseated me, I felt my stomach churning, and knew I was going to be sick, as I had often been sick on the tramcars in Wishaw. I told Gertie, who told Daddy, he grabbed me and hauled me quickly up on deck to the side of the ship. Gasping the lovely fresh air, I soon felt better and Daddy said to stay there, he would leave Gertie with me.

We watched with interest the beautiful coastline slipping away from us, and the steamer calling at other ports, Innellan and Wemyss Bay. Someone pointed out the Cloch Lighthouse, strikingly white in the summer sun. Now we came to Rothesay; it seemed a very pretty town. The sparkling sea, the screeching of the graceful seagulls, as they wheeled and swooped, their cries mingling with the shouts of the crew and porters. My spirits rose. Here was light, colour and space and hopefully a real home!

Daddy kept telling us how lucky we were to have sailed in such a fine boat, he expected us to be able to write a good essay about our journey when we went to our new school. We left the pier, a cab was called, Daddy said 'Port Bannatyne'. We piled in, but after a few minutes my stomach threatened to throw up. Daddy scowled, pushed me to the door, and asked the driver to stop. Just in time, I retched painfully, and stepped back into the cab.

Beatrice said, 'Disgusting brat.'

Daddy looked angry. We arrived at Pointhouse Crescent, and as we stepped down, I sighed with relief. It had been a very long journey.

Pointhouse Crescent

The house was large, with tall windows, and built of dark-grey stone; it looked old and was just across from the seashore. A stream ran down by the side of the garden which had a high wall round it. Daddy took keys out of his pocket and opened the heavy front door, then a glass panelled inner door, leading into a narrow hall. We laid our packages on the tiled floor, near a tall coat-stand which had mirrors and cupboards. Everything smelled damp and musty. We entered a large kitchen, table, chairs, sink and dresser were all scrubbed wood. They should have been white, like those in the orphanage, but were mildewed and grey. We did not like our new house at all.

Beatrice went upstairs to change and rest, telling Daddy to put the kettle on, she was sure as dry as dust, and wanted a drink. Money was put in a small meter under the sink, a gas ring was lit and soon the kettle whistled, just like Granny's.

One side of the kitchen wall was filled with a huge old-fashioned black range. Black iron kettles and pots sat on the side of it. The fire was set, ready to be lit. Steel (rather rusty) fender and fire-irons completed the fireplace, but there were no carpets or rugs on the grey wooden floor. A box bed in another wall reminded us of our beds at home, but this one had very dingy curtains and no valance. A lavatory, just inside the back door, a very dark box room, comprised the kitchen. One tall dark window, the shutters three-quarters of the way down, let in very little light. Six chairs and a table occupied the centre of the bare floor.

Daddy bustled about, taking a tray up to Beatrice, he changed into old trousers and shirt. We were given weak tea and bread with jam. We were very hungry, but he said we would get dinner later.

Taking us round the house, we were pleasantly surprised to see how nicely the sitting room was furnished. The walls were of embossed silk paper, a cream and pink carpet covered only the centre of the floor, polished wood round it. The chairs and chaise-longue were covered in pink and cream striped silk. Half a dozen little tables were dotted round the room, laden with many trinkets and ornaments, which Beatrice had collected from her travels. Pink velvet curtains hung from the windows, with heavy gold tassels.

A small round table, holding a great bowl of flowers, sat in front of the window, with two easy-chairs on either side. We were to learn that Daddy and Beatrice sat here on sunny days talking about the view, visible to traffic and passers-by. Beatrice dressed prettily, smoked little cigarettes from a long holder, and Daddy smoked a pipe.

The View

The windows looked out on Rothesay Bay and the islands beyond. Daddy could not wait to show his visitors 'the view'. I found his absurd pride in the view very puzzling. Opposite the sitting-room door was another room, the door of which was locked, and was to be kept locked. We were allowed to peep inside the large empty room. The curtained windows made it quite dark. On the floor lay boxes and trunks, and, with a pang, I recognised Mama's old trunk, the one that Gertie, Granny and I had packed after Mama left us. Daddy was explaining that he could only afford to redecorate the rooms they were using. He would have the rest of the house done later.

There were two empty and locked bedrooms upstairs. The bathroom was really pretty, with a great many bottles and little jars in front of a large round mirror. Pink mats on the floor, pink towels on a hot pipe which ran round the wall, and a lovely white bath which had just been installed. We felt it would be lovely to have our baths in it!

Downstairs again (not having seen Beatrice's room), we were impatient to see the garden. Beds of roses in front of each bay window were in full bloom, but the back of the house was old and neglected. A dilapidated summer-house in one corner of the garden, a twisted old tree in another, a square of grass which held four clothes poles. Daddy said he would have the rest of it dug over in the autumn to grow vegetables.

We wanted to stay outside, wanting to run over the road to the seashore, but Daddy said we were not to play in sand, as 'Mother' would not permit sand to be walked into the house. He told Gina to take off her new dress, and put on that 'silly' velvet dress. We unpacked our uniforms under his watchful eyes, laid them on the shelves or hung them up in the kitchen cupboard, which also did duty for brushes, step-ladder and cleaning materials. We were never to enter the bathroom or sitting room unless told to, there was no need, as we had a toilet in the kitchen, where we found a tattered towel, and put our toothbrushes in a cracked jar.

The bedcurtains, when opened, revealed two army blankets, one long bolster which had a white slip on it. Another blanket served as a sheet. I was told to sleep at the bottom of the bed. I said, 'There isn't a pillow,' to which Daddy replied, 'It's much healthier to sleep without one,' and proceeded to tell us that when he was a prisoner of the Germans, he had no pillow. We were to learn that everything we wanted was met and answered in the same way, 'When I was a prisoner. . .'

We were now very tired, and Gina was falling asleep at the table. He roused her to pick at some bread, drink her milk, gave us bread and jam then sent us to bed telling us we would have to rise early as there was a lot to do tomorrow. He would be in the kitchen at some time during the evening, 'So don't be frightened if you hear noises.' We climbed into the bed recess, the army blankets itched after the soft cotton sheets of the orphanage, but we slept soundly. So much had happened, but how I wished Mama was upstairs instead of the pretty lady.

It seemed very early when we were wakened by the milkman, hanging a can of milk on the front-door handle. Daddy appeared, told us to put on these 'rags' as he called our velvet dresses, and help him to get breakfast. We were going to church and he hoped we had not picked up any 'Popery' from the nuns. He pulled out a small trolley, showed us how to arrange it. A silver tray was placed on it with silver cream-jug and teapot. The cruet, sugar bowl and jam dish were of crystal. A lace napkin was folded neatly on the bone-china plate, with matching cup and saucer. These were to be washed very carefully in the first of the washing-up water.

Beatrice came downstairs, went straight into the sitting-room and closed the door. Grapefruit was cut and placed in another crystal dish, a plate of bacon, eggs and sausages were added to the tray, with toast and little pats of butters. Gertie and I were told to wheel the trolley through to the sitting-room. She was sitting beside the fire, dressed in a robe with pink feathers all down the front and round the hem. She had lots of little curling pins round her head, she did not speak, so we left hurriedly.

Daddy had made Gina help him set the table in the kitchen, and we sat down eagerly to a plate of egg, sausage and fried bread. After breakfast he showed us how to boil the kettle, fill the basin with water and a teaspoon of washing powder. When all was cleared away, and Beatrice's tray covered with a white lace tray cloth, ready for her afternoon tea, Daddy supervised our getting dressed in our new uniforms, showing us how to make the knot in our school ties, all the time saying how 'lucky' we were. Telling us not to get dirty, he went upstairs to dress in the same pale-grey suit, with a fresh red rose in the jacket. Beatrice followed him downstairs wearing a different dress in heavier material, but similar in style. Her new hat matched her dress and she carried a beautiful Moroccan leather handbag with a gold clasp, and soft leather (maybe kid) gloves.

Daddy said, 'We don't want to be too early.' We were to find out that they liked to make an impressive entrance when the church was full. How proud he was of himself, his lovely wife and pretty Gina (she wearing her new sailor dress), Gertie and I followed in our new uniforms, feeling shy with all these prople staring at us. There were nods and glances in our direction. Our pew was near the front, where we could see and be seen all round. After church the minister shook hands with every member of his congregation, and when we reached him, the minister shook hands with Beatrice, Daddy and the three of us in turn. He asked us to join the Sunday School next Sunday at 3 o'clock.

Daddy and Beatrice stood around, talking to all and sundry. We asked to visit the toilet, Beatrice was so sweet about it, excusing herself to the couple they were talking to at the time, and holding Gina's hand, led us into a small hall, putting us in to a door marked 'toilets'. She herself stayed outside, glancing coyly at the men, and seemed very free with them, seeming in no hurry to join Daddy. He was relating his war experiences, with many 'ohs' and 'ahs' from his audience.

We walked home very slowly, with another couple, both of them talking all the time! Once home, we were made change into our 'rags' and severely told we must take off our uniforms immediately we entered the house, unless told not to. We were to hang them up carefully on the hooks and hangers in the brush cupboard. Daddy, looking very serious, now placed a sheet of paper in front of him, told us to sit down and listen carefully. This turned out to be a timetable, listing jobs to be done, and how long it should take us to do them.

We were to stop calling him 'Daddy', that was childish, and Beatrice was to be addressed as 'Mother' at all times. I was not to be called Mary as it reminded him of my mother whose name was Mary, my name would be 'Minnie' from now on; anyone heard calling me Mary would be punished. He made Gertie and Gina say 'Minnie' over and over again making me really angry. I cried, 'I don't like that name, Daddy.' He rose and smacked me across the face twice. Once for calling him Daddy and again for speaking back, saying 'That will teach you to do what you are told, and let it be a lesson to you two.'

Next he put us to scrubbing potatoes, scraping and dicing vegetables, complaining all the time the stupid nuns had not taught us anything useful. Gertie and I had to fill four large pails with coal. When Beatrice 'retired' for her afternoon rest, we were shown how to mend the sitting-room fire, and sweep up the hearth without making any dust that would settle on the furniture. We were a little shocked and unhappy to see the musical box that should have been Mama's now amused Beatrice.

She also had a gramophone, and a pile of records of the latest tunes, often dancing to them to Father's great pleasure. She only tidied her bedroom and did a little cooking. She explained she was not a servant, we would have to attend to ourselves, saying Father would be better off without us. We secretly agreed with her, and hoped we would be sent back to Mama or St Joseph's.

Father boasted at every opportunity of his fine house, his lovely new wife and how his children would attend a fee-paying school. He was quite well off at this time, having received a gratuity from the army, plus back pay and war pension. A cleaning woman came in on Monday to wash everything but Beatrice's underwear, stockings and see-through blouses. These were of flimsy tulle, muslin and lace. She washed these by hand; her silk stockings, gloves and so on would drip from the kitchen pulley into a chipped enamel bath.

We were now beginning to realise that neither Father nor Beatrice had any idea of how to look after children. The first washday (a week after we arrived) we had put our dirty clothes in with father's shirts. We could not find any clean ones. Slipping on our old dresses, we had to tell him we had no clean clothes, and no nightdresses. They had all been left in St Joseph's, we only had one set of underwear and stockings each. Father muttered angrily, he had paid them well. He had a pension of 5/- (five shillings) per week for each child, which he could claim till we were sixteen years old, or started work. This money they had asked for and he really grudged it. He made us take out our dirty clothes, put them on and sent us off to school, saying he would have to buy us some new underwear and stockings.

We had gone to school for just one interview with the rector of Rothesay Academy, Father paying our fees for the term, even for Gina, who would be in Primary 1. The rector spoke kindly to us, then sent another teacher to show us our classrooms, the cloakrooms, the drill hall and toilets. Roll call was taken in a huge assembly hall, after which we said prayers, then dispersed to our various classrooms. The school was beautifully situated on the hillside. A steep road led to the gates. This road was named 'The Serpentine'. I was pleased to hear Father saying to the register-keeper that my full name was Mary Stirrat Morton, Gertrude and Georgina were also called by their proper names by their teachers. However, I was soon to acquire the nickname of 'Skinny' Minnie.

Most summer evenings we went for a walk along the prom, dressed in our uniforms. Father sporting a suit of plus-fours, Beatrice in her newest dress. Father took up golf, playing on Saturday afternoons, but Beatrice soon put a stop to that. She created a 'scene', screaming that he had his 'brats' to look after, she was not going to be saddled with them at weekends.

Apart from the washer-woman, no one came to clean up the house, though both of them told others they had a maid. We worked in earnest now. When the washerwoman went off, she left a boiler full of soapy water. We were given a pail and scrubbing brush, and cloths to scrub every corner of the kitchen. Little Gina had to have cloths wrung out for her to dry up the place we had just scrubbed. Our arms ached and our knees hurt, kneeling on the hard floor. Beatrice stood over us till we had cleaned out each pail, hung out each floor-cloth, and dried out the boiler. We were glad to go to bed, we were so tired.

During holidays and weekends Beatrice kept us working non-stop, polishing floors, dusting, sweeping, cleaning silver and cutlery. My heart ached for Gina, she had to wipe each stair-rod with Brasso, then polish them. There were eighteen rods and her arms ached so much she began to cry. She was only five years old.

Beatrice would lift a rod, and strike her across the legs with it. Gina would flee into the kitchen and crawl underneath the bed. Beatrice sent me to finish the job, poor Gina would not come out till Father came home.

The tramcar rails came to an end just in front of our house. We travelled to school and back every weekday, a distance of two miles. Father started work at 9.00 a.m. too, so we all left the house together, and took the same tram into Rothesay. Now we had real school books, and real jotters, no more slates and slate pencils. We had to learn how to write with pen and ink. The pen nibs were a nuisance, sometimes they made big blots on our work. Girls were chosen each day to wash out the empty ink-wells and refill them from a messy bottle.

Father showed us how to cover our books neatly with new brown paper and write our names, class, school and home address on the outside. Fearing to offend him, I did not know whether to write Mary or Minnie, but he said to write down my proper name. After school, and after finishing all our 'wee jobs', as Father laughingly spoke of them, we had twenty minutes to do our homework before going to bed. We would strip off our uniforms the minute we came in from school. Put on the potatoes (scraped the day before) start on the next days vegetables for the soup. Gina set the table, while we filled coal-pails and mended the sitting-room fire.

After dinner (which never varied, except on Sundays), which consisted of soup, bread and a potato, we would wash everything, and clean *all* the shoes. Gertie had to clean out and black-lead the range (an extremely dirty job), then polish it. Gina rubbed the steel fender and fire-irons with emery paper. We tried to help her as much as we could, but dare not let Beatrice catch us. My jobs were to scrub out the toilets, clean the shoes, and fill coal-pails, sometimes chopping up firewood.

At this time the parents entertained a great deal, and went out visiting. Sometimes when we came in from school Beatrice would be sitting in the window seat, daintily drinking out of tiny coffee cups, with two or three ladies round her. If she wanted us to go into the sitting-room, she would beckon us in before we stripped. She would make a great fuss of us, especially Gina, and the ladies would say what a wonderful mother she made, how well she managed with us, and her so young! Beatrice would hand us her box of 'bon-bons' and we gingerly took the smallest one, having previously been well warned about being greedy, then said we had our 'little jobs' to do, and we escaped to the kitchen.

All the edible food, like sugar, jam, cakes, biscuits, bread, oatmeal and flour, was kept in a huge, gleaming 'chiffonier' in the sitting-room. This was a massive piece of furniture which had been sold with the house, as it was too large and heavy to move. It contained cupboards, shelves and drawers, every one of which locked. Beatrice said the kitchen was damp and there were a few mice around, but it meant we could only eat what we were given, not helping ourselves like we used to do at home or at Granny's.

By scraping all vegetables and potatoes we could not even eat potato peelings. Beatrice saw to it we did not eat one piece of vegetable. By the time Father came home, we were starving. He doled out a slice of bread and dripping each for our lunch at school and 6d (sixpence) to pay our penny-fares each way, we dare not spend or lose the money. If we walked the two miles home, we would have been too late to put on the potatoes (scrubbed the previous day) and Beatrice would have been furious.

Gina was very nervous, kept wetting herself, so we had to resort to devious ways of hiding this. One was to carry our clean knickers to school with us (we only had the one change). We would dry her wet ones in the back of the warm oven after Gertie cleaned it out.

One afternoon Beatrice called her into the sittingroom to meet her lady-friends. Gina was too shy to say she needed to use the toilet and wet herself. The dark stain showed up plainly on the pink and white chair when she rose and ran fearfully from the room. Beatrice called me to fetch a towel from her bedroom to put over the offending stain. She continued to talk with her friends, while Gertie and I tried to soothe the shivering, crying child. We took off her uniform, and wet knickers, put on her velvet dress and coaxed her to start setting the table, although we feared for her.

The ladies left, Beatrice came storming into the kitchen, pounced on Gina, sat down and pulled her over her knee, threw up her dress and spanked her as hard as she could. Gina's squirming body and terrified screams alarmed Gertie and me; the woman had worked herself into a frenzy and could not stop. We looked at each other, dived on Beatrice, each catching an arm. Gina dropped to the floor, Beatrice pulled her arms free, and sent Gertie flying across the room, hitting her head on the chair. She then turned on me, but I ran, twisting and dodging her flailing arms, her eyes were streaked with red veins. She could not contain her anger, and threw anything she could find at me.

Fortunately for us, she tired (her tight corsets made physical effort almost impossible). With a, 'Wait till your father hears about this,' she left us. Poor Gina lay on the floor, sobbing miserably, lying on her side. Her little bottom swelling scarlet by the force of the blows rained on her. We had to leave her, to get our work done, but we set the table for her, and put away all the things which Beatrice had thrown. Father came in, to be met by a tearful Beatrice: 'George darling, these awful children attacked me just because I had to smack Gina for wetting our lovely chair.'

Father demanded why we had upset our poor mother so. We told him we had tried to stop her hitting Gina, she was never going to stop. He just laughed and said, 'You will just have to get used to being punished. Gina had to be taught a lesson.' That he did not look to see if Gina was hurt, or believe a word that we said shocked us into stunned silence.

It was weeks before the bruises faded on Gina's bottom. At first she could not sit down properly. We would fold some dusters to put under her. At school, sitting at her desk was so painful that she wept and was sent to the sickroom. Cross-examined by the nurse, she refused to say who had thrashed her, and was given a letter to take home. We told Gina to say she had lost it, and threw it away, after tearing it into little pieces. Nothing more was said at school so we surmised it had only been a warning.

A month later, we were given a routine medical inspection. Gina was given a letter to take home to Father, quite unaware of what it contained. He read it, his face growing red with anger. He shouted to Beatrice, 'Come and hear this!' the letter said some supervision was required over the toilet of *all* the girls.

Beatrice was angry, no doubt feeling guilty. 'I wish you would get the dirty brats out of my life!' she screamed at Father. We were terrified when she said she would, 'supervise us all right, leave this to me, George, I'll have the skin off the filthy brats'.

Father lifted our hair, saw the tidemarks on our necks and wrists. We had not had a bath since we left the orpahange, six weeks ago, or had our hair washed. As there was only the cold tap, coarse soap and thin hand towel, we had managed as best we could. Our work was dirty, coaldust flew in our faces as we filled pails and emptied ash-pans. What else could they expect? Gertie and I said we had once washed Gina's hair, but our hair was too long and heavy. Father said we will soon cure that.

The next two hours were ones we would rather forget. The memory of the immersion in a rusty tin so small we could only kneel haunts me still. Kettles of hot water were poured in as they boiled, we had to jump out of the way, and were slapped for doing so. Gina was stripped first. Father discovered we had a no flannel or sponge, so he threw me a duster. Beatrice held poor Gina's head under the water, rinsing it, she said. Father asked her to fetch some decent towels, but she flounced out and we heard her playing records.

He had to go upstairs himself, and bring his own towels. We rubbed soap on Gina's body, the strong yellow soap stinging her eyes. She cried all the time, and shivered, as much from fear as from the cold. It was cold, the fire was out, and Gertie was cleaning the range. I rubbed Gina down as well as I could, squeezing the water out of her hair. Father said, 'That's enough,' inspected her neck, ears, nails and toes, then sent her to bed naked, though her hair was still wet. She was blue with cold. He threw a comb to her, telling her to get the tangles out of her hair.

I was next. He put another kettle of water in and I rubbed every part of me with the rough cloth. Trying to wash my long heavy hair was difficult and he told me to hurry up, he did not want to sit there much longer. He dipped my head underwater to get rid of the soap, which stung my eyes. At last he said I could get out. I tried twisting my hair to get rid of the water. The towel was damp but I was glad to jump into bed, also naked (for we had no nightdresses.)

Then it was Gertie's turn. I was lucky that Beatrice had left the kitchen, but now she returned and said she 'would see to it that Gertie would never be dirty again'. Father walked way, his newspaper in his hand, no doubt keen to sit by the sitting-room fire. Beatrice put in another kettle of water, ordered Gertie to kneel down and bringing out the scrubbing brush (used for the floor), pulled up her sleeves and scrubbed Gertie's back till she howled. Father heard her and came in, saying to Beatrice, 'Let her get on with it herself, I will inspect her when she is ready.' Beatrice laughed, she seemed to be actually enjoying herself. She pushed Gertie's head under water, holding it down till Gertie scrambled out of the bath in great fear. Again and again Beatrice forced her back into the water, making her wash her hair, over and over again.

Father came in, looked her over, and said we could empty the bath outside in the morning. Gertie was only half-dried, her hair dripping wet, her skin bright scarlet with the strong soap and scrubbing. Next morning we took a handle each and carried the bath outside to the drain. We hung the very wet towels on the pulley. A few days later father brought home two thick dark towels, a face flannel and a nail-brush. He decided we would have our bath every Monday. The laundry woman would be told to leave the soapy water in the boiler. Beatrice had a bath every day. A hot water cistern had been installed in her bathroom, but it did not heat water in the kitchen. Father had his bath on Sunday evening or if he was going somewhere special. I don't think Beatrice liked him to use her bathroom too much either.

They entertained quite a lot, inviting people (couples especially) to supper. Beatrice loved to sing and dance, captivating the company. We could hear them clapping and shouting for an encore! Sometimes the men came into the spotless, clean, scrubbed kitchen (by us). They would sit round the table, drinking and smoking. We would peep round the edge of the drawn curtains, but not if Father could see us. He had caught us once, and belted us with the back of his hand across our faces. So now we listened, smelling the smoke from the pipes and cigars, mingled with the odour of beer and whisky.

Father would start on his experiences as a prisoner-of-war. That the stories never seemed twice exactly the same did not deter him. He had them all laughing at his descriptions of the fat, stodgy or pretty 'fräuleins' he had had. The French nurses were the best, he said, 'You took all you could get as you did not know what would happen to you from one day to the next!' Thinking of these tales when I was older, I wondered why Father was so bitter at Mama, was he not even more unfaithful?

A Visit From Granny

A letter arrived from Granny, she wanted to see us before winter settled down. She would come on the September holiday weekend, Father's sister (Aunt Mary) would bring her. She would not stay, and would leave Granny with us, catching the last boat, as she was a very busy person, attending meetings and sitting on committees. How we polished and cleaned for Granny's visit! Father wanted everything to be just perfect. They were the first visitors from home.

A single bed was bought and placed in one of the empty bedrooms, also a piece of carpet on the floor, and a net curtain at the window. One of our blankets was taken for her bed, and she only had a very thread-bare bed-cover. The room smelled damp and musty, even though we had polished every inch of it. We asked Father if we could pick some roses. He cut them himself, we put them in a jam jar, and thought they made the room look nicer.

That we had such lovely roses was the result of the horses' dung (manure) which we had to pick up every day after school. There were less cart-horses here than at home. We kept our uniforms on to shovel up the dung, as we were not allowed to be seen at the front of the house unless we were 'properly' dressed. It may seem unthinkable to the reader, but we were not allowed to play or paddle on the sea-shore, like the children we saw from the windows. Beatrice detested sand. Father said it was a waste of time, there were more useful things we could do than play like babies!

When Father left to meet Granny and Aunt Mary coming off the steamer Beatrice set the table in the kitchen with a large white damask table-cloth (a wedding present) with matching serviettes. We were all going to eat together till Aunt Mary left. Beatrice lectured us on what we should do and say, saying Granny was a 'nosey old bag', and we were to tell her nothing about ourselves, 'just talk about your snooty school, that will please his "holier than thou" sister.'

Dressed in our uniforms, we met Granny at the door. She looked just the same, her shiny bonnet all askew as Gina leapt into her arms and hugged her. We scarcely looked at Aunt Mary. Beatrice and Father had gone to the gate and they were showing Aunt Mary the 'wonderful view' and the splendid roses. We pulled Granny into the kitchen and whispered, 'Where is Mama?' but she put her fingers to her lips, saying, 'Later, I am here for a whole week, you know.'

Aunt Mary came in, gushing over us, a stout, pompous, but good-looking lady, very like Father. Well-dressed and extremely talkative, she looked us over, said how smart we were, and followed Beatrice into the sitting-room. We were sent upstairs to Granny's room with their coats and hats and Granny's black hold-all. Talking went on all through lunch, the first time Beatrice had ever sat down at the kitchen table to eat with us. We were very nervous, as her black eyes would turn on us if we spoke, with sour disapproval.

It was a good meal for us and we ate all we were given. Aunt Mary exclaimed about our hearty appetites, our school and our good behaviour, praising Beatrice for looking after us so well. Granny did not say much, just mentioned how all her family were getting on and smiling at us all the time. After lunch Granny said she would go to her room to unpack and rest. We ran with her to the door, but Father said we had to clear the table and wash up the dishes, taking Granny upstairs himself. Beatrice took her tray through to the sitting-room, where Father joined her a few minutes later.

We had changed into our 'rags' immediately Aunt Mary had gone out of the kitchen, and started on the great pile of dishes. We put the sugar, milk, sauces and remains of salad on the dresser and ate up everything else we could find, a few potatoes, scraps of steak pie left in the dish, bits of bread and butter. We put butter thickly on the crusts, it was so long since we had tasted any, as it was always kept in the chiffonier, and only used by Father and Beatrice. He kept the bulk of it in a meat safe in the wash-house (as cold as any ice-box) along with meat, fish and milk.

By the time we had cleaned everything in the kitchen, we heard Aunt Mary getting read to leave. She came into the kitchen, said how well trained we were, gave us each a silver threepenny piece and was off, Father taking her to the pier to catch the last steamer, which left about 5.00 p.m. Beatrice told us to mend her fire, let the kitchen range fire out, and we could get it cleaned before Granny came down. Gina and I washed up the cups, reset the tray, and started to clean the fender and fire-irons with emery paper.

Granny came down to the kitchen, and was surprised to see the fire out. She went into the sitting room, where Beatrice was sitting in her favourite armchair, eating chocolates from a large box which Aunt Mary had given her. We had told Granny we were not allowed into the sitting-room, especially with our working dresses.

Granny said to Beatrice, 'What a lovely fire you have in here, will we bring the children in?'

Beatrice said, 'Of course not, children should neither be seen or heard.'

Our father had promised her, before she married him, that he would see the children would not be a burden to her.

We had been listening to every word, as Granny had left both doors open. Granny said she would like a cup of tea, and would take it in the kitchen. Beatrice said, 'Just as you like,' and continued to read her magazines. These were delivered with the daily newspaper, and we would devour the contents when we were given them to cut into squares for toilet paper, or hiding them under newspapers while we cleaned the cutlery and silver. Father derided her magazines, 'Tuppenny Horribles' he called them. They were all romantic short stories, I remember some of the titles, *True Romances, The Red Letter, Women's Own*. Beatrice loved them and Father indulged her every whim.

When Father returned, he told us to get 'dressed' and we all went for a walk except Beatrice. We each held Granny's hand, but Gina pushed me away, and took a firm hold of Granny, refusing Father's proffered hand. We spent one penny on a 'pokey hat' (ice-cream cone) and had two pennies each in change, which Father put in his pocket for safe keeping. How we enjoyed that stroll on the promenade on a rather cool and misty September day. Most of the holiday-makers had gone, the beach was almost deserted.

Father talked of his fine house, his good job, his daughters' expensive schooling and how Beatrice was a real lady She would entertain his colleagues, and was not tied to a 'grubby' sewing machine, but a real companion to him. They had a wonderful social life, and were looked up to by all the people they knew. When Granny said, 'Who keeps the house clean?' father said they had two maids, which made Granny say, 'My, aren't we gentry!'

After tea, having done our 'wee jobs', we settled down to our school books, Father showing them with some pride to granny, who asked why we could not read our books in the sitting-room, as it was quite cold in the kitchen. Father answered that Beatrice would not like that, poor girl, she sees enough of them and weekends are a great trial to her. Granny suggested we should visit the 'matinee' on a Saturday afternoon at the cinema. All her other grandchildren liked to go there, and it took the children out of the way on Saturday afternoons, when the men attended football matches, and the wives could do some shopping on their own. Father said he would talk it over with Beatrice. We wondered if he would.

Granny had tea with us in the kitchen, so Daddy stayed to have his, but took Beatrice's through to the sitting-room. We made the most of the chance to eat more bread and jam than we were usually given. Granny brought out a box of cakes, Father said, 'We will give your mother first choice, she will like these,' but Granny put a large cream cake on each plate, leaving one in the box. Father looked slightly put-out, murmured that Granny was spoiling us.

He sent me to Beatrice with the cake still in its box, and I knocked on the door before I entered. Beatrice looked at the cake, said, 'Where's the rest of them?' and I told her we had all had ours. She lifted the box, squashed it flat on the cake, and threw it into the fire.

I darted from the room, and fearing to anger Father, I said nothing. He went to Beatrice, we heard her shouting at him, saying that, 'she was not accustomed to left-overs, and the rotten old hag could keep her bloody cakes!' Father was a long time soothing her, so we took the opportunity to ask about Mama, Kiki, and the new baby. Yes, Kiki was well, but we must not talk about Mama just now. The kitchen was now quite cold, Father said when we had washed up and finished our 'wee jobs', we were to get into bed. He asked Granny to come through to the warm fire, and enjoy some music.

In bed by 7.30 p.m., Granny came through to say goodnight. She asked us when we got up in the morning, she would come down early and we could have a long talk. We slept happily that night, having talked of happy days with Mama and Hughie. Gina said she wanted to go home with Granny, but we said Father would not let her go.

In the early hours of the morning when it was very dark, we were wakened by a slight noise, and found Granny had lit the gas, and put the kettle on to boil. The poor soul was shivering and her teeth were chattering although she had a blanket wrapped round her, and over a heavy flannel nightdress. She whispered to us not to make a noise. She had been so cold in that damp, empty room with no hot-water bottle and not enough bedclothes. She was further amazed when she found we were all naked. She filled two large breakfast cups with hot water, and we sipped at one, while she drank the other.

We were wide-awake now, and pleased when she climbed into bed with us, lying between Gertie and Gina, somehow I managed to squeeze half-way up the bed, so we could talk in whispers. Mama had had her baby boy, his name was Hughie, too, they both sent their love, and prayed for us every night. Now living in Belfast, the only news Granny could get was through Kirsty, as Mama did not want Father to know her address, nor would she write to Granny's house. She sent letters to Kirsty, who would send it to Granny, with the Belfast address cut off. Mama must have been very afraid that Father would find out where she lived, and do something to hurt her or Hughie.

We soon had Granny warm, she stopped shivering and we said she had better go to her own bed, we would not tell she had been in ours, but Granny said she would get her death of cold in that room. She would certainly have something to say to our parents in the morning.

It was daylight when Father came downstairs as usual to get us up, and make tea for Beatrice. We climbed out of bed, dressed quickly when he went up with the tray. Granny was still sleeping. She had not heard him, and he did not look behind the drawn bed curtains.

We hastened on with our work quietly, soon the fire was crackling merrily, the table set, the coal-pails filled, and the sitting-room cleaned, dusted and the fire set. Father bustled in, as it was Sunday morning he was wearing old clothes. He was quite startled when Granny sat up in bed. He said he was about to take tea up to her room. Granny asked him where the tea was kept, she could not find any when she arose during the night, she also told him she could not sleep another night in that poor bed, she would squeeze in with the girls, and why had they no nightdresses, that kitchen was cold even before they went to bed.

Father just laughed, saying, 'You're too soft, mother, you would have them wrapped in cottonwool, you should have seen how they treated the solders in Germany, you were lucky to have a bed at all!' Father had this peculiar idea that personal comfort was to be despised (except Beatrice's), how he sneered at 'dodgers' in 'cushy' jobs as feather-bedded scum, while he was fighting for *his life and theirs!*

Granny went upstairs and came down fully dressed, carrying her luggage with her. We were dismayed when she said she could not stay another minute in that house. It was a 'whited sepulchre' if ever there was one. She was angry with what she had seen, that the children were just servants. Beatrice appeared and accused her of trying to make trouble, whereupon Granny told her she was a lazy good-for-nothing, that never had a penny till she married George. We trembled, for Beatrice to be spoken to like that, we knew things would happen and they did.

Father was powerless as the two women argued. Beatrice beside herself with fury, Granny not loud, but very, very angry.

Turning on George, she yelled, 'Get that interfering old hag out of here, and send your brats with her, just get them out of my life!' Granny told her she was just a tart, and the sooner he got rid of her, the better, she would put him in the gutter! Soon Beatrice was throwing everything within reach, the final insult came when she smashed a beautiful marble clock, shattering it into a thousand pieces on the tiled floor. The clock had been Granny's wedding present to them.

Screaming abuse, Beatrice ran into the sitting-room and locked the door. Father said, 'I'd better get you out of here, I'll take you to the boat!'

We pleaded with him, 'Father, don't leave us here, can't we go home with Granny?

He turned to his mother, saying, 'Now see what you've done. You can't bear to see me as a gentleman, you are all jealous of Beatrice.'

I can't describe the look on Granny's face as she gazed at Father, as though he were a stranger. 'Why, in God's name, did you keep the children? What a miserable existence they have with that awful woman.'

But Granny went, and we tried to work, dreading the moment when Beatrice would come in the door. When she did, it was only to have us clear up the broken pieces of glass and ornaments, and warning us not to mention 'that nosey old bag's' name, and proceeded to make herself some coffee. When Father returned, all was quiet. The Sunday stew was on the fire and a rice pudding in the oven. We were told to get dressed, and we all went for a walk along the promenade. They walked in front of us girls, and we could see Beatrice was being very pleasant to Father. We did not always go to church, often helping Father in the garden, or working in the house.

Our stockings were a problem, all wool in those days, and holes appeared faster than we could hide them. Plucking up courage, I asked Beatrice if we could get darning wool and a needle, as we had been taught to darn at the orphanage. Strangely enough, she did not rebuke us for wasting her money, but produced a packet of needles, wool, scissors and a great pile of Father's socks, which pleased him mightily, saying we could be of some use after all! Sometimes our stockings were so thick and lumpy with constant darning, they hurt our feet when walking.

A few days later Father received a letter from Uncle Johnny. His mother (Granny) was seriously ill, suffering from rheumatic fever, he thought her visit to our house had brought it on – we did not hear the rest of the letter. A week later a parcel arrived with three flannel nightdresses, and three pairs of black stockings. Granny had asked Aunt Mary to send them to us. Beatrice just sniffed when the parcel was opened, saying it was about time they were putting their hands in their pockets, *that* family had never helped George in any way! To our great astonishment, Father agreed with her.

At school we were happy, all of us quite smart, keeping in the top row. Hunger made us sharper, and we started to do our friends' homework at playtime or lunch-time, for a biscuit, an apple or even a crust. One morning I asked Father for a bit more bread, as we were very hungry at school. He gave us another half-slice each. We only drank water at school, from a well, built into the school wall, a heavy iron cup attached by a chain was used by all.

Burnt Porridge

Being a little behind one morning, I turned the gas on full under the pot of porridge. I stirred till it boiled, turned down the gas flame, and hurried through to clear up and set the sitting-room fire. Coming through the kitchen with the ash-pan, I noticed I had turned the gas so low it had gone out, and the porridge was not cooking. Lighting it again, I returned to the sitting room, where I worked for another ten minutes. I heard Gertie call me, 'Minnie, I think the porridge is burning.'

The acrid smell of it was spreading through the house. Gertie had turned off the gas. I took the pot off, the top looked all right, Father was upstairs, now he came running, 'Can't you do anything right?' He slapped me several times and stood over me as I poured the porridge into bowls. The top was put in Father's and Gina's, Gertie and I got the burnt black bits at the bottom of the pot. No one could eat it, not even Father. The pot was left soaking, to be cleaned by me that evening, the porridge put in one large dish. Father ordered me to eat some at every meal till it was finished, there would be no other food for me till then.

He made toast for all, but I got none. A plateful of burnt porridge was put in the oven for my evening meal, I was so hungry I ate it, but got nothing else. Next morning I made fresh porridge, but was again forced to eat another plateful of the burnt stuff. On the way to school I was sick, and again in school, messing up the skirt of my uniform. I was more afraid of Father seeing this than facing the rest of the awful stuff.

Lunch-time was spent trying to clean my skirt in the cloakroom, using the roller hand towels dipped in water. It remained very wet and uncomfortable, Teacher noticed it, and sent me to sit by the hot pipes which ran the length of the room. I hoped the skirt would be dry before I got home. Alas, Beatrice spotted it whenever I entered the house by the front door. Father would not let us come in by the back door, he said it was just for poor ignorant peasants, pedlars and tradesmen!

Beatrice called me a 'disgusting brat', made me hang my clothes outside, and get on with my work. When Father came in, he was angry with me, telling me if I must be sick, to keep it off my clothes. At night, I was presented again with the awful mess of burnt porridge, my stomach revolted and I fled to the sink, retching on an empty stomach. Father told Gertie to put the porridge down the lavatory pan, saying he hoped that would be a lesson to me for wasting valuable food. I had no food that night, fortunately my stomach was too upset for hunger to bother me. I certainly enjoyed my fresh porridge next morning after two days almost without food. I changed the wooden 'spurtle' for a wide wooden spoon, which stirred the oatmeal much better, and Gertie stirred occasionally, but she had very little time. We were very careful, keeping an eye on the gas flame all the time.

Father's wounded hand prevented him from helping us, very occasionally he drew the carpet-sweeper over the sitting room and hall carpets. He would watch us closely, down on our knees polishing the surrounds (the wooden part of the floor not covered by carpets). I shall never forget his impatient, 'Hurry up,' and, 'Why can't you be as smart as 'so and so!' He started nearly every sentence with these words. He could use his 'gammy' hand when necessary, I think he used it as an excuse to avoid helping us.

My Long Hair

About this time I found my hair a great burden to me. I asked Father if he would let me have a bob. A lot of the older girls at school had their hair cut short, it had become very fashionable just after the war. Father was very proud of all our hair. Gertie's and Gina's thick curls entranced him; he would often sit and play with their curls. My hair was plaited from Monday to Saturday, but on Sunday it cascaded in shining ripples down to the hem of my coat, and was commented on by the congregation when we were at church.

Sometimes I sat on it, which was painful, and would put my plaits inside my blazer when going to school. Children on the tramcar took a fiendish delight in tugging them as hard as they could. In the playground it was the same, and I began to resent having it. After prayers one morning, we went to our respective classes. When Teacher came in, we had to stand up quickly to say 'Good morning, Miss Wilson.' Just before this, two girls dropped a pencil case on the floor, the pencils rolled under my seat, the girls got down on their knees, scrabbling about behind me. Just in time they seated themselves, Teacher came in.

We all stood up quickly, except me, I let out a yell, and fell to my knees. Pain shot through my head, then I realised my two long plaits had been tied together under my seat to the iron legs of the desk behind me. I saw the two snigger, rage, pain and frustration filled me. I did what I had seen Beatrice do, and shouted abuse at them. 'You lily-livered bastards, you bitches of whores, you rotten swine, filthy pigs,' and more. Suddenly I was brought to a stop by a ruler stinging my hand. 'Stop using that kind of language here, at once, do you hear?' I just glared, still vainly trying to loosen my hair. Teacher demanded to know who did this? I left her in no doubt, and accused the now red-faced and deflated pair.

When they made to come near me to loosen my plaits, I screamed at them to get back to the 'stinking hell holes' they came from. Teacher, white-faced, sent a girl for the headmistress, and she untied my hair. Still defiant, I shouted, 'I'll get you two for this!' I sat down with my aching head in my hands, my elbows on the desk, aware of an ominous silence in the room. The door opened, to admit the headmistress.

Miss Wilson talked to her in low tones. The two culprits were called out, then myself. I rose slowly, we followed the headmistress out of the classroom, along the corridor, and stopped at the rector's room. I would not look at the other two girls, as we all stepped out in front of the rector's desk. The headmistress gave him an account of the disturbance in class, but refused to repeat the language I had used. It had been written down by Miss Wilson, and she now placed the sheet of paper in front of him. His eyebrows shot up, and he looked at me as though I were a being from another world. Turning to the two girls, he told them they could expect to be severely punished for creating such a disturbance in class.

I thought he was much more concerned about the disturbance than my suffering. He gave them two of the belt (tawse), one on each hand. They were also to write a complete chapter of history, to be handed in to him next morning. They went out, I was left standing there, wondering what he would say to me, but with no thought of being punished.

He looked at me sorrowfully, saying, 'Where did you hear language like that?' I was about to say, from my stepmother, but knew if she heard I had blamed her, the consequences could be worse than I could imagine. I remained silent.

'I am shocked and very disappointed in you, Mary, your work at school has been excellent, but do you know what this means?' He went on to say that parents sent their children to the academy to avoid hearing that kind of language, and now, if they hear what their children have heard today, they could remove them from this school. 'You could be expelled. I will have to speak to your parents, no doubt they will punish you, but now you will receive six of the tawse.'

Shocked, I cried out, "That's not fair, I did not start it!" The headmistress forced my hand out, the stinging leather numbed my arm, another and another, then the other hand. I kept saying through my tears of pain, 'It's not fair, it's not fair.'

Out in the corridor I dropped to the floor, sobbing, the burning injustice in my heart as great as the pain in my burning hands. The janitor lifted me to my feet, and led me to the sick room. I stayed there till playtime, when the headmistress escorted me back to the classroom, my hands so swollen I could not hold a pencil or book. Before leaving she warned the class that any more incidents like that, the culprits would be expelled.

At lunch-time the girls avoided me, talking in little groups. Gertie heard about it, and hoped Father would not get a letter, but he did. He was asked to visit the rector next day on a very serious matter. Of course, Father asked a lot of questions, saw the weals on my hands, and seemed quite angry at the punishment I had received. I told him about the girls who had tied my hair, that I had called then names, but he did not ask for details.

School went normally the next day till 4.00 p.m. when I was told to go to the rector's room. Father was there, looking quite angry, 'What's this? I hear you have been using bad language,' and he glanced at the paper put before him by the rector.

Standing dumbly before him, the rector glared at me, saying I would not be expelled *this* time, but any more 'trouble' and I would be. It was only for my 'parents' sake that I was allowed to continue my education at the academy. 'Your father has promised to punish you "suitably".'

Going home with Father, he did not seem very upset, smiling, saying, 'You certainly gave them a few home truths, didn't you?'

We had tea as usual, had finished our housework, when Father came through to the kitchen, saying, 'I don't really blame you, but I have to thrash you to please the Rector.' Crying out that I had already been punished, that it was not my fault, he just said, 'Get on the bed.' Beatrice came in to 'witness' the punishment. Father had a heavy leather belt, and proceeded to hit me with it.

I could not escape. A box bed has walls on three sides, I clung to the farthest corner, as the belt stung my bare legs and buttocks, I had no clothes on. Gina was howling, turning my head I saw Beatrice actually smiling! Father tired eventually, I crawled under the blanket, fiercely rebellious, hating school, Father, Beatrice and the life we led! Next day, I was given a note to say I had been given a good sound thrashing. The headmistress and nurse examined the weals in the sick room just to make sure, and report back to the rector.

I now pleaded with Father to cut off my hair, but he said he liked it long. However, my troubles in that direction were about to be solved. Just before Armistice Day (1919) a school medical officer examined the pupils, giving some of us a pink card. When handed to Father, he exclaimed, 'Good Lord!' and called Beatrice to show her it. Apparently we had an 'infestation' (of lice) in our hair, were to purchase a box of Rankin's Ointment, and our hair to be 'treated' and washed every night, also combed with a tooth-comb.

Beatrice was furious, as Father said 'she' should have noticed, with one movement she lifted one of my plaits, and hacked at it with a kitchen knife, sawing at it, it was so thick. Father sent Gertie for the scissors and finished the job himself. Beatrice removing herself from the 'lousy' brats! He cut my hair off to just below my ears, saying he had helped to cut his fellow prisoners' hair in Germany. Gertie's and Gina's curls dropped to the floor, poor Gina, white-faced with terror till Beatrice went out of the room. I felt a great relief, no more painful tugs.

Now we sat for hours, our heads over a newspaper, Father watching, showing us how to kill the tiny insects with our thumb nail, which made a little sharp crack. We did not mind doing this, although our scalps were red and raw with the tooth-comb. Or hair was much easier to wash and dry. Beatrice was sure she had lice in her hair now, and made us comb her long hair for hours till our arms and legs ached. We discovered she had black roots in her hair, she must have got the red-gold colour from her bottles of henna.

She spent many hours on her 'toilette', and (as Father would say) getting 'dolled up'. We thought she looked quite ugly before she was dressed, her eyelashes were false, her skin sallow and spotty, telling each other Mama was far prettier. Beatrice was also getting fat, no doubt due to the indolent 'lady's life' she now led. Appearing at school with our hair cut short, smelling of Rankin's Ointment, a few girls called us 'lousy', but I gave them such a look they left off, remembering how the two girls had been punished for tying my plaits. We were not the only ones anyway to receive pink cards.

Winter closed in, it was quite dark in the kitchen. Father kept the light as low as possible, saying it cost money. During the night we were in pitch dark, and the scurrying feet of the mice grew louder.

We were afraid to go to the toilet, having to cross the kitchen floor. Our parents were entertaining as usual one Saturday evening. Father brought in a tray, in the dim light from the hall we could see some of Beatrice's cookies on the plates. When he left, I jumped out of bed, grabbed two chocolate ones, my fingers sticking to the cream. Back in bed, we ate the cakes, not waking Gina, who slept, hiding under the blanket. I licked my fingers clean, but they still felt sticky when we fell asleep.

It must have been about 4.00 a.m. when I waked to a sharp pain in my finger. I put out my other hand to touch it, when my fingers came into contact with a warm furry body. It was quite big, this was no mouse! Yelling and screaming, I jumped out of bed and smashed my hand against the table, but still the 'thing' hung on to my finger. I ran screaming to the foot of the stairs, the 'thing' twitched and I went into hysterics. I knew little of what happened then, but Gertie had followed me out of bed, and saw it all. Father ran downstairs, slapped me across the face, which stopped my screaming.

He laid me on the floor, quivering with fear, stretched out my arm with the 'thing' on it and put his foot on my hand, trying to disengage the big, black rat! Apparently smashing my hand on the table was the worst thing I could have done, as the rat was stunned, its teeth firmly embedded in my finger. Father could not get its mouth open, sent for a poker, and cracked the skull of the beast. He then had to force open its jaws, levering them open with the heavy poker.

I was only semi-conscious, when he carried me through to bed, and he forced a sip of whisky between my lips. I shuddered at the taste of raw whisky, and realising what had happened, started screaming again. Father pulled and pushed me to the sink, letting the cold water run over my sore finger. I stopped crying, but still had to endure more pain as Father put my finger in a cup of iodine, after which I realised the rat was really gone, and I crawled as far back into the bed as I could. As Father was about to leave, I pleaded with him to leave the light on. Muttering about the expense, he put more pennies in the gas meter, and left the light on low. He had tossed the body of the rat in a coal-pail.

Next morning, I got out of bed, my legs buckled under me, and I felt sick. Father told me to stay in bed, as I seem to have got a 'bit' of a shock. I could not eat, and was sick when I tried to.

Fortunately, it was Sunday morning; Beatrice's parties were usually held on Saturday evenings. I never did get over my fear of rats, and always wondered if my sticky fingers had attracted the rat! Father contacted a rat-catcher, he put down little cans of poison in all corners, warning us not to touch them. He said the rats liked the poison but it would make them so thirsty they would drown themselves in any water they could reach. We had peace for a while, the scurrying ceased, and we were able to sleep in the dark.

Armistice Day, 1919

Armistice Day came. Gertie, Gina and I remembered everything about Armistice Night on 11th November 1918. It seemed so far away, so much had happened to us, and so much had changed. We all attended the service in church each wearing a poppy. Father had spent a long time cleaning his uniform belt and buttons. At 11.00 a.m. he paraded with about a hundred other men in uniform before the war memorial. Some men were in wheelchairs, many wore black armbands.

There was a ball to be held in the evening. Beatrice had ordered a new gown, Father was resplendent in his uniform, they made a handsome couple as they left for the ball, Beatrice also wearing a new fur cape. We always marvelled at the change in Beatrice when she was going to an evening function. She loved dancing and drinking, smoking her tiny cigarettes in a long holder. She was always in a good mood, but I don't think Father was keen to go out *every* evening.

Beatrice hid the accounts for her clothes, often throwing them into the fire. All the bills came at the end of each month as Father was receiving a monthly salary. When he questioned Beatrice about the price of her clothes, she would be very loving to him, sweetly reminding him that she wanted to look nice just for him, and didn't all the other men envy him, their wives were such frumps! We envied the attention Father gave her (we were not aware of sex and no children were allowed inside our house) we could not talk normally about family relationships. Father was desperate to have a son, he showed no emotion to us other than impatience and anger, but he was the only person we could talk to especially in the early morning, as Beatrice seldom rose before midday.

I did not feel well at school, either too hot or shivering. I got through the day. Once home I started to fill the coal-pails but had to sit down on the floor. Gertie helped me (though she had so much to do) by chopping up the firewood for me. Beatrice came through with her tray and demanded it to be cleared and the dishes washed up. I stood at the sink, my breathing hurt my chest. I was so slow that when she returned for the tray, she was about to slap me for not having it ready.

Gertie said, 'She is not feeling well.'

Beatrice looked closely at me, saying I had better get into bed, 'We'll see what your Father says.'

When Father got home, he felt my forehead, said I had a temperature, and 'We will get a doctor to look at you.'

Next minute I was whisked out of bed, clean sheets were produced, and 'Granny's' bed stripped to provide another pillow and blanket. Father told Gertie not to clean the range yet, and to keep the fire in. She and Gina were sent out when the doctor called. He diagnosed pneumonia, and said I looked comfortable, the kitchen was warm and, looking admiringly at Beatrice, said I was in good hands.

He had no sooner gone than Beatrice ordered Gertie to take off the sheets, pillowslips and bed-mat, but left the extra blanket. I tossed and turned all right, Father came down at some time and gave me medicine, then wrapped the blankets round me. He blamed my having diphtheria for causing my weakness, of course, blaming 'that woman' (meaning Mama). Until the doctor stopped his daily visits, the sheets and pillowslips were taken off as soon as he left. Beatrice would show him into the kitchen, all dressed up and appearing to show great concern for the poor motherless child. Once the doctor said I could get up for a little while each day, she had me at the sink, scrubbing potatoes and vegetables, or washing up her friends teacups! She held her afternoon teas as usual, and warned me not to speak or make any noise. She did not want her friends to know I was there.

Poor Gina, she tried to carry the heavy coal-pails, she could only half fill them. Gertie was forced to work longer, she now had my work to do as well as her own. Father 'thoughtfully' got her up an hour earlier to get everything done before school. It was three weeks before I was able to return to school and it was a great relief. Beatrice had found me all kinds of work to do, such as washing and polishing the bric-a-brac in the sitting-room and polishing the floor with Mansion polish, the strong smell of turpentine from this nauseated me.

Deciding I needed more to do, she spring-cleaned her bedroom. We washed the pretty curtains, cushion covers and lace bed-mats, lifted the carpet on the day the washer woman came, who beat the carpet outside. We swept down the walls, Beatrice holding me on a high chest of drawers to reach the ceiling, and to re-hang the curtains. Starting to wash the paintwork, I became dizzy, and Beatrice said, 'Go to bed, we will finish the room tomorrow.' I would be sound asleep when Beatrice would shake me furiously, and order me to make myself useful. Going on and on about these 'lazy, useless brats' till I felt like answering back, but was too weak even to try.

A week before Christmas Father announced we were going to Glasgow. He had a great treat in store for us, having bought tickets for the Kelvin Hall Circus. We were to visit Aunt Mary, who lived in Glasgow, have lunch with her and her family, before going to the circus. No, we were not going to see Granny, poor Granny was not too well.

What an understatement that was! Granny had been bed-ridden since her September visit to our house, almost crippled with rheumatism, and suffering from the effects of rheumatic fever. We thought Father would not have been welcomed. He got round that by saying she was an old woman, could expect ill-health, and needed peace and quiet!

The great day came, once again we sailed in the paddle steamer, but now the sky was dark, the sea rough and the wind cold. I stayed on deck. 'We don't want you sick today, do we?' said Father, but we enjoyed the sail although the hills around were shrouded in mist. Sailing up the Clyde, past the noisy shipyards, seeing the huge cranes swinging almost over our heads was very exciting. Arriving at Aunt Mary's house, we had a sumptuous spread laid out in the dining-room, it was warm and cosy. She exclaimed at the loss of my beautiful hair. Beatrice quickly explained that it was necessary for my health. Seeing my look of astonishment, she glared at me, and said loudly, 'Now, eat up, dear, you must build up your strength!' offering me more trifle, this pleased me so much I soon forgot the incident.

Our cousins, two boys and three girls, played with us, but not for long as we were soon on our way to the Kelvin Hall. They had remarked that *they* did not wear their school uniforms in the 'hols'. They attended private schools in the city, as they lived near Charing Cross in a very imposing terrace of red sandstone. The journey through the city made us gasp with wonder, there were coloured lights, and glittering signs above the shops, whose windows were radiant with masses of tinsel, Christmas trees and toys of every description.

Aunt Mary gave each of us a small textbook, and Father presented her with a very large box of chocolates. She had not mentioned her mother's visit to our house; she seemed very worldly, important looking, and extremely charming, so like her brother (my father).

The Circus

Arriving at the circus, we entered a huge tent and looked for our seats. Beatrice did not come with us, but took the opportunity to visit the many and wonderful shops. She was to meet us at the railway station after the show, and what a show it was! Clowns in funny clothes kept tumbling head over heels, knocking their hats off. A tiny dwarf man threw buckets of water, making them slip and fall about. We were in stitches, the three of us; Gina, so happy, was squealing with delight.

A cage was erected inside the tent, six lions came running out. The ring-master, dressed in red and gold breeches and jacket, cracked a long whip. The lions obeyed him, each sitting on a separate stool, all but the last one, he growled and shook his heavy head. I thought I would die with suspense, was it going to eat him? He spoke sharply, and with much whip-cracking, the lion jumped on a stool. After the lions came the horses, resplendent in purple plumes and chiming bells. A dainty girl in a tutu stood on the bare back of a beautiful white horse. She could jump from one horse to another, then all the horses bowed to the audience before they left the ring.

Next came the chimpanzees, they made us laugh helplessly at their antics, they had a tea-party, stealing each other's cake and clapping their hands. A great big elephant came next, we had never seen anything as huge as *that!* It did not look so happy, but we cheered up when the acrobats came, swinging from the roof of the 'Big Top'. We were thrilled and alarmed, sure that one could miss the swinging bars, as they turned and twisted above our heads. Some little dancing poodles enchanted us with their clever tricks. Now the clowns threw custard pies at each other, picked flowers and chickens out of their hats, or the dwarf's trousers. We clapped or booed as we chose.

Soon it was all over, balloons fell from the roof, we managed to catch two, we gave them both to Gina, I don't think I ever saw Gina as happy as she was that day. I gave her a hug, loving her happiness. With burning cheeks, and full of excitement, we talked of all we had seen, all the way to the station. We had to wait for Beatrice to show up, when she did, she was laden with parcels, and complained her feet were killing her!

It was dark when we sailed back, seeing only the twinkling lights on the coast. We caught the last tram home. The house was cold. I helped Father to light up the sitting-room fire, and we were told to go to bed. We heard Father making tea and toast, the smell made us hungry, and he gave us each half a slice, saying he did not know how we could be hungry, having such a good lunch at Aunt Mary's house. Sheer excitement kept us awake, as we talked far into the night about all we had seen. Father had told us we were to tell all our school-friends about our visit to the circus, and we must write out essays, ready to take to school when required.

Two days later we jumped out of bed, it was Christmas morning. We searched round for presents, even in the sitting-room, but there was nothing. We just could not believe it. We comforted ourselves that Father would be giving us a surprise, and talked about the happy Christmas last year with Mama and Hughie. Our new velvet dresses (now soiled and torn), the small gifts of sweets, toys and Christmas crackers. Father rose quite early, he got us up and made Beatrice's tea.

Before he took up the tray, he said he had a present for Mother, we must come up to see her open it! We followed him upstairs, outside their bedroom door was a large box wrapped in gold paper and tied with a large red satin bow. He told us to wait till he called us, and went in with the tray. We were to bring in the box, hand it to her and wish her a 'Happy Christmas'. She was sitting up in bed, eyes smudged, hair all about her on the large lace-trimmed pillows. Smiling to Father, she said, 'What's all this?'

If Father noticed we missed out 'Mother' when we said Happy Christmas, he did not prompt us. He was watching Beatrice open the box, taking something out of many folds of tissue paper. She exclaimed, 'George, just what I wanted!' as she drew a beautiful fox-fur to her, the head so real-looking we drew back from the glittering gaze of its shiny brown eyes. Beatrice was delighted, and hugged and kissed Father. He told us to run downstairs and get on with our wee jobs. We were in a ferment of expectation, surely he had something for us – no one *ever* forgot Christmas!

Father appeared later, dressed and ready to attend the Christmas Day service in church, Beatrice wanted to show off her present. We were not going, we would have breakfast when they returned, and could get on with our darning.

Summoning up al my courage, I asked him if we were getting any Christmas presents. He looked at us with real astonishment.

'You have had a wonderful Christmas, do you know how much it cost to take you to the circus? I am sure none of your friends will have had such a wonderful time. I am really surprised at you, thought you would have been more grateful.'

We hastened to assure him, saying we had always had something in our stockings. 'H'm, if that's all, here are a few sweets,' which tasted of tobacco, but we were quite happy now.

Father had only one day's holiday at Christmas, we dreaded being left alone with Beatrice for the next ten days. She drank a lot of spirits while she sat in the sitting-room, sometimes she was in a good mood, but more often in a vile temper. She bullied and slapped, found the dirtiest jobs for us she could think of, never let us out of the house, or be seen at the front windows. When the washerwoman came, she polished the name-plate and bell, scrubbed the doorstep and cleaned the front windows. We were locked in the spare room upstairs, told not to speak or make any noise. We sat on 'Granny's' bed, wrapped the cover round our legs, and whispered to each other, till the woman left the house. Beatrice had afternoon teas, or visited other's tea-parties, which was fine for us.

The New Year Party

Father made plans, he was really going to celebrate his first New Year at home for *four* years. There was to be a big party on Hogmanay. We spread butter on many slices of bread, Beatrice filled each sandwich with cold meat, tinned salmon, cheese and egg, strange patés and pastes, large fruit cakes were cut in fingers, lots of shortbread and black bun were arranged on patés with lace doyleys. Dozens of glasses were laid out on the kitchen table, now covered with the silk damask table-cloth. Gertie was told to build up the fire in the range. We were allowed to eat up the crusts and fat off the cold meat which were left. We hoped there would be some bits of cake left over the next morning.

Holly branches and mistletoe were hung in the hall. The guests were expected to arrive about 9.00 p.m. We were in bed by 8.00 p.m. and warned severely about peeping out of our bed curtains. Father had bought records of Scottish songs and reels, and the music could be heard all through the house. We heard feet moving round the kitchen table, but dared not look out through the curtains. As midnight struck on the hall clock, we heard glasses being filled, people kissing each other with great hilarity under the mistletoe. The noise grew louder, the hall carpet was lifted and dancing went on there, with many hoochs and skirls, just like the night when Father came home from the war! We heard Beatrice giving one of her dance 'routines', she would be kicking up her legs, and singing 'bawdy' songs.

It was quiet in the kitchen now, I heard strange noises. After the horror of my encounter with the rat, I was acutely aware of furtive sounds. Peeping through the edge of the curtains, I saw father kissing and cuddling a pretty young woman, who was gasping and moaning very softly. Suddenly the door flew open, Beatrice took in the scene at a glance, and jumped on the woman, burying her hands in the woman's hair, knocking her head against the wall, screaming abuse all the time. Father arranged his clothes hurriedly, pulled Beatrice off the poor woman, she turned on him, mouthing the most awful oaths. The young woman fled, shouting to her husband to get her coat and handbag. He just stood in the doorway, wondering what was going on, she herself running upstairs to get her things.

Beatrice broke away from Father, and chased the woman upstairs, and again fought with her. I could hear a man's voice ordering Beatrice to leave off. An avalanche of coats and bags were hurled downstairs, Beatrice locked herself in her room. Father said she had had a drop too much, and helped the guests to pick up their coats, hats and bags. The clock struck 4 a.m. as they left.

Father took one of our blankets, and went to sleep on the sofa in the sitting-room. He did not waken us next morning as usual. We built up the fire, put on the porridge, and started to clear the table, which was covered with empty bottles, half-filled glasses, and remnants of food. We found the remains of a large steak-pie in the oven. Although dried-up, we promptly scraped it out, soaked the dish and ate all we could. The kitchen cleared, we ventured into the sitting-room to clean and light the fire. Father was snoring loudly, his feet sticking out of the blanket, but opened his eyes when we came in. He till had his socks on, only his trousers lay on a chair. Pulling the blanket round him (he wore long salmon-pink woollen drawers), he went off to climb into our bed, and was soon snoring again.

The room was in turmoil, glasses, plates, cutlery, teacups were everywhere. What a feast we had! Half-empty plates of cakes, shortbread and sandwiches, partly open boxes of sweets, chocolates and fruit jellies. We had some of each, not daring to quite empty the boxes. We carried dishes, washed them, eating all the time, listening for either Beatrice or Father waking up. We polished, swept, dusted and arranged the room as it usually was, closed all the boxes, covered the cake and shortbread with table napkins.

We were full of food, and emptied the porridge down the lavatory, washed the pot, and decided to tell Father we did not know whether to make it or not! Father wakened, asked if Mother was down yet, made her tea, and carried the tray upstairs. We listened at the kitchen door, heard Father saying he was so drunk, he thought it was her he was holding in his arms. This mollified her, and when she came downstairs, saw we had worked hard to clear up the room, she made no mention of the food that he been left. Neither of them felt like having breakfast. It was just as well we had stuffed ourselves.

We had no food that day till 6.00 p.m., then only a slice of bread and jam and a half-cup of milk. They did not eat as they were going to another party. Both were a bit subdued that day.

We noticed a distinct falling-off of Beatrice's afternoon tea-parties. We think her bad language and behaviour that night turned a few of her 'friends' against her. She began to drink quite a lot, hiding a bottle in the kitchen, telling us not to dare let Father see it.

We were now forced to scrub out the kitchen on Friday evenings, the range would not be lit on Saturdays. Father said if we worked well we could go to the picture house matinee on Saturday afternoons. This pleased us and we worked as hard as we could on Saturday mornings. Father and Beatrice always shopped on Saturday afternoons, bringing in either meat pies or fish suppers, as Beatrice disliked cooking. Gertie was relieved of the cleaning of the range, and filling the coal-pails, though Father found her something else to do, and I still had the sitting-room fire to attend to.

Spring came, and Father bought two cheap pails and spades. Every afternoon when we came home from school, and before we changed, we were to pick up all the dung from the street, put one spadeful between each rose bush, mark where we left off by sticking the spade at the spot. There were many horses in those days, not many motor vans. That Father had the loveliest roses in the area was no doubt due to this exercise. On Saturday mornings he would hoe and rake with his one good hand, speaking to all who passed, showing his roses with great pride.

After a lunch of bread and dripping we were given a shilling (sixpence for our tram fares, and twopence each for a seat upstairs where we would be among other children from the academy). On no account were we to just pay a penny, and sit among the riff-raff in the stalls. He gave us two boiled sweets each in a piece of paper (they were very sticky). We were thrilled seeing the big screen (black and white) following the adventures of Pearl White, Charlie Chaplin, Jacky Coogan and others. We lived every moment with the actors and actresses, but the serial always finished with the hero or heroine in great danger! The evil face of Doctor Fu Manchu came to me in dreams, and I would shout in my sleep. Gina loved it all, but we had to read out the words to her as they appeared on the screen. We were usually in bed by 7.00 p.m. Father would lock us in before they went out, or if they had company.

Easter holidays came round, we wondered what was in store for us. Beatrice wanted to shop in Glasgow, Father always did what she wanted. He had a long weekend (Good Friday and Easter Monday). We finished school on Thursday, and arrived home to find Beatrice had made a round sweet pudding. Father called it 'Spotted Dick'. We had a slice each for tea, it was full of currants, and very solid. As we ate, Father told us they were going to Glasgow for the weekend. They would take Gina. We were to stay in the kitchen, eat a slice of pudding for each meal. He would not leave any matches, so we could not light the gas, or the fire. We were to be in bed before dark. Gina was now 5 years old, I was 7 years and Gertie 9 years.

To our great surprise he produced a game of Ludo, we had played this game before and were happy to be left at home, though Gina wanted to stay with us. Father promised her a nice new dress, but she would rather have stayed at home. Since Beatrice had thrashed her, and still did on the slightest pretext, she was afraid of her, becoming withdrawn and silent, living in a fantasy world of princesses and pussy-cats. We could hear her whispering to them in bed, or while cleaning the banisters on the stairs, her thin little fingers mechanically pushing the duster in and out through the scroll ironwork.

On Friday morning, Beatrice actually appeared early, dressed to go out. Gina was wearing her sailor dress, now too short for her, and by 8.00 a.m. they had gone to catch the steamer. Father had locked all the doors, we were not to attract attention by showing ourselves at the window, nor answer the door, we could not get to the door, anyway. We were given a list of jobs to be done, were warned that they could come home at any time, so we had better get them done, and we could improve on our homework when we had nothing to do! We would miss our visit to the picture house, that was why we had been given the game of Ludo, also a few coloured pencils and some sheets of plain paper.

Waiting till the front door closed, a few minutes till they should be out of the street, we let out yells, danced round the table, jumped on the bed, on the chairs, and rattled the pot lids. Suddenly we thought, what if they missed the boat! We washed up the dishes, cleaned out the kitchen, dusting and sweeping, not till all was clean and tidy, did we bring out the Ludo. It was a relief not to have Gina, she had to be shielded from Beatrice's anger, and we had to coax her to do her 'wee jobs'. She would be thrashed if they were not done, and often we would fit her work into ours.

At lunch-time (we knew it was one o'clock by the chime of the hall clock) we drank half a cup of milk and ate one slice of the pudding. We cleaned the cutlery, cut up toilet squares from newspapers, had another slice of pudding, and then another, till it was finished. Feeling happy and satisfied, we were in bed by 8.00 p.m. I liked sleeping in Gina's place at the top of the bed with Gertie. We talked and sang, told stories and made up guessing games. Alas, through the night, I knew I was going to be sick, the pudding lay heavy on my stomach.

Waking Gertie, we crossed the floor together to the sink, in pitch darkness, I would not go myself, still terrified I would meet another rat. After I threw up, Gertie was sick too, we sat on chairs till we shivered with cold, then crawled back into bed. Next morning we hurried to clean up the mess, which did not take long, and we jumped into bed again, having a wonderful lazy morning. When the clock struck midday, we rose, drank a little milk, but did not feel like eating.

We played Ludo, or drew little 'party' dresses to fit on the form of a 'cut-out' figure which I drew. We coloured the dresses in the brightest colours we had. I think the drab, grey kitchen in which we lived and slept made us appreciate colour and light. I could never get enough, and would take a chair to the window. By standing on it, I could see the blue sky and white clouds, envying the lucky children out there in the beautiful world. We finished the milk, but still could not eat, feeling the effects of our greed.

We began to get a little fearful, imagining footsteps in the empty rooms, huddling close together and actually wishing we could hear Beatrice playing her records. Sunday passed, we heard people talking as they went to church, but could not see them, as the kitchen window only looked out on a dark wall at the side of the house. It was heavily barred and no matter how we tried, we could not open it. It must have been nailed down, even if we had been able to open it, we could not have got through the bars, though we worked it out that, being so thin, I could have gone through sideways.

The silence was now frightening. We clung together in bed, listening, unable to help ourselves, having exhausted everything. Monday morning came as a relief, we cleaned, tidied and scrubbed with cold water, everything spotless, hoping they would come home early. We had a slice of bread left after our breakfast of water, bread and dripping, the milk was finished. We played Ludo rather aimlessly, studied our school books, just waiting for the sound of the key turning in the lock of the front door. We combed our hair a dozen times, wearing our old velvet frocks, now sadly washed out, the lace collars torn off, and most of the buttons missing, but we felt that by wearing them we still had a link with our dear Mama.

Night came, no sign of them, once or twice someone had knocked at the door, and the milk-man hung a can of milk on the handle, but, of course, we could not reach it. We waited up till it grew very dark, and we knew there would be no boats arriving at the pier. We became really fearful, what if something had happened to them? What if we were left to die here, locked up without food, and if we died, would the rats eat us, maybe even if we were not quite dead?

Tuesday morning, we often cried, but in the afternoon, with great relief, we heard the key in the lock. Beatrice unlocked the kitchen door, we stood staring at them. Gina was wearing a pretty print dress and carried a large doll. Beatrice said they had missed the last boat on Monday evening, and that Father had gone straight to his office. Gina told us that Beatrice wanted to see a show, they had not even tried to catch the last boat. They had stayed in a hotel, and a maid had kept an eye on Gina. Beatrice had bought the doll for her 'to keep her company', she said. We had been locked in that kitchen for nearly four days, yet all Father said, when he came home, was that he hoped we had 'behaved' ourselves.

We now worked in the garden for long periods, each of us having a piece of ground to keep clear of weeds. Beatrice started taking Gina out with her (we had her work added to ours), dressing her up, having bought her quite a few outfits. When we were given old magazines to cut up for toilet paper we would hide the 'exciting' love stories under our pillows to read at night, as it as now daylight till nearly 9.00 p.m

We were happy that Beatrice was treating Gina better but it did not last long. Gina was happily occupied one day, taking the clothes off the doll. Beatrice came in, saw the clothes on the floor, ripped the doll from the now trembling girl, and sent her sprawling with such force that she cut her head on the steel fender. She marched out of the kitchen (with the clothes and the doll). We picked Gina off the floor, washed the blood off her forehead, and tried to comfort her. She was never given the doll to play with again, but when visitors came, Gina would be dressed up, put into the sitting-room and given the doll to hold, all to impress her friends.

A little girl came with one of the friends, Beatrice did not like children running about, and did not encourage the mothers to bring them, but there must have been a reason for this child's appearance. Gina was told to play with her in the sitting-room. The child dragged the doll from Gina, refusing to part with it. Gina had not owned anything of her very own since Kiki, and tried to get the doll back. The little girl refused, and started to cry. Beatrice said she must let the child have it, whereupon Gina, getting hold of the doll, smashed it on the floor.

The kitchen door flew open, Beatrice, eyes blazing, threw Gina inside. 'Ungrateful brat, just you wait,' she hissed, and turned back into the sitting-room. Gina was shaking with fear, how could we save her? Gertie and I planned to distract Beatrice's attention when she started on Gina. No sooner had her visitors gone, then Beatrice made straight for the cowering Gina, and began slapping her relentlessly. We both jumped at the same time, grabbed those fat, flailing arms, and held on tightly. She was powerless to hit us with her hands, but took us completely by surprise by running us into the wall, her hefty bulk wedging Gertie's head and face against the cupboards.

Gertie struggled free and we ran round the table. Beatrice, unable to catch us (too tightly corseted to run) walked out, 'Wait till your Father hears about this, she flung back.

Poor Gina, she stared at the door, expecting Beatrice to return, her eyes dilated with terror, the red marks on her face showing up her white face. When Father came home, Beatrice told him that Gina had humiliated her, fighting with her friend's daughter, and smashing the doll in a fit of temper, these two 'bastards' had attacked her, and what was he going to do about it?

She flounced out, he asked us what happened. He looked quite worried about Gina, she could not speak, just sat staring at the door. He said maybe we were right to stop Mother, though he could not understand why Gina should want to break her beautiful doll. Gina ignored the doll completely, it had not broken, but had a crack round its neck. Beatrice dressed it up, and sat it on one of her little tables, would explain to her ladies about the pretty doll she had bought for her stepdaughter and would sigh as though Gina was a great burden to her.

About this time, Gertie complained of a sore neck. Father wrapped a clean sock round it, but the swelling grew larger. Eventually he took her to the doctor, who gave her black ointment and a bandage. She was to apply the ointment every day, keep the bandage over the swelling, which would reach a certain stage, when the gland would have to be lanced.

When that day came, a nurse and Father had to hold her steady, it was very painful and she came home in tears, (no anaesthetic was given for 'minor' operations then). She visited the doctor's surgery every week to have it dressed, but what with the soot, coal and ashes from the range, the bandage got very dirty. Beatrice had to take her to have it dressed. She disliked the dirty bandage, and forced Gertie's head into the sink to wash her neck with strong soap, having ripped the bandage from her neck, blood and matter oozing out of the wound. Gertie was crying loudly, and twisting herself away from Beatrice, who threw me a clean bandage, and told me to get the filthy brat's neck cleaned up.

I would put the ointment and bandage on as gently as I could, but we both knew the blood would make it stick. However, the nurse was gentle, and when the doctor asked why the first bandage had been removed, Beatrice said we had been fighting, that I had torn it off. She said the same to Father. Father was very cross with me, but Gertie told him the truth. He only said, 'What am I going to do with you?' It was a year before Gertie's neck healed, having to be lanced twice again. What she suffered with every fresh infection impaired her health, she looked so ill even Father noticed.

He now sported a fine, tweed sports suit with breeches (plus fours) and took to playing golf on Saturday afternoons, sometimes in the evenings too. This so infuriated Beatrice who hated being on her own, especially on Saturdays, that she picked up the new golf clubs, smashed them in two, and packed the fire with them, before burning them. He gave up golf, but sported the new suit at weekends, only changing for church. We did not attend church so often now, Beatrice preferred to lie in bed on Sunday mornings. Father would read his Sunday papers or work in the garden.

At the end of our first year at the academy, Gertie and I walked out with an armful of prizes. Father, beaming to all around him, embarrassed us by showing everyone near him our books. Beatrice never visited the school, only coming with Father on Sports Day. He expected us to be first in everything, and I know I made every effort to win. Gertie and Gina did just as well, and at sports I could outrun the rest. I know now it was fear of disappointing Father that made us try so hard.

The Farm

Now that school had closed for summer, Father announced he was about to let our house for two months to a doctor and his family. We would be sent to a place called Craigberach Farm, on the island, while Beatrice and he visited her people in America. As he only had three week's holiday time, he would take lodgings in the town, till the summer boarders had gone.

We knew a farm would have a lot of animals, but were apprehensive about the owners; farmers were known to be very gruff and did not like children 'messing' about. Father said it would be good for us, especially Gertie, whose neck still pained her, she looked dispirited and ill.

The following week was a flurry of changing round furniture and beds. The boarders had a maid, who would sleep in our kitchen bed. We had to hang curtains, clean carpets and even paint, under Beatrice's watchful eyes. Father had picked up some carpets cheap (about 4 yards square). Gertie and I beat them outside, the dust choking us, then they were laid out on the kitchen floor, to be scrubbed with special soap, till our arms, knees and backs ached, even Gina had to have cloths wrung out of clean water for her, to rub on the piece we had just scrubbed.

Beatrice locked away her records and gramophone, her pretty things from the bathroom and bedroom. She visited a second-hand shop in the town and came back with three faded print dresses for us to wear at the farm, even packing our velvet 'rags' to change with them (our uniforms were to be sent to the cleaners). She said farms were dirty places, anyway, we could run in our bare feet, but were allowed to take our canvas gym shoes.

At midday a high-sided hay cart stopped at the gate, driven by

Jimmy, a ruddy-cheeked lad of sixteen years. He jumped down, put our trunk inside, then lifted us inside. Father told us to behave, to wave goodbye to 'Mother', who was standing inside the sitting-room window, looking very pleased to see us go. At the last moment Father ran out with the box of black ointment for Gertie's sore neck, and some bandages, telling me to see she used it, and he would visit us when he returned from holiday.

Dobbin was the horse's name and with a, 'Come on, Dobbin,' from Jimmy, we trotted out of sight of Father's waving hand. It was a lovely day, we passed through narrow lanes edged with sweet-smelling hawthorn hedges, and wild pink roses. At the sides of the lane, pinks, poppies, daisies, buttercups and honeysuckle grew in abundance. Men and horses toiled in the fields and Jimmy pointed out places of interest.

We arrived at a long, low, red-roofed farmhouse, surrounded by numerous outhouses and barns. Hens strutted about the wide yard, an old dog lay across the doorstep, while another came running to meet Jimmy, who said her name was Meg, she was about to have pups. The other dog was Duke. A third dog, Bess was out with the farmer. The door opened, a stout rosy-faced woman shooed Duke off the doorstep. Jimmy lifted us down, saying we weighed 'no more than a hen'!

The woman who greeted us with a wide smile of welcome, said, 'Come away in bairnies, you look as if you could do with some good feeding and our fresh air.' She ushered us into a large sweet-smelling kitchen, and told the two women there who we were, introducing us as the young ladies from the academy.

They wore large white aprons and caps (dolly caps) with a little frill round them. She said one was Kate, the other Rose, and everyone called her Jean, even though she was the farmer's wife. They sat us down to a large glass of fresh warm milk, and laid plates of scones and pancakes, with butter and jam spread over them. How it reminded me of our Sunday visits to dear Granny!

When we had eaten our fill, we followed Jean up a narrow wooden stairway, into a low-ceilinged bedroom. Three narrow beds were lined up on one side of the wall, where the eaves seemed to drop very low. They were covered in pretty, patchwork bed-covers. A marble wash-hand stand, with basin and jug in a pretty design of birds and flowers stood on a marble slab. A rail had three thick white towels hanging from it. There were shelves to hold our clothes, they also held books and photographs.

We were enthralled by the warmth and, to us, luxury. Soft mats lay on the polished wood floor, their bright colours matching those of the curtains. When Jean turned down the beds, we saw with delight that they had white sheets and pillows. She explained the photographs were of her three sons, one of whom had been killed in the war. It was through the business of paying this son's war pension that Father had become friendly with them. The other two sons were married, and lived in cottages nearby. This had been their bedroom when they were on the farm, but it had been empty for a while now. Jimmy was her grandson.

We were anxious to go outside, where we met Farmer and Bess. He showed us round the byre, holding Gina up on the high bars of the gates to see the cows, and the grunting sow with many piglets. The cows were lined up for milking; Kate, Rose and Jimmy doing the milking, sitting on little three-legged stools. We had to force ourselves away to see the tiny, yellow, fluffy chickens in the hen-hose, Gina almost beside herself in ecstasy. Two goats were tethered near the house, one had a long beard, There were horses in the stable, Farmer said he would tell us their names, but after the milking when we would be having dinner.

What a dinner! So much we could hardly eat for admiring and wanting to taste everything. Steaming bowls of soup, followed by great plates of meat and vegetables, floury potatoes in their skins, sauces and pickles, home-made bread and farm butter. Pies of all kinds, apple, raspberry, rhubarb served with lashings of thick cream. Ten of us sat at the table, Farmer, Jean, Rose, Kate, the two sons, Jimmy and ourselves. Farmer said, we, 'ate no more'n a sparrow', and indeed we had difficulty tasting everything. We did manage to eat a tiny piece of chocolate cake.

We offered to wash and dry the dishes, but Jean gave her great hearty laugh, and chased us outdoors to see the calves being fed. We laughed at the calves sticking their heads right inside the pails, and we all leaned over the gate to stroke their hard boney heads. In a small pond some ducks were cackling, they had baby ducklings, who struggled valiantly to keep up with their mothers, cheeping furiously. All too soon we were tucked up in bed, Jean giving each of us a great smacking kiss. It was so long since we had had that kind of attention that I said, 'Let us thank God for sending us to this farm and these kind people.'

Each day that followed was a source of wonder and delight, Gina changed remarkably, running with the dogs, watching the chickens and ducklings. All of us developed sharper appetites, doing justice to the splendid food, which seemed to be of limitless abundance. A few days after we arrived, Meg had six puppies, all black and white like herself. One was smaller than the others, Gina claimed it for her own, and named it Craigie. At first Meg would growl when we went near her, but in a week's time, she would leave them to go out with Farmer. Then we would cuddle and play with them. Jean said we could think of names for them, but four would be sold, they would only keep one, and we could take Craigie home with us.

The farm was noisy in the morning, cows mooed, calves called, cocks crowed, and the rattle of milk-pails and churns being loaded on the milk carts, had us up early and eager to join in the activity. Our first delicious strawberry out of the field was gathered at 5.00 a.m. A crowd of school children appeared then, and we ran to join them, helping to fill baskets and trying not to eat too many. farmer said 'too many 'ud bring out spots,' so he would know who was stealing them, but he laughed as he said this, though we believed him. The raspberry-picking followed the strawberries, then red and black currants. Big yellow gooseberries were not so easy to pick as they had very sharp thorns, though the rich sweet taste of them tempted us sorely.

The kitchen filled with the smell of boiling jam, great 7lb jars made of earthenware were filled, left to cool, then covered with muslin tied over the wide tops. The jam was 2/- (two shillings), with 6d (sixpence) deposit on the jar. We were left to do just what we wanted, there were no restrictions, except one where we were forbidden to visit the field where the big black bull was kept. His name was Kaiser Bill, he did not like anyone (said Farmer) and looking at his wicked little red eyes we could well believe him. He would snort and paw the ground, and we darted away in fright!

I loved watching the horses, the great 'shires' as they ploughed the fields, so strong and patient. In a field close by were some 'carriage' horses. One in particular I made friends with, he was young, very lively, with a shiny coat and tossing mane. His name was Prince, and I would stand on the gate stroking his face and neck, feeding him with fresh grass from the road-side. He would come running when I called his name, Kate gave me sugar lumps to feed him with, and he would nuzzle into me as I sat on the top bar of the gate.

I told Gertie I was sure he was friendly enough to let me ride on his back, but she thought it would be dangerous. However, I persevered, and one day I put my leg over his back, keeping my hold on the gate. He looked round mildly, so I slipped right on his back and said, 'Come on, Prince.'

He stood very still, Gertie's hand to her mouth, saying, 'Don't Minnie, he's never been ridden.'

Even as she spoke, Prince gave a kind of shudder, then ran off with me clinging to his mane. He ran round in a circle, put his head down, and I sprawled right over his head into a bed of nettles.

Wondering which was worse, the fall or the stings, I forgot both when I saw Prince galloping straight at me. I made a bee-line for the gate, scrambling over as he stopped sideways at the gate, kicking up his back legs. Jimmy had seen what happened and came running. 'You should na' hae done that, he might 'a broke your neck!'

He pulled me into the farm kitchen. Kate sent Gertie to pick dock leaves and she rubbed my blistered arms and legs. Jean, although concerned, was quite worried saying, 'I was not to try that again, what would your parents have said if you's broke a leg or arm when I am supposed to be looking after you?' I still went every day to feed and stroke Prince, but I would not have had Jean troubled for all the world.

Kate or Rose bathed and washed our hair so gently, enveloping us in soft towels. Jean did not put the ointment on Gertie's neck, but said the sun and fresh air would heal the wound much quicker. She cut Gertie's hair shorter so that none would stick to her neck, in a few days a scab had formed. She told Gertie not to knock it off when washing, it would fall off when new skin had formed underneath.

Time just flew, we dreaded the day Father would visit us. Jean got a letter from him saying they would come on Sunday. We inquired anxiously if were were going home, and were happy to hear we had another three weeks before school began, what we did not know was that she had asked Father to let us stay longer, and he would not have to pay any more. We were tanned, rosy-cheeked and full of energy, but Gina's was the greatest change. She had 'literally' blossomed, her cheeks pink and rounder, her yellow curls bleached by the sun, as she laughed, sang and played with Craigie. Jean said she was a little princess, but we told her our Mama had called her 'Angel'. Having no girls of her own, Jean took a motherly interest in us; I think she would have liked to keep Gina.

Father and Beatrice arrived on Sunday stepping from a small local bus, which took the children to school. We could seen them from the farm, each of them carrying baskets. Jean and Farmer said we should run along to meet them, we did not want to go, and Gina clung to Jean's apron, hiding her face. No amount of persuasion would induce her to move, so Gertie and I ran down the road. Father was very pleased at our much-improved appearance, though Beatrice just sniffed and handed us her basket. They were to buy some eggs as they would be cheaper at the farm.

When Beatrice met them, she was all sweetness and charm, to the farm folk. After tea and cakes, she said we should show her our bedroom. Once there, she produced our sewing aprons (lap-bags) which we had made at school, they had two very large pockets. She ordered us to put all the eggs we could find in them, and put the bags under the hedge near the bus stop, even showing us how to tie the lap-bags under our dresses. We tried to say no, saying we were frightened to steal, but she said, 'Don't come home without them.' We were to gather a few every day, hide them, then collect them nearer the time of their next visit. Gina had not come upstairs with us (she avoided Beatrice as much as she could) and we were to tell her.

Once downstairs, Beatrice praised the pretty bedroom, and actually looked concerned about the sore on Gertie's neck, though it looked cleaner and healthier. Father took us all down to the bus stop, asking us a lot of questions. Beatrice pointed to a thick bush, and drew Gertie's and my attention to it, whispering it would be a good hiding place for the stolen eggs. We waited till they went off in the bus, then scampered, danced and shouted all the way back to the farm. How we wished we did not need to go home at all.

Now Craigie was running with us, he tired easily, and we would argue who should carry him. We had shown him to Father, who did not seem very pleased. But when the Farmer said he was ours, Father pretended to be quite overwhelmed with such generosity, saying, 'What lucky girls you are.'

Hay-making and harvest came round; what fun we had! We carried jugs of 'barley bree' to the men and women in the fields, who followed the cutting machine, tying the hay in large bundles, and forking them on to haycarts. We would help Jean to make the barley bree, by cutting up about twenty lemons, into quarters. The barley was soaked in fresh spring water, in barrels, the lemons thrown in, the whole stirred briskly every time we filled the jugs. All would empty a jug at a time, and we would drink some too when we felt hot and thirsty. One woman said it tasted 'like nectar from the gods.'

The day before we were due to leave, Gertie and I slipped down to the hiding place, and left our bags full of eggs. We hated doing it, but it was more important to please Beatrice. That last night we said another prayer, asking God to forgive us, and let us come back to the farm next year. I lay in the field next morning, drinking in the sweet smell of new-mown hay, listening to the sounds of the many insects and birds around me. I was about to leave this paradise and my heart was heavy.

We were ready and waiting for Father when he arrived by himself. With many hugs (and some tears from Gina) we took leave of these kind people. Even Farmer said, 'am I not to get a wee 'cheeper' [kiss]?' We kissed him too, Father looking on rather impatiently. He had brought two large baskets and Jean filled them to capacity. As Father was very profuse in his thanks, we thought she did not charge him for the contents.

Gina led Craigie on a piece of rope, blowing kisses and waving till we were out of sight. Reaching the hedge, we lifted the bags of eggs very carefully placing them in one of the baskets. Father stripped a cabbage, and put the leaves on top. We never knew if they found out, but I was sad that we had so badly returned their great kindness to us.

Craigie

Once home, the eggs were counted, there were about six dozen, but we had also picked some 'wally' ones. These were clay, white-glazed egg shapes, and when put in the hen-house, the hens were induced to lay eggs beside them.

Father had tied Craigie to the door of the old summer-house, saying he must never come into the house, not even the kitchen. He barked and whined to be free, and Gina gave him water out of a tin can. We asked for food for him, only to be told we would just have to give him some of ours. We saved our crusts, and some vegetables out of the soup, wrapping them in a newspaper. He jumped for joy when we gave him the food, straining and biting at the rope, whining pitifully when we had to leave him. Beatrice said dogs were dirty, smelly animals and if we let him indoors, she would have him destroyed.

All that night we heard Craigie barking and whining, but we were powerless, as Father always put the back-door key in his pocket when he locked up.

We returned to school on Monday, even the headmistress remarked on how healthy looking we all were. Our first objective was to beg scraps for Craigie, managing to fill a bag with pieces of cake, sandwiches and biscuits, tempted to 'nibble' some of the 'choicer' scraps ourselves. Reaching home, we ran straight in the front door, through the kitchen and into the garden. How joyfully Craigie greeted us, his eyes shining, his tail beating the ground. He gobbled up every morsel, we untied the rope, and he raced off round the house, getting among the roses.

Beatrice knocked sharply on the window, making signs to get him out of there. We hastily tied him up, hurried into the kitchen to find

Beatrice standing there looking very angry. She told us to get changed, the kitchen was filthy, the boarder's maid had not cleaned it properly for two months, and we had no time to waste on that stupid mongrel! When Father came in, she complained that we had played with the dog, instead of getting our work done. The entire evening was spent cleaning, scrubbing and polishing, not even having time to examine our new school books. We should have had them covered with brown paper, and each of us received a stroke of the belt for not having done so.

Next evening we had to turn out the sittingroom, clean the bathroom under Beatrice's wrathful gaze, forcing us to work till darkness came down, again having no opportunity to cover our schoolbooks. We told Father we would be punished again, so he wrote a note to teacher saying he would buy brown paper, that was the reason the books were not covered (he said). Beatrice saw to it that we did not go near the poor dog, who whined when he heard us moving about, keeping us working inside the house.

Father brought paper that evening, but Beatrice said that the books were a waste of money, and refused to let us bring them out, or look at them. Father had ordered us to have them done by the time he got home, so between jobs we brought our books out, and started to cut the shape to fit each book. Beatrice's friends had just gone, when she came in with a tray, demanding the dishes washed immediately. Telling her that Father had said we must have them covered before he came home, she said, 'Bloody books, I'll show him,' and lifting my new history book off the table, she threw it into the fire.

I jumped up, put my arm out to catch it, but the book landed in the fire, Beatrice's clenched fist came down on my outstretched arm, pinning my elbow to the hot bar. I screamed in agony, the pain was cruel, the smell of burning cloth and flesh was in my nostrils. Holding my arm, I fell backwards against the table. Beatrice shouted, 'Serves you right, stupid books, what right has he to spend good money on them?' Forcing me to get on with my work, she watched as I tried to with only one hand, but made me use the other by slapping the burnt elbow.

It seemed ages before Father came, to be told we had been fighting, that I had thrown my book in the fire, tripped over the fender and burnt my arm, He replied, 'Why can't you behave like other children?' I was in too much pain to answer, Father cut off what was left of my sleeve, and ran cold water over the burnt elbow. He had to take me to have it dressed, the doctor said I was to attend the surgery twice a week. Father repeated what Beatrice had said about us fighting, and the Doctor tut-tutted, saying that it was the kind of thing that happens to 'naughty' children.

That Father should believe Beatrice was quite beyond my comprehension! We *never* fought each other, our efforts to pacify our parents controlled every moment we were in the house. As visits to the surgery cost money in those days, Father dressed my arm himself. It was very painful, throbbed all night and gradually got worse. A week later I was sick with pain and had a temperature. The doctor was very cross with Father, and said he would send a nurse in every day to dress it. Beatrice said she would have none of that, I could go to the surgery after school, and get a later tram home.

All this time poor Craigie had been tied up, he only flicked his tail slightly when we fed him the scraps. He must have been starving; he was so thin. Scrabbling in the mud, he was dirty and his once shining coat was dull and lank. He had been with us for two weeks, and tied up since the first day. One Saturday morning the parents were out shopping, Gertie and I took off his rope, his legs were so weak he fell over, but regaining his freedom, he found new strength and ran wobbly round the garden.

We heard our parents coming to the gate, and made a grab at him, but sensing he would be tied up again, he darted off to the front of the house. To our great dismay, he fled into the house, the doors to the hall and sitting room had just been opened, he ran in, leaving dirty, muddy footmarks on the cream carpet. Beatrice screamed, Father swore, the terrified dog made for the door, but did not reach it in time. Father lifted his foot, kicked the poor animal outside, then booted him all the way to the summerhouse. Beatrice flew at us, slapping screeching all the names she could think of.

We fetched hot water, and had to clean every mark off the carpets and floor and were punished for letting that 'filthy mongrel' loose. I was locked in the coal cellar, Gertie in the dark lavatory, and poor Gina in the empty bedroom. We were to be kept there all afternoon, there would be no visits to the matinee either that day, or for the next four weeks.

In the cellar, I listened for Craigie, but all was silent. By standing on the coal, I could see through the top of the door. The wood was pretty rotten, and there were gaps. My arm ached under the bandages, Beatrice's hefty slaps were usually direct on to our most painful and vulnerable areas.

A Shaft of Sunlight

The cellar was damp and very cold, a few spiders and beetles lived there, but I was not so afraid of them as I was of rats. Sitting miserably on the coal, I felt the heat of a ray of sun which shone through a gap. I spread out my hands, and held them in the light, bringing back the memory of sunny days at the farm. Closing my eyes, I went through each happy day, shutting out the awful present. I am sure that shaft of sunlight saved my sanity at this time. I must have fallen asleep or was in such deep reverie, that I was roused by a key being turned in the lock. Gertie stood there, said we had to fill the pails, and were to get no dinner. Gina had been screaming to get out of the dark bedroom. Father thrashed her, and threw her into bed. We had been locked up for five hours; Beatrice said we could 'rot' for all she cared!

Next morning, whenever we got the back door open, we ran to Craigie. He did not move, or wag his tail. My heart nearly stopped! I had seen Farmer with dead hares and rabbits looking just like that.

Gertie said, 'I think he is dead.'

Poor Gina, she cuddled that poor, frail, starved and battered little creature in her arms, trying to make him respond.

Father came to look for us, pulled Gina away, said, 'Good riddance,' telling us to get on with our work. We could not stop crying, the tears falling in to our porridge. Father got really angry, said it was our own fault for bringing him from the farm, and we could help bury him, when he came home next evening. We were not to near him, and as they were having friends that evening, he did not want to change his clothes.

Poor Gina sobbed most of the night, looking quite ill next morning. Father said she could stay at home, but fear of being left alone with

Beatrice made her dress herself shakily. We were a subdued trio in the tram that morning. The whole enormity of Craigie's death began to overwhelm me, and in the middle of a lesson, I broke into uncontrollable sobbing. Nothing the teacher could do or say had any effect on me. I was sent to the sickroom, Gertie was called out of her classroom. She told them about Craigie's death.

The headmistress was kinder than I expected, saying that maybe it was better for him to die, than to be tied up for such long periods. This I had not thought of, and managed to get through the rest of the day much as usual, and without having to search for scraps. Beatrice was waiting on the doorstep when we arrived home, forbidding us to look at Craigie. She locked the back door, the coal-pails could be filled when Father came home. We worked in silence, which seemed to make her very angry. She started to hit us with a wooden spoon, and wished we were as dead as the 'dirty mongrel'. Utterly dejected, Gina took on the blank stare we had come to know. She rubbed at the steel fender, but we knew she had retreated into her 'fantasy' world.

After our meal, Father announced we had better get rid of 'the beast'. We followed him out, each carrying a shovel or spade. He dug a large hole, told us to lift the dog, throw him in, and left us to fill in the tiny grave with our spade and shovel. When he went off to read his newspapers, we let our tears flow again, and I promised Gina I would write a farewell note, put it in one of Father's tobacco tins, and bury it with him, which we managed to do next morning:

To Craigie, who died 15-9-1920

Craigie now lies still and cold,
Dead, yet not three months old,
Eyes, like windows of an empty house,
That used to shine with eager welcoming.

My tears fall like drenching rain,
But do not ease the cruel pain
within my heart.

I wish that I could die,
In spirit then we both would fly,
Back to the barn, so sweet and warm,
Your joyful bark, our happy laughter,
Such memories can never die.

I will not love a pet again,

Could not face this parting pain,
Our love for you was all in vain
But we gave it all to you, Dear Craigie.

Our uniforms had been cleaned when we were on holiday, but
our beautifully polished 'brogue' shoes were now too small. Father
was dumbfounded, 'I buy you the very best shoes, and you can't
wear them!' He had so little experience and real interest in children
that it showed up in many ways. We were supplied at school with
canvas shoes (the cost of which must have been included in the
school fees). These were to be worn at all times inside the school to
preserve the polished oak floor in the assembly hall, and to cut
down on noise. We crushed our feet into our shoes to go out in the
morning, but when Father left the tram to go to the office, we
immediately changed into our canvas shoes with great relief. We
did not wear our brogues again till next morning.

Now our parents were having fierce arguments about money.
They had been living well above Father's income. Father's 'war'
money had gone, bills were not being paid, and he said we would
have to cut down. Beatrice demanded he should send us to the local
school, but Father would not hear of it. She threatened to burn
every school book she saw. Now we could not do our homework,
so Father got us up half and hour earlier, about 6.00 a.m., when
Beatrice was safely in bed.

Ornaments began to disappear, Beatrice maintaining we broke
them, but when the silver service disappeared she had to admit she
had pawned it. Father threatened to give her no more money, he
would pay the bills himself in future. He handed her a few pounds
for herself, but she demanded her housekeeping money, throwing
the notes on the floor. Father picked up the money, laid it on a
small table, but she grabbed it and tossed the lot onto the fire,
telling Father what he could do with his 'pittance'. Father's rage
was terrible, he pulled Beatrice by her hair, and slapped her with
his good hand. She fought to free herself, but he dragged her round
to the fire, saying he would put her hair where the money went!

We stared in silence, afraid to draw their anger on ourselves.
Beatrice tore herself free, dashed upstairs and locked herself in her
bedroom. Father put on his coat, hat and gloves and left the house.
We worked hard, hoping to please Beatrice. She came to the top of
the stairs, and asked us where Father was. We told her he had gone

out. Beatrice left shortly after, carrying her fox-fur in a paper bag; it looked as though she was going to sell it.

We were alone, and without food. All the cupboards in the chiffonier were locked, and we hunted for the key. Her bedroom was locked too. The coalman came, and was not paid, he told us he would not leave any more till the account was settled. The milkman did likewise, but at least he left milk, so we had half a cup each. We were worried should Father not come home after that fearful row. However he turned up with fish and chips, and as Beatrice was not there, he divided her share between us.

He could not get into the cupboards either, for sugar, tea, butter and so on. So we just had water, and no bread. Father did not say where he had gone, but was more talkative about Craigie's death. He told neighbours the dog died of distemper, we did not know what that meant, but whatever it, it was certainly not that which killed Craigie. We did not blame him entirely, it was Beatrice's screeching that had made him lose his temper and vent his anger on the poor dog. I asked him what America was like, he had not mentioned their holiday. He said it was fine, then changed the subject. Gertie did not think they had gone very far. We had seen a large bed in the empty front room and a pile of clothes belonging to Beatrice.

Beatrice returned very late (we were in bed) Listening intently, we only heard the murmur of their voices. We did not go to church that Sunday, Beatrice stayed in her room, and we helped Father most of the day in the garden, cleaning up for winter. It was now October, Father said the auditors were coming, so he would be working late at the office. We were to 'behave' ourselves and not provoke Mother! He seemed to believe everything she said about us. We were too frightened of her temper to provoke her at any time, or in any way. I pleaded with him to come home as quickly as possible, we were frightened when he was not there. He just laughed and said Beatrice would not 'dare' hurt us! He did not come home till the last tram left Rothesay, about 10.00 p.m., once he came home in a cab at midnight. Beatrice accused him of having another woman. She locked him out of her bedroom, after a furious quarrel. He slept on the sofa, and sometimes we were late when he overslept.

After our soup one evening, Beatrice went out, saying she would catch the rotten 'bastard' with his fancy woman. Apparently she had gone to his office, found it closed, and looked for him in a nearby restaurant, where she found him having a meal with a young woman. Beatrice had created such a scene that the girl fled, and Father was asked to remove both himself and his wife. He brought her home in a cab. She was crying when she came in, he telling her that he had given the girl a meal as they had been working together till late at the office. The following week he came home as usual, but after many arguments about money, he started to stay out late again.

The Bathroom Episode

After one particularly violent row Beatrice threatened to kill the 'bloody brats' if he left her with them, unless he promised to take her out on Friday evening. She was now drinking heavily, hiding the empty bottles in the kitchen cupboards. He did not come home that Friday night.

Beatrice drove herself into a frenzy, suddenly said to us, 'You are a dirty-looking lot, get undressed, and go to the bathroom.' We froze with sheer terror, watching her remove all her pretty things. Once in the bathroom we were pushed into the empty bath, the cold water was turned on and splashed on our shivering bodies.

We struggled to climb out, but Beatrice kept pushing us in, laughing like a maniac. Gertie managed to get out, Beatrice cornered her, catching her across her shoulders, with a stair rod, after which she lost all control, hitting us all. Gina had slipped so far into the cold water, I thought she would drown, her lips were blue, the rod had caught her across the chest and forehead.

I dodged about, but could not escape. Gertie jumped on Beatrice's arm as the rod descended once more on my bare back. Beatrice dropped the rod, grabbed Gertie by the hair, and forced her head down the lavatory pan, pulling the chain. Gertie's head came up, she was gasping for breath, but Beatrice, using both hands, forced her head into the bowl, blood spurted out, the sight of which galvanised me into action.

I pulled the plug out of the bath, turned off the tap, lifted the rod and literally fell downstairs, out through the front door into the street. Stark-naked, I felt nothing but desperation to get help, the house facing me was lit up, and I banged the door-knocker, using both hands, never stopping. An angry-looking woman opened the door, but when she saw my naked body, she drew me inside. I caught her arm, 'Come quick, come quick, she is killing my sister,' repeating my plea over and over.

Two men hurried out, the woman put a jacket on me, but I ran outside begging them to 'come quick'. I dashed upstairs, looking back to see the two men and the woman following me, and made straight for the bathroom. What a sight! Gertie was lying in a pool of blood, her face swollen, the rod marks scarlet on her white skin. Gina was staring at the wall, red weals over her face and head. Cradling Gertie's head in my arms (she was moaning piteously), I heard her say, 'Let me die, I want to die.'

One of the men was sent get blankets out of the kitchen bed; the other to get help. There was no sign of Beatrice, she must have locked herself in her bedroom. An ambulance came, they wrapped up poor Gina, her eyes still wide-open and staring, and she was carried downstairs. A doctor was examining Gertie; her eyes were closed, her face a horrible mess. As they carried her out, I picked up my clothes, wanting to go with them. The woman took my arm, said we would go to her house, as I would have to talk to the police.

Sitting at the fire, sipping cocoa, I was too distressed to take in my surroundings. Would Gertie and Gina die? Two policemen arrived, by which time I had dressed myself, and given the woman her jacket. I thanked her, and saw she had tears in her eyes. The policeman took me home, and to my great astonishment there stood Beatrice, her make-up fresh, and wearing a new dress.

She looked puzzled, and smiling, 'Why Officer, what ever is the matter? I have just come in and the children are not here!' Then she looked at me, saying, 'I hope you have not been fighting again?' The men listened gravely, while Beatrice told them she was our stepmother, we would do anything to discredit her with Father, we were wicked, deceitful children. 'God knows I have tried to be a good mother to them.' She sighed deeply and dabbed her eyes carefully with a lace handkerchief.

The men looked at me doubtfully. I could sense, like Father, they were going to believe her awful lies. She sent me to put the kettle on, and they talked for a long time. I was glad when Father arrived, yet apprehensive. When told two of his girls were in hospital, he turned to go out again, but I caught his arm, and refused to be left at home. Beatrice, showing great concern, put on her pretty fur cape and followed Father and the two men out to the police car, and in a few minutes we arrived at the hospital.

The nurses moved about very quietly, leading us to a ward where children were sitting up in bed. Gertie lay in a cubicle, her dark curly head on the pillow, her face already discoloured by the mass of bruises. Father gasped, leaned over her then looked at Beatrice. I looked out of the curtain and saw Gina's yellow curls. She too was sleeping (they had been given sedatives), her head was bandaged, but did not quite cover the weal across her forehead. Father was told she was in shock, and a specialist was on his way to examine her. I ran back to Gertie's bed, leaned over, saying, 'You will be all right now!' The journey home was made in silence. It was strange having to go to bed by myself. Once I heard Beatrice laugh, and wondered what story she was making up now.

Next morning, two men and a nurse came to see Father. I was told to take off my vest, when Father saw the weals criss-crossed on my back, he whistled, 'You must have had some battle, did Gertie do that?'

I could only shake my head, conscious of Beatrice's stare. She told them we were quarrelling so much, she just had to get out. She knew nothing of what had happened. I cried out to Father, 'Please, please, we did not fight, we would never hit Gina.' An idea flashed through my mind, 'Look at her dress, there is blood on it.'

Beatrice said, 'She's lying, I have worn this dress all day.'

One of the men went out of the room, he must have gone upstairs and found the lace cream dress she had been wearing. It was indeed spattered with blood, and water, but Beatrice declared she had skinned and cooked a rabbit the previous day. It was then I saw Father looking suspiciously at her, he knew she had never cooked (far less skinned) a rabbit in her life, and detested messy jobs.

No more was said or done about that event. I was hard-pushed to get through all the housework. Father helped me carry the coal-pails, he attended to the sitting-room fire while I tackled the range. Pleading with him not to be late at the office, he said he would come home early till the 'girls' came home from hospital. He also took Beatrice out in the evenings, seemingly posing as the caring parents of 'uncontrollable children'.

A Broken Leg

Gertie came home in ten days, but Gina was sent to another hospital. I think Father was afraid for her sanity; the last two and a half years had all been too much for her. With Gina absent, Gertie and I felt a great sense of relief, she had been our responsibility, except at the farm.

The quarrelling started again, how we hated to hear them! Father started to stay out late. Beatrice vented her anger on us – often locking me in the coal cellar till he came home (though making sure the housework was done first). Deciding I would try to get out of the cellar, I left an old knife inside, and packed some paper in the bolt hole. As Beatrice was usually in a temper when she pushed me in, I guessed she would only push the bolt as far as it would go. Next time, I started pushing the bolt along with the edge of the knife and it slipped out. Closing the door carefully behind me, I crept into the kitchen, which was empty, and hid under the bed.

When Gertie came though with a dust-pan, Beatrice was with her, and told her to take the pails and let me out to help her fill them. Gertie returned, saying I was not in the cellar. Beatrice did not believe her, and went out to see for herself. Coming out from under bed, I ran past them to the garden wall and tried to scramble over it. Beatrice came at me, hands outstretched just as I reached the top, and catching my ankle, threw me to the ground. My leg twisted under me, I tried to rise, to escape the blows raining down on me, but the pain made me yell, and fall down again. Gertie took one arm, Beatrice the other, and dragged me screaming into the house.

Gertie said she thought my leg was broken, to which Beatrice replied, 'It's a pity it wasn't her neck!' and walked away. Gertie put a pillow under my head, but I still lay on the floor, the pain too great if I moved. When father came in, my leg had swollen to twice its size, but felt numb. Once again the ambulance came, once again Beatrice said it was my own fault, but Gertie said later she told Father what had really happened.

I lay in bed with great thankfulness, no more at the mercy of my stepmother, quite glad my leg was broken. It was a double fracture, just below the knee. My stay in hospital lasted three weeks, then I was sent home with a crutch, the leg in plaster.

Christmas and New Year came round, and we were not surprised when Father told us he was taking 'Mother' to town (Glasgow). He said he could not afford to take us to the circus this year, and I could not go on crutches anyway.

Once again we were locked in the kitchen without heat or light, going to bed if we felt cold. We managed to keep quite happy, huddling together to keep warm. My leg, itching under the plaster, made me uncomfortable.

Bread had been sliced and put in a tin box with half a jar of dripping. We finished the milk, but this time we rationed out the bread, though, unlike the 'Spotted Dick', it would not have made us sick. At night I lay afraid, sure the rats were coming back. We kept thinking that father and Beatrice might not come back and we would die in that cold gloomy kitchen, with rats eating us. This was a very real fear, and when after two days (and nights) our parents returned, I told Father I heard rats. He pooh-poohed the idea.

We started school in January, my plaster was off, but my leg was heavily bandaged. Wearing our tight shoes we had chilblains, when these burst, Father cut the toes out of our shoes, to let our bandaged feet get room. At school we took lot of nasty remarks, and the more mischievous tried to step on our toes.

I was still wearing a heavy bandage, but being so much on my feet, the leg had not healed straight and looked funny. Beatrice never let up with the housework and I often collapsed in tears with exhaustion.

Dunoon

About the end of January, Father announced we were leaving Rothesay. He had asked for a transfer and hoped to move to Dunoon at Easter. We knew he owed money to the tradesmen, and since the bathroom episode, we had few visitors and were being talked about. Beatrice gave up all her afternoon teas, and started to pack up, and sell off. She sold the pretty silk suite in the sitting room. Father also sold the huge chiffonier, and it could not be moved till two joiners had taken it apart. It had been in the house when Father bought it, and as it was a beautiful piece of furniture, he must have made a profit.

How empty the house looked, all the doors were thrown open to let would-be buyers see the empty rooms. Gertie and I swept down cobwebs, washed floors and windows, even cleaning out the coal cellar. Now the two of them visited Dunoon at the weekends, either house-hunting or buying furniture.

We moved out during the Easter holidays with many boxes, but no heavy furniture. Gertie and I said a last farewell to Craigie, putting some primroses on his tiny grave, and thinking of Gina. Arriving at Dunoon, we were taken to a much more modern house in Auchamore Road, with 'Hetherington' painted on the gate-post. The sun shone in the kitchen, and we were delighted to see there was no boxbed and only a small range. We dashed upstairs to see our bedrooms, in which there was a double and single bed, one chair and an old-fashioned wardrobe. Beatrice's bedroom was across the landing, which made me nervous.

The next few days were spent hanging curtains, and filling cupboards, or helping Father in the garden. We looked forward to our return to school. As the year's fees had been paid, we would travel to Rothesay till the end of June, leaving earlier and arriving home later. Father would be home about the same time.

We enjoyed the trips across the bay, got to know the sailors well and they teased us – Gertie especially, she was nearly twelve years old, and really pretty. I was my usual skinny self, but uninterested in my looks. Beatrice's false make-up and finery revolted me, as did the smell of whisky, which was to remind me for ever of her cruelty.

We did very well at school, Gertie gaining first prize for French, German and English. I also gained a few firsts and seconds, the highlight of which was a beautiful wrist watch with my initials engraved on the back. We did not take part in the Sports Day that year: it would have meant an extra journey as they were held on Saturdays. Our parents did not come to the prize-giving either, in fact I can't remember them ever returning to Rothesay.

As summer drew near, we hoped we would be sent to the farm, but Father said it was time we paid a visit to Granny, which made us very happy and excited. Father enjoyed working in the new offices, there were some very pretty typists, he would say with a wink, when Beatrice was not there.

Our routine was much the same in the new house, and as it was screened from the outside, we could scrub the doorsteps, and clean the outside of the windows. Our old velvet dresses had disappeared, and we were given knitted ones, not new, which I disliked; the wool was draggled and stretched when wet, especially at the knees. Losing our old velvet dresses, we felt we had lost touch with Mama, yet somehow I felt better. Having lost Craigie was so final I could still live in hope of seeing Mama.

Gina came home to Dunoon, she looked well and happy, though avoided Beatrice as much as she could. She had been given a furry toy cat, which she would not let out of her sight. Beatrice could not make her speak, and disregarded her as a 'stupid brat'. We were not so isolated from our neighbours, which meant our parents would have to keep up their outside image at all times.

A path led from the back garden, through a small gate, and down to a place called the Waterworks, a part of which was known as Fairy Glen. Here we played when we could during the following summer. Beatrice entertaining new friends, or visiting, would send us outside. We made a little shelter of twigs and branches, naming it the 'Authory'. We spent happy hours making models out of clay, or writing on such paper as we could lay hands on, paper bags, wrapping paper, newspapers and so on, with stubs of pencils we had collected at school. Gina gathered daisies to make chains, talked to her toy cat, so content we felt she was not quite natural. We wrote little stories and read them to her, and she would rest her head on our knees.

We played hide and seek round the trees. The wood stretched quite far out, we explored every bit of it. Sometimes other children would come, but we hid in our little 'Authory' and were not discovered. Beatrice let me wear my new watch, so we would know when to come home to get our work done. We would have loved to play outside during the long summer evenings. We could hear other children running about the trees, and wondered why they had no housework to do. Father said they were frivolous, useless and pampered.

More and more children seemed to have bicycles, approaching Father timidly, I begged for one to use between us only to be told it was only 'Hoydens' and boys who got bikes!! Beatrice had no washer woman now, but put the two of us into the wash-house every Saturday morning very early. We learned how to fill the boiler with water and light the fire underneath. Beatrice supervised the first morning, showing us how to separate the whites from the coloureds. The whites were boiled rapidly, but the rest were washed in two tubs. These were squeezed in soap suds, by using the 'dolly; which looked like a giant potato masher.

We quite liked it, although the sheets were heavy and awkward. We took turns putting the washing through the wringer, which was fastened to a board between two tubs. On good days the washing was hung out, if wet it was hung on a rope put up in an empty bedroom. Shirts and Beatrice's 'specials' were sent to the laundry.

Sundays were spent ironing, and helping in the garden. Father dug some of it, and we raked it smooth planting vegetables. He had brought the best of his rosebushes over, and with some new bushes, we had a wonderful show in front of the house, Father having bought some manure from a local farmer. Afterwards he took us into the fields to fill the coal-pails with manure.

Beatrice raged at Father for enrolling us at Dunoon Grammar School, as it was also fee-paying, but Father insisted he could not have us brought up at the 'local' school, mixing with riff-raff, or, as he often called them 'the great unwashed'. We were given new blazers, and hat bands, a different colour from the Rothensay Academy ones.

Our baths were just as uncomfortable as in Rothesay , only now we had them on Saturday. After the washing, the boiler fire was allowed to die out, the boiler itself left full of hot water and washing soda. This nipped and stung our eyes or any cuts and scratches we had. There was an outside lavatory, so we were *still* banned from using the bathroom.

Gertie now moved to senior grade, and made friends with bigger girls, who giggled a lot. She told me to make friends of my own. At this school, we actually had boys in the same classes, though they occupied only one side of the classroom and had separate playgrounds. I would walk Gina home from school, Gertie lingering with a group of older boys and girls.

It was not long till Beatrice started her former extravagant way of life, and soon they were quarrelling about money. Sadly, we had not seen Granny during the summer holidays. The parents travelled to Glasgow quite often leaving us locked up in the kitchen. As the lavatory was now outside, we were given a pail to use, but they stayed only for one night in town. Father, to Beatrice's annoyance, had joined a 'committee', having to attend three or four nights weekly.

Beatrice was very suspicious, accusing him of being up to his old tricks, running after other women. He taunted her, saying she was no use to him, not giving him a son, what did she think he had married her for? At this she threw a pot of stew at him, and said she would make his 'brats' suffer if he left her with them. He ducked the contents of the pot, and we had to clean up the mess.

She was also quite jealous of Gertie, who had filled out, had a beautiful pink and white skin (which we all had) and a wealth of curls, which shone like black satin. I loved to twine them round my finger, when we dried and combed each other's hair. Poor Gertie was verbally abused, beaten and worked to exhaustion at every opportunity. Nothing she did could please Beatrice. Only at school she was happy. Gina and I had our work to do, but I tried to help Gertie through her work-load.

One day I came home, changed, and started to clean the vegetables, pulling a towel from the rail above the fireplace, it caught on the gas pipe, breaking the mantel. These were made of very fragile filament. When first lit, they turned black, then white.

Father was the only one who could balance them carefully on pins under the glass shade. They were lit by tapers, a bundle of these lying on the mantelpiece.

Just at that moment, Beatrice came in with her tray, saw the broken mantel which lay like snow-flakes at my feet, and putting down the tray, she went out, returning with the heavy leather belt. She told me to get down on my knees and pick up every piece. Each time I bent over, the heavy belt lashed my bare legs. (Our stockings came off with our uniforms, we were often told to scrub our 'filthy' knees, which were really black and blue from kneeling on the stone floors or when cleaning carpets and polishing floors.

Gina screamed with fear, Beatrice turned on her, and would have struck her if Gertie had not come in at that moment. Beatrice handed Gertie money to run to the shop for a box of mantels, warning her she was in for it if she broke any. By this time I had brushed up all the tiny pieces, and took the shovel outside to empty it.

Beatrice ran after me, tried to push me in the coalcellar, but I dodged her and ran away. She went inside, and called to me to get on with my work. I entered warily, did not see her till she jumped on me from behind the door, gripped me by the shoulders, and ran me to the cellar, pushed me in, turned the lock with a big key, then took the key away.

When Gertie returned, she was made to do my work as well as her own, and when Father did not come, Beatrice lit a candle for her to work by. Gina had all the dishes to wash and dry. When it was time to fill the coal-pails, Gertie was told her 'bloody' sister was in there and could stay there till she would rot, playing with the key in her pocket.

When Gertie and Gina escaped to bed, they meant to tell Father where I was. It was very late when he came, everyone was in bed. I heard him locking up and shouted as loud as I could. This was a well-built shed, with a solid and well-fitting door. The coal was more than half-way up, and I could only crouch, not having room to sit properly. My stinging legs cause me to weep for a while, then I tried to find a way out. The roof was covered with corrugated zinc or tin sheeting, I could not budge it an inch. I forced myself to drift off in my memories of Granny, Mama and the farm, but my cramped position and pangs of hunger kept me awake and miserably cold.

If Gertie had fallen asleep, I realised that father would not know I was in the cellar, and he would go to bed. That thought filled me with sheer panic.

Picking up lumps of coal, I banged on the roof, my arms ached trying to lift the heavy coal. The sound was very loud, but I kept it going, as each lump of coal broke, I picked up another. Then Father's voice, 'Who's there?'

Almost hoarse with dust, I beat at the door, shouting, 'It's me, Father, let me out.' There was no key, he said, and I told him Beatrice had taken it.

He went away, he seemed to be gone for a long time, surely he would come back, or would he? If Beatrice had lied to him, he maybe would not want to let me out. He did return, this time with a torch, looking at me, he said, 'My God, what a mess.' My face was streaked with tears and black coal dust, my legs red and swollen. I was shivering and coughing up coal dust. He lit the candle in the kitchen, and by its meagre light, he placed the mantel under the gas shade. He helped me to wash myself, gave me a drink of milk, and some cold potatoes. Beatrice had told him I had broken the mantel deliberately.

Running Away

During my spell in the cellar, I resolved to run away, return to Rothesay and find my way to the farm. I would stay with Jean, and plead with her to bring Gina and Gertie. Sure of her help and kindness, I vowed I would never never return to Beatrice.

Next morning I rose with the others, Father still woke us up at 6.00 a.m. I managed to slip an extra slice of bread into my lunch bag, which gave me two and a half slices, afraid to spread it with dripping as Father might notice. To Gina and Gertie I said nothing, fearing they would stop me, or tell Father where I had gone. After spending the morning in school, I saw Gina and Gertie at lunch-time, waited till they were out of sight then walked out of the gate.

Reaching the pier, I produced my out-dated weekly ticket from the previous term when we had travelled to Rothesay. Smiling at the ticket-collector, whom I had come to know quite well, I handed it over to him.

He looked at it, then said, 'It's the wrong ticket, Missy.'

'Oh,' I said, 'I must have picked up the wrong one, I will bring the right one tomorrow'.

He asked me why I was travelling in school-hours, and I said we had been given a half-holiday.

'Off you go then, be sure to bring the right ticket tomorrow,' he replied. I could have jumped for joy as I walked up the gangway.

I had struck a blow for freedom, and had achieved the first part of my journey. Once in Rothesay, I took all the side roads, not wishing to meet anyone who might know me or the family. Reaching a bench in the corner of a quiet country lane, I ate all my bread, but wished I had something to drink. Hunting around, I found some sourocks and chewed them happily, reflecting I would not be really missed till 4.00 p.m. when Gina and Gertie would be looking for me. I hoped to be at the farm by then.

Climbing to the top of the hill, I looked for a familiar road to the farm. I had only travelled once there and back, and should have taken more notice. All the narrow roads looked the same, the farmhouses, fields and meadows similar. The fields were alive with 'tattie howkers', bands of men and boys who came from Glasgow. They wandered from one farm to another, a good meal and a few shillings their reward for ten hours of back-breaking work.

A man passed, wheeling a bicycle. I inquired what time it was, and the way to Craigberach Farm. Frowning, he replied, 'It be near 6 o'clock, you be a long ways away from that farm. It'll be dark soon, you'd best move yourself, Lassie.' Hurrying in the direction he pointed I must have walked for another hour. Feeling very tired and with darkness falling, I decided to sleep overnight, and continue my journey in daylight. Gathering some ferns, I made a bed under some trees, put my school satchel under my head, my hat over my face, and was asleep almost immediately.

It seemed only minutes when I woke to the touch of a tongue licking my face, and saw the face of a collie dog close to mine. Behind him, I saw three pairs of legs, one in gaiters, the others in moleskin breeches. Looking upwards I found myself being scrutinised by three brown wrinkled faces. One man drew out a spotted red hanky and wiped his forehead, knocking off his cap. 'What a turn you gave us, to be sure, we thought you be a goner! What are you doing here on your own, you'd best come home with us.' Feeling very hungry, the prospect of food and drink made me jump up and join them quite happily.

In the labourer's cottage I was given hot cocoa, and all asked me questions. I would not give my name, or where I lived, just that I was looking for Craigberach Farm and had lost my way. While I was in the lavatory my school bag was searched, every school book had my name, address and school neatly written on them. I had to tell them I had run away from home.

As I ate cheese and oatcakes, one of the men went off on his cycle to contact the police in Dunoon, who would inform Father of my whereabouts. His wife scolded me, saying that my parents would be worried, and soon I was sobbing out the whole story. Apparently a man and his dog had been walking on the nearby road. The dog spotted me and fetched his master, who, thinking I had maybe been murdered, ran back to the cottages for help, then contacted the gamekeeper. They were about to look under my hat, when the dog woke me.

It was now about 8.00 p.m., Father had been making inquiries; Gertie and Gina were out looking for me. When the police arrived at our house, only Beatrice was at home to take the message, she made no effort to let Father know, but he managed to catch the last ferry boat sailing that night. When he did come, he was amazed at my getting over to Rothesay without my fare. Full of anxiety, I dreaded to meet him, but he looked so relieved that I felt sorry for causing him so much trouble and expense.

His hair was tousled, he said they had been worried sick at home, and where was I going anyway? The farm folk said I was trying to find Craigberach Farm and he told them I had spent a holiday there, and was very fond of the farmer's wife. He also said I did not get on with my stepmother, that I had exaggerated the punishments, the marks on my legs and wrists were just strap marks received at school. He said that my being locked in the coal cellar for hours had been an accident, my sister had locked the door in a spirit of mischief, and had fallen asleep, not telling anyone.

I gave up in the face of these denials and when we were alone told him I would never go back to Beatrice, could he not just give me to Jean? Angrily he told me not to be so stupid, it would be against the law for them to take me, or my sisters, and he certainly could not afford to pay them for looking after us. We slept in chairs and were up at dawn to catch the first boat, calling first at the police station, where Father had a long serious talk with the inspector. How I dreaded going home, they would punish me. The rector would punish me, truants were severely dealt with by the rector.

Thankfully Beatrice was in bed, Gertie and Gina pleased to see me safe, but disappointed as much as I was at not reaching the farm. On our way to school, I told Father I would not go home till he came from the office. I was terrified to be alone with Beatrice, that I would just run away again if I was locked in the cellar. Whereupon he gave me a frightening account of what could happen to a young girl out in the world on her own.

At home-time we all came home together, Beatrice was standing in the doorway, in her fashionable clothes, all smiles for Father. he pushed us into the kitchen and went into the sitting-room with Beatrice. She had actually cooked the soup and potatoes, set the table, and now inquired why Gertie and Gina had not come home straight from school. Father said they had wanted to stay with me, and I was afraid to come home without him.

He gave me a note for the teacher to say I had felt sick and gone home at lunch-time. We were not to mention any of this outside, or at school. Although I did not now fear the school punishment, I knew Beatrice would not forget, or forgive.

At school I made a new friend, Martha Stirling, whose mother was a war widow, and had a small newspaper and sweet shop. Martha had one brother, David, about three years older than us. He often spoke to Martha at playtime. He had the same wide smile and frizzy fair hair as his sister. The family were very religious, spending most of their spare time at services and meetings in the Gospel Hall. Martha begged me to join, and I asked Father if we could go there on Saturday afternoons. He seemed quite pleased, said it would keep us out of the way, and were given a penny each for the collection plate.

On Saturday, Gina and I went into the hall, but Gertie took the opportunity to be with her friends, arranging to meet us later at the tram stop. We were taught to sing some very lively hymns, given texts, and hymn books. Father had not joined the church in Dunoon, Beatrice preferring to lie in bed and Father pottering about the garden. We still wore uniform, but Martha and others wore plain coats over dresses after school and at weekends. Father knew Mrs Stirling. Her husband had died from tuberculosis, brought on by the effects of war wounds. She had had business with him about receiving a war pension.

Next Friday evening there was a soirée in the hall. Father gave us 6d (tickets cost twopence each) and let us go. Unfortunately on Friday evenings we scrubbed out the kitchen, polishing the range, the windows and cutlery. Beatrice refused to let us go, but Father said we could do all that on Saturday after noon, after the washing was done. Daunting thought! We would have to tell Martha we could not attend the meeting on Saturday afternoon.

We really enjoyed the soirée, when we handed over our tickets we were each given a bag of buns, and a tin mug. The service started with prayers, we sang, 'My cup's full and running over' with great gusto, just waiting for the moment we could open our paper bags. The three of us exchanged buns and scones; Gina wanted my sugar bun and gave me her scone. It was a feast, especially to us as our diet seldom varied!.

Martha never seemed hungry, and gave me most of her buns. She always went home at lunch-time, David would wait for her at the gate. Both Gertie and I fell in love with the handsome boy, but we never spoke to him; he was probably quite unaware of us.

Armistice Day came round, Father once more marched on parade to the War Memorial. We all attended the service. Mrs Stirling and her children stood silently near us, I saw David give his mother such a look of love, before placing his arm protectively round her thin shoulders.

Shortly afterwards we had a visit from Father's brother, Andrew. He arrived with four children, who either sat on his knee, or on the floor at his feet, very shy, smiling all the time. His wife had died of cancer, and he was bringing up the children on his own.

Father said, 'You should marry again.'

Uncle Andrew replied, 'I don't think that would be a good idea, from what I hear.'

Father coloured to the roots of his hair and spoke of other things. Beatrice had gone out, not caring to meet any of Father's family. We all had tea in the spotless kitchen (cleaned by us), Father having bought pies and teabread.

After we had washed the dishes, we walked along the sea front together. The girls talked to us, saying that we spoke funny, and that we talked panloaf. Asking Father later what that meant, he said we spoke English properly, they used 'slang' because they attended a council school, what else could you expect? He implied they were inferior to us, but we thought Uncle Andrew disapproved of Father's life-style just as much.

We were longing for news of Granny, and hearing Father say to his brother we would see him at Christmas when he visited his mother, we hoped he meant it.

Before Christmas, Martha was absent from school, and meetings in the Gospel Hall. Plucking up courage, I stopped David and inquired why.

He looked down at me saying, 'Martha is ill, but she would like to see you. Come to the shop at lunch-time.'

Martha lay on a narrow bed near the fireplace, so pale and thin I hardly recognised her. The room was behind the shop, so her mother could attend to her between customers.

Now she greeted me with her wonderful wide smile, asked a few questions about school, then said, 'I am going to Jesus, won't that be wonderful?' I was struck dumb, and looked at her mother, who said she was easily tired, but would I come again? I went there on Saturdays for three weeks, putting Gina into the meetings. Father found out, and was not pleased; maybe Martha had TB and he did not want me to catch *that* disease.

He would go with me next Saturday and see what was wrong with her, which he did, and was utterly charming to Mrs Stirling, shaking his head sadly when she confirmed Martha had TB, and had only a short time to live. This he told me almost as soon as we left the shop, and I was never to go there again. Feeling sad, but rebellious, I vowed I would. Two days later David told me she was very ill, and asking for me. I braved Father's anger, and ran to the shop after school.

Martha was propped up on pillows, breathing loudly, her nose and lips blue-tinged, her smile feeble. She just held my hand, 'I am going to Jesus now, remember me in your prayers.' She seemed to fall asleep, and I left with David. He talked about how he was going to medical school, as he wanted to become a missionary doctor. At home, Beatrice had visitors, and did not seem to notice I was late. I felt sad, but could not accept that Martha could die, just like that.

A few days later, our teacher announced in class that Martha Stirling had died. David met me, said Martha had left me her Bible and hymn book. I told Father, and we both called into the shop after the funeral. David was serving behind the counter (his mother, too upset, was resting). He handed me the well-worn books; I hugged them close, meaning to treasure them. Reaching home, Father put them immediately into the fire, said I would get tuberculosis from them, making me scrub my hands.

Not long after that, Mrs Stirling sold the shop, put all the money in David's bank account, and went to live with an ailing relative, so that David could go to medical school.

The Carpets

Beatrice was now drinking heavily. She had fewer and fewer visitors, not seeming to make so many friends. Father took her out much more often for meals and drinks. Beatrice was furious if she did not get out. They attended local dances, and every new show or film in Glasgow and Dunoon.

Father was looking for ways to make more money. He brought home a thick hall carpet, which he had bought cheaply in a Glasgow sale room. We were given a carpet beater each, and Gertie and I beat it as it hung from a rope in the yard. A cloud of choking dust spread over the garden and into our neighbours. They banged their windows down, to keep the dust out, then complained about it.

The carpet was laid on the kitchen floor, and armed with two pails of water, two scrubbing brushes, carpet soap and clean cloths, Father directed us to clean a small square at a time. Gina was to rub the clean part with dry cloths. The carpet came up beautifully, Father sold it for much more than he had paid for it.

Now he scoured sales rooms in Glasgow, and as many as four carpets were delivered every two or three weeks. Father found a derelict barn in the Waterworks, tied a rope across, and in the evenings we all helped to carry a carpet there, and Father would help to beat it when we tired. This way we had no trouble with our neighbours. No sooner had we cleaned one than we had to start again. We were now so occupied with cleaning carpets that Beatrice hired a washer woman.

We would have preferred to wash outside, than to be constantly kneeling and scrubbing, with bare feet, our dresses tucked up in our knickers, as the skirts got very wet. Discovering our sore knees,

Father bought us kneeling pads. The patterns on these carpets were quite exciting, especially the ones with Egyptian figures and scrolls. The colour came alive as we scrubbed, beautiful Turkey red dyes and brilliant blues. We were quite sorry when they were sold.

After a good sale, he would take Beatrice to town, often staying overnight in a hotel, but leaving us to constant scrubbing. As each carpet was cleaned and dried, it was placed in the hall (we dared not walk on it), and it was sold from there on Saturdays, Father having advertised. Beatrice would have nothing to do with them, never letting up on our housework, our hands so rough and swollen we could only scrape the vegetables with great difficulty.

Our bedroom was much colder than the box bed in our old house, but we were so tired we usually slept right away. Father had a few days holiday over Christmas and New Year, and he and Beatrice left the three of us with two carpets to clean. There were fewer locks on the doors inside this house, and we would have to use the bathroom. With strict instructions not to show ourselves at the windows, or mess up the bathroom, we were to have both carpets ready for Father when he returned.

He put pennies in the gas meter, to get hot water for washing the carpets, telling us to be very sparing or the gas would run out, and to use candles to work by. There would be no fires, if we worked hard all day, we could go to bed early. We had no Ludo now; Beatrice had put it in the fire in one of her tempers. Our fear at this time was that she would take Gina's toy cat from her, which she never let out of her sight. Father said Beatrice would not *dare* having been warned that any more shocks to the child would affect her badly, though poor Gina still had to work constantly.

It was easier to work without Father scolding us, and for a time we worked hard. Gertie wanted to get out. We discovered we could open the bathroom window, at the side of which a rhone pipe led to the ground. Putting her coat over her old dress, and brushing her hair till it shone, we helped her out, and strained to watch her as she climbed down quite easily.

She had no money, but put a jam jar in each pocket; the jars were worth a penny each. Having made contact with her friend, she returned in an hour, clambered into the window we had left open and shared the bar of toffee with us which she had bought for a penny. We worked very long and hard next morning, so that she was able to slip out for the afternoon. The descent was too dangerous for Gina, or we would have gone too.

We did not want Gertie to leave us next day, as our parents could arrive home at any time, but she was sure she could be back before them. An hour after she climbed back, we heard Father's key in the lock, we got down on our knees, purposely having left the last square of carpet uncleaned. Father was not pleased with out work, and we had to go over the carpets again.

Imagine our dismay when he boasted of a great bargain, *eight* hall rugs were on their way (each 5 yards by 3 yards).

We were given new stockings and a packet of sweets for Christmas. Beatrice had new records, jewellery and dresses, Father a new suit and gloves.

Having closed the bathroom window carefully, leaving no signs of climbing out, we went outside to fill the coal-pails, and were startled to see muddy smears on the pale grey-surface of the pipe, while on the ground Gertie's foot prints were plainly visible in the soft earth! Our hearts in our mouths, we got cloths from the wash-house, rubbed off the tell-tale marks, and smoothed the footprints out. What a relief! If either of them had seen that before we did, God help us!

What with the cold in the bedroom, the dust and wetness of cleaning carpets, I went down with pneumonia again. Doctor said I should go to the hospital, as my room was too cold, he wrapped me up in a blanket, and minutes later I was in a warm bed. I loved the time I spent in hospital, and never wanted to go home. I had pneumonia every winter, five times in six years from when I left St Joseph's. Father, of course, blamed my troubles on Mama; if *she* had looked after us better, we would have been stronger.

Gertie was kept cleaning carpets, and was glad when I came home from hospital. Father, now anxious to have them finished, beat them himself with her help. Once home, it all started again, but to keep me from getting cold, the range fire was kept on, the table pushed back, and the carpet spread out in front of the fire in the kitchen.

He now bought a few at a time, and advertised once a month, boasting he made more money by the sale of the carpets than he earned in a month! To repay *us* for our hard work he bought a fish supper for *each* of us, instead of between us. It was certainly warmer working in the kitchen, but Gertie had to clean the range in the early morning, having to rise at 5.30 a.m. Both of us had to lift heavy pans of hot water to put in the pails.

Gertie hated it all; she longed to be out with her friends, and worked slowly. Beatrice belted her and shouted at her, but she just sat hunched up on the floor and cried. She would soon be of school-leaving age, and vowed to leave home. Father said she would have to stay with him till she was fourteen years of age, or he would lose the war pension allowance for her; if she left before then, he would bring her back.

One afternoon, on the way home from school, Gina and I left Gertie with two or three girls at the corner of our road. They were giggling and laughing, when who should come round the corner but Beatrice. She ordered Gertie home and followed her inside. Running upstairs to change, Gertie never reached the top stair. Beatrice dragged her down, punching, kicking, accusing her and her friends of laughing at her.

Pushing Gina into our bedroom, I ran downstairs yelling, 'Stop it, stop it,' but Beatrice smelled of whisky, and I knew it was hopeless to try to stop her.

Lifting Father's walking-stick I let fly, shouting to Gertie to run out of the still open door. Gertie dodged and twisted, but Beatrice caught her again, bashing her head against the wall. Again I hit Beatrice with the walking-stick and this time she felt the blow. Her face livid, her eyes full of hate, she jumped on me, squashing me against the stairs, punching and swearing. I managed to twist away, made for the door, but Beatrice could move very quickly when angry. She put out her foot, tripped me up, and would surely have killed me if she had not seen Gertie and her friends watching from the gate.

Even as she slammed the door shut, I had fled upstairs into the bathroom and locked the door. Just as I managed to open the window, and climbed out on the sill, Beatrice burst the door open. Running forward, with both hands outstretched, she sent me flying off the sill.

I knew no more. Gertie, not knowing what was happening to me, ran all the way to Father's office. He came at once, found Beatrice laughing like a maniac, boasting she had finished off one of his 'bloody brats'! Gina was huddled under our bed, white with fear. It was Gertie who found me unconscious on the back green. An ambulance was called, and I was admitted to hospital with concussion and a broken wrist. Fortunately I fell on grass, or it could have been worse.

Shapes and movements became clearer, and in a few days, I was sitting up, my wrist in plaster and supported by a sling. A doctor and a nurse looked at me, saying, 'So this is the 'tom-boy' that jumps out of windows!'

When Father came he seemed to be annoyed. 'Why did you jump out of the window, just when we had so many carpets to finish?'

I got home in a few days. Gertie said Beatrice had told Father we were chasing each other, and said I had jumped to get away from Gertie.

No more was said about the matter, Beatrice was a little subdued for a time. Father wanted to believe her story, and refused to accept the truth. For all our difficulties in getting homework done, we did well at school, acquiring a good many first prizes. Gina loved painting, her work was often displayed in the art room. As I could only use one hand, Father helped me with the dishes and coal-pails.

Beatrice blamed Gertie for what had happened, and made her life a misery. She would be fourteen years old in August, but told Father she wanted to find work when the school term finished in June. Gertie said she knew a girl who was going to work in a hotel in Girvan, and if she (Gertie) said she was fourteen years, she could work there too, hating to stay a day longer than was necessary with Beatrice. Father realised this, and accompanied her to the hotel in Girvan. I was not to see her for nearly a year. She did not write and had made Father promise not to tell Beatrice where she was. We missed her so much, Gina and I, we now slept together; Gina was still terrified of Beatrice.

We were working in the kitchen when Beatrice came in, she saw Gina trying to dry dishes with her toy cat under her arm. Shouting 'You can't work properly with that 'thing,' she threw it into the fire. Gina screamed, Beatrice slapped, I lifted the tongs to retrieve the toy, but Beatrice pulled the tongs from my grasp, and pushed the toy as hard as she could into the heart of the fire.

Gina's screams annoyed Beatrice, who, lifting the heavy tongs, threw that at her. She stopped screaming, stood there gazing, then started to twitch, her arms and legs all twisting up, her mouth working soundlessly, her eyes rolling in her head. The tongs had only grazed her hand, now she fell over them, writhing and twisting on the floor. Even Beatrice stopped to look at her, saying, 'She's in a fit,' telling me to get cold water and throw it over her.

The twisting subsided a little, we lifted her up on a chair, but she just fell to one side, like a rag doll. Beatrice grabbed my shoulder, telling me I was to say I had put the toy cat in the fire, or they would send her away. Fear made me promise and only then did she send for the doctor.

Gina was taken away, it was to be many years before I saw her again. She had lived for six terrible years with Beatrice, and never regained her mental health, suffering from persecution complex for the rest of her life. Beatrice told Father *I* had thrown the toy in the fire, and this had caused Gina's convulsions. Later, he came to me as I cleaned carpets alone, and I told him exactly what happened, begging him not to let Beatrice know, or she would kill me.

Then he surprised me be saying he was leaving her, he had applied for a transfer to head Office in Glasgow, but it could take some time. We would finish the carpets we had, and he would not buy any more. Beatrice decided to take 'boarders' that summer. With a burst of activity, rooms were changed round. (A mattress in the attic, with my few clothes, was to be my room for the summer). The following months were a nightmare of constant drudgery, though now I had only myself to look out for, and watched Beatrice like a hawk.

She 'cooked' for the first couple, an elderly lady and gentleman; but the lady soon asked if she could cook her own meals. Beatrice was about to explode, but I pulled her out of the kitchen, saying, 'That's great, we can go shopping.' However, Beatrice told me to stay to 'keep an eye on things' and went out alone. When she returned, she smelled of drink, and I led her upstairs to bed to sleep it off.

When the couple had had their meal, they went in to the sitting room. Scraping potatoes and vegetables, washing up and cleaning kept me busy till Father came home. He bought some cold ham, which we ate with our potatoes, then he joined the couple in the sitting room. I was just starting to clean the range, when Beatrice appeared, bleary-eyed and dishevelled. Coaxing her to sit down, I made a fresh pot of tea, a sandwich with a piece of cold ham, and left her.

Knocking on the sitting-room door, I asked Father to come to the kitchen. He took Beatrice upstairs, put her to bed, and gave her a sleeping pill. When he came downstairs he was jauntily dressed in his plus-fours, offering to guide the boarders round the town, telling me to hurry up, get finished and go to bed.

This pleased me, as I had been given a book prize at school, titled *Mary Slessor of Calabar*. I had had no time to open it but was able to hide it in the attic, with a candle and a few matches. I dreamed of the day when I would be a missionary too, having heard that one of Aunt Mary's daughters, also named Mary was training to be a missionary. I would ask them for help and advice if I could. (Two years later Mary went as a missionary to Kenya, and within a few weeks of her arrival she was accidentally shot by a 'bearer' while on safari. Her trunks, still unpacked, were returned to her parents' home.)

The elderly guests departed early. Beatrice was quite pleased, as she always took their money in advance. A younger couple came next. Father and Beatrice went out with them quite a lot. After them, came a family of four. The young wife brought a great deal of food; Beatrice was to cook for them.

There were a lot of arguments, Beatrice was accused of mixing oatmeal with the mince. I knew this was true, I even helped her to take out enough cooked mince for our dinner, and fill the pot up with oatmeal. They left after three days, maintaining they had been swindled, leaving some bottles of sauce, pickles and jars. Beatrice filled these up with water, wiped the outsides, then sent me into the shops to say I had purchased the wrong article and wanted my money back. Making every effort to pleas Beatrice, I tried all the shops till I succeeded, sometimes having to accept sugar, butter or tea in exchange.

To my great relief, school started, and Father said he would only pay a term at a time, as he could get his transfer through any day now. (As war-wounded pensioners were dying off, small regional offices were being phased out.) I was on no account to let Beatrice know, he would arrange for a separation soon.

It was this news that kept me going day after day, forcing myself to keep Beatrice in a good humour, not always succeeding. She often threatened to get rid of me too, but did not shut me in the coal cellar for so long, as she had no one else to do the housework! She slapped me if I was slow, or late home from school. Father was staying out late and she vented her anger on me.

Christmas came round again, Father told me he was going to visit his mother. I begged him to take me, but he said I would have to keep an eye on 'Mother'. She was furious when she heard this, and threw things at him, but he told her to 'behave herself', he would be back by evening. Beatrice took a bottle of whisky to bed with her. I did not take my clothes off, feeling that if she attacked me, I could run out of the house.

Next morning, I was surprised to see her up and drinking coffee. Father had not come home, as he had promised, she was going to see 'what your rotten Father is up to!' An hour later she came downstairs, her make-up fresh, wearing her smartest coat and hat and without even looking at me, walked out of the door. I tidied everything up, fully expecting her to come back, then locked all the doors and rummaged round for some food. Making myself tea, I was ready to pour it down the sink if she returned.

Roaming from room to room, looking out of windows, I hoped Father would come home. As darkness fell, a great silence settled on the house. I did not like that, but was not too frightened. Before I had had my sisters, and now I was alone, and would be for three days and two nights. As Beatrice had not bothered to lock the doors, I could go out. Woolworths was warm, and I hung about for a long time, till a man asked me what I was looking for, I was acting suspiciously.

Running home, covered in embarrassment, I did not venture into town again. After cleaning the range and sitting-room fires I did not light them, but filled a hot-water bottle, and hid under the blankets, straining my ears for the sound of a key in the lock. Next day I read and re-read *Mary Slessor*, and studied my school books, ate up all the bread and finished the milk. There were some cans and jars, but felt I dare not open them.

On the second night, the silent darkness closed in on me. I felt a rising panic, wanting to scream as Gina had screamed when shut in the darkness. Gloomy thoughts entered my head, nobody wanted me, I would be better dead, and began to work out how I should die. A woman had gassed herself recently in the area, but there would not be enough pennies in the meter to make certain. If I walked into the sea, I would drown, being unable to swim, but what if someone saved me?

Sinking into deeper despair, I wept long and hopelessly. Some small part of my mind brought me a picture, Mama standing over me when I had diphtheria, saying, 'Fight, Mary, fight!' Yes, Mama loved me, *she* would want me, and was waiting somewhere out there for me to find her. Peace in my heart, I slept till morning, to be wakened by an insistent knocking on the door. Scampering downstairs, I turned the heavy key to find Father on the doorstep.

I had locked the door from the inside, so he could not use his own key. He dashed in, asked where Beatrice was, then ran upstairs to change into his office suit, talking to me as I stood (rather bewildered) at the bottom of the stairs. He was pleased when he knew Beatrice had gone looking for him, and told me to tell her he had come home early on the following morning. He had spent the holiday with a very nice young lady, and intended to marry her when he had got rid of Beatrice.

As he hurried out, he told me to meet him at midday in the Dairy (a small dairy and tea room combined). He had something to tell me; if I was not there, he would know Beatrice had returned. As the house was as clean as I could make it, I hurried out too, afraid Beatrice would come home, and wandered round the shops till 12 o'clock. We had a glass of milk and a sandwich each. I could have eaten more, but Father gave me a 10/- (ten-shilling) note, to buy food for the evening meal.

He had not had time to visit his mother, but he heard she was well enough, and Gertie visited her on her day off. His big news was that he had had an interview at Head Office and would move to Glasgow in April to take up his new appointment. Everything in the house would have to be sold. He would just take digs in the meantime, till he had seen a solicitor about a separation from Beatrice. Gazing sternly at me, he made me promise not to breathe a word of his plan to 'Mother'.

Feeling happier, I arrived home half an hour before Beatrice. When she heard Father had (supposedly) returned next day she became calmer, and asked if I had any money. The money was for food, I said, holding out the 10/- note. She just pulled it from me, turned on her heel and went out. Scraping some potatoes, I boiled them on the gas ring, to be ready for Father. He came home first, followed a few minutes later by Beatrice.

She asked him where the hell he had been (having promised to be home the evening of the day he left). He had not gone to his mother's (poor Granny) or his sister's, as she had gone there to look for him. He just said he had attended an important meeting, which did not break up till 11.00 p.m., and had stayed the night with a colleague. Somewhat mollified, she sent me out for sausages, and we sat down to the potatoes I had already cooked. It was the first hot meal I'd had in three days, finishing my plate before Father had even started!

He seemed unconcerned that I had been alone, but Beatrice noticed how hungry I was and asked what we had had for dinner yesterday. Taken aback, I looked at Father, he gave me a warning look, before saying we had had hot pies. Beatrice had become very stout; Father's lips would twist in disgust, telling her 'she was no use to him, he wanted a son, a fresh young wife, she was a burnt-out old hag', making no secret of wanting a separation, even divorce.

He now stayed away nearly every weekend, leaving me to cope with the drunken Beatrice. She spent every penny on drink, and I became so used to cleaning up her sickness that I stopped retching. Washing her towels, pillow slips, and nightdresses almost daily, cleaning up vomit from floor and sink, gave me a life-long revulsion to drink. I avoided and despised anyone who smelled of drink for the rest of my life.

At the end of term, just before Easter, Father was asked to attend an interview with the rector, who wanted to enroll me for the next three years in the Senior School. They discussed all the possible subject I could take, Father seemingly very interested. I should make the top grade, and with 'hard work' could do extremely well. Father smilingly agreed with everything suggested, but said he would have to talk thing over with his wife.

On the way home from this interview, Father calmly told me he would not pay for next term, that he would help me to find work. It was impossible for him to keep me, he had found rooms in a men-only establishment. The house sale was now in the hands of his lawyer, but Beatrice was not to know anything about that. We were going away for a week's holiday, as he wanted her out of the way while prospective buyers were inspecting the house.

It was very nice in Auldgirth, Dumfriesshire. Father hired a rowing boat to fish in the River Nith. He would take me, but Beatrice was too heavy, and disliked the idea, preferring to spend most of the time sitting in a tea room, smoking and drinking tea or coffee, complaining that the coffee was like dirty dish water.

Father took her out every evening to a small hotel nearby. She was extremely bored, and he was afraid she would go home before the house had been sold, so he bought her all the magazines and novels that she wanted. On the last day of our holiday, I joined

Father as usual on his fishing trip, Beatrice lying late as usual. He rowed to a spot under some over hanging trees. The water here was still and deep, the colour muddy and dark, just like Beatrice's eyes, I thought with a shudder.

He caught a few brown-speckled trout, though I disliked the way he put the poor squirming worms on a hook. Suddenly the line tightened, Father shouted he had caught a 'big one', tossing his catch into the boat. I recoiled in horror. A snake-like slithery body, an open mouth revealing rows of sharp teeth, a pointed face, so resembling the face of my nightmare rat that I would have jumped out of the boat, but, even in panic, I realised the water would have been full of these monster rats. I screamed hysterically. Father stood in front of me, unhooked the 'eel' and threw it away as some men ran to the bank.

They pulled the boat in, and Father pushed me out, trying to steady the boat. Still screaming, a woman threw her scarf over my face, and ran me into a field, telling me I was safely away from the river. When I had calmed down, Father took me back to the cottage. That night I had a terrible nightmare. I dreamed I was being overwhelmed by a multitude of rats, their weight was smothering me, and struggle as I might, sharp teeth and claws seemed to pull me into deep dark waters, as I tried to escape. In the morning they found me curled up on top of a chest of drawers, where I had climbed in my sleep to escape from the imaginary rats.

We came home next day. Father wanted the last carpet finished, to sell with the rest of the furniture. My wrist was quite weak, and ached with the heavy scrubbing. How glad I would be to see the last of them. Father confided that he had seen his lawyer, had taken out an inhibition order, which meant that Beatrice could not buy goods in his name, or molest any of us including himself when he was at work.

He had many debts to pay, and would have to live carefully for the next few years. Beatrice was told that he had applied for a 'trial' separation, had found her nice lodgings in Glasgow, and she could start packing, as the carrier would call for them in two days. She screamed, swore and smashed everything within reach, accusing Father of getting rid of her to live with his 'fancy woman'.

They went away early one morning, Father threatening that she would receive no money if she stayed – which meant no drink. As I watched them, I felt a twinge of pity for her. She had looked so lovely that first day I saw her, a real show-girl, now she was fat, blousy, and (without make-up) ugly and bad-tempered looking. She did not even look at me as Father bundled her into a taxi. He returned in the afternoon, and told me we were going as soon as possible, before Beatrice could come back. He had paid her rent for a month, given her money and a bottle of whisky, but *that* would not last very long.

Working well into the night, we filled two trunks, one to be sent to Granny's house, and one addressed to Glasgow Central Station, where it would be uplifted by Father. After the trunks were filled with Father's most personal belongings, we attached prices to the furniture, and everything else, even the carpet I had just finished cleaning. A price tag of forty pounds was put on it, which was a good month's salary in those days.

We finished every scrap of food, and had no breakfast on the day we left Dunoon, Father putting the house-keys into the lawyer's office. Carrying my school-bag, containing all I owned (a change of underwear, a nightdress, toothbrush and comb), I began to wonder what was in store for me.

Arriving in Glasgow's Central Station, Father told me to go to the 'Ladies', wash myself, comb my hair and use the toilet, which made me feel quite grown-up. We then entered Crawfords' tea room in Argyle Street, and had a huge breakfast. We were both very hungry.

How well I remember the pleasant dining room, all scarlet and gold, with pure white napkins, and table-cloths, even flowers on the table. Plates of bacon, egg, sausage, potato scones and black pudding were placed before us, with plenty of rolls, butter, marmalade and a large pot of tea. Looking back now, it must have seemed like a condemned man's last meal (in my case), but ignorance was bliss, as satisfied and happy we left the restaurant to walk up Buchanan Street.

Midway along, we stopped at a door with a sign above it, which read, 'SERVANTS' REGISTRY'. Opening it, we walked up a stairway, and entered a dismal room, which contained rows of dilapidated benches. Some women were sitting, apart from each other, mostly fat, greasy and poorly dressed. Some leered at Father, who led me quickly over to a woman sitting behind a desk.

She asked for my name, age and what experience I had. (Father had told me to say I was fourteen years old, which I would be in five weeks.) After paying the fee of 1/- (one shilling), I was told to sit on a bench, and Father left, telling me to work hard, not to leave the job, and he would contact me through Granny, the 'lady' at the desk would see me 'all right'!

More women came, some to sit, others to look at us. I was too young, they wanted an experienced cook, or cleaner. A small sharp-faced woman came over to me, looking like a 'moose (Scots for mouse) below a divot', as Father would have said, swamped in a large velour hat and fur coat. She required a girl to help her in the house, and be able to run up and down stairs. She also paid 1/- fee, and we left the dreary room together, walked up the Sauchiehall Street, and crossed over to North Frederick Street.

Tenements

High, grimy tenements blotted out the sunshine as we entered a white-tiled close which had an iron gate at the other end. We climbed four flights of stairs, Mrs McBride stopping for breath on every landing, all having doors facing each other. Reaching the top landing, she opened the door on her left, and I followed her inside, pleased and surprised to feel the warmth, and see the rich furnishings.

Mrs McBride took off her coat, and still wearing her hat, she led me into a small kitchen, made a cup of tea, over which she gave me some instructions. I was to call her 'Ma'am', would receive one pound per month, from which breakages would be deducted. No half-day, but I would have a Sunday off every four weeks, to be taken the day before I was due to be paid. I said I had no money, how would I be able to visit my Granny, who lived in Motherwell? She said she would give me my fare, and take it out of my wages when I returned. (I was not to know that her servants would not return if she gave them their full wages.)

We toured the house, surprisingly large, with four bedrooms, a sitting room and lounge. A very large, ornate bathroom next to Mrs McBride's bedroom, and a huge utility cupboard, with washing baskets, pails and brushes, occupied all that floor. A few steps led to a small dark landing, which only contained two doors. This was to be my area, I would use the dark, cell-like lavatory (not the bathroom). The other door revealed my bedroom. After seeing all the well-filled and comfortable rooms, my heart sank. Inside was a single iron bed, on which lay two wrappers, two aprons, and two dust-caps.

Ma'am left me, to get dressed in a wrapper (a striped dress with buttons down the front). This was much too long and wide, but I tied an apron tightly round my waist to keep it from tripping me up. Looking round the room at the small grimy window (half-open to reveal a sea of roofs and chimney tops), I saw a rickety table on which stood a discoloured basin, cracked jug, a saucer with sticky soap still in it, a candlestick, and rough towel. A small rusty grate in one corner could not have been used for ages, though the fire place held an old heavy poker and tongs.

Inspecting the bed, a stained pillow (without cover), two grey blankets, a large sheet of brown paper on a very thin mattress, did not appeal to me, and I knew I would not stay in that room for more than the month. A bell rang, and I ran downstairs, where Ma'am showed me a row of bells above the kitchen door, each one denoting the room to which I was summoned. When 'Gaffer' came in, he would show me the coal cellar, and wash-house at the foot of the stairs.

At the sink I was scrubbing potatoes, when Ma'am saw them she laughed, saying it was a lazy way, she liked her potatoes peeled. I replied that I had always scrubbed or scraped potatoes at home, Father thought it was wasteful to peel them. I could not use the peeler, tried a knife, cutting too deeply; Ma'am grew quite angry, saying I would have to practise. We went round all the bedrooms, making beds, she talking all the time. Ronald, her son, was seventeen years old, and attended a private school. Two daughters slept in another bedroom, an elder daughter in a smaller one, then came her own bedroom, the fourth and largest.

All had fires in the winter, but only in hers would I need to clean out the fireplace every morning. Fires were also to be attended to in the sitting-room, lounge and kitchen, which filled me with dismay. That meant filling and carrying heavy coal-pails up all these stairs twice a day.

The 'family' bathroom (as she called it) had plenty of thick soft towels, numerous jars of cream and powders, the walls lined with pretty green tiles which would be easy to clean. Ma'am did all the cooking, saying the Gaffer had his meals in the kitchen, as he liked to eat before he got bathed and dressed in clean clothes; 'plumbing' was a 'dirty' job. Their son, Ronald, came home from school, tall, spotty and cheeky, I did not like him, then Gaffer came in, took off his overalls, threw them in the brush cupboard, and sat down at the kitchen table after washing his hands and face at the sink.

Ma'am laid out a knife and fork, lifted food from all the pots simmering on the range, and placed a huge plateful in front of Gaffer. He ate noisily, then wiped his lips with a big, red-spotted handkerchief. Speaking with a broad Irish accent, I was reminded of Kirsty's husband ('Himself'), having the same squat, strong build and cheery manner. Finishing his meal, he sat down in the rocking chair, with a glass of beer and his newspaper, there was only one other chair in the kitchen.

I helped Ma'am to set the large table in the sitting room for five people. The three daughters came home from work, and I was kept busy taking the crockery between kitchen and sitting room. When all was cleared, I carried through a teapot, a plate of cakes and biscuits, and was told to fill my own plate from anything that was left in the pots.

How glad I was to sit down, though Gaffer was snoring almost beside me. Minutes later, Ma'am wakened him, telling him to light her bedroom fire. He got a large shovel, emptied the hot coals from the range into it and carried them to her bedroom. This would cool the range and I was to black-lead, and polish it, then scrub the kitchen table, sink, chairs and floor.

As if that was not enough, he showed me where three large keys were hung behind the front door, and taking them, four pails and a shovel (he handed two pails to me), he led the way downstairs. Unlocking the iron gate, then the coal cellar, the other key was for the wash-house. After filling the pails and locking up, we climbed those stairs again. My arms ached so much I had to rest on each landing, but Gaffer went on, leaving me to climb the rest of the stairs.

I spent the next three hours washing dishes and pots, cleaning the now cool range, setting it for the morning, finally scrubbing out the kitchen, reflecting sadly that nothing had changed, only now I could not escape to school. Surprised at the warmth of the brown paper sheet, which I spread over the pillow, I dropped wearily into the narrow bed, and slept soundly.

It seemed but a few minutes when Gaffer knocked on my door, it was only 5.30 a.m., apparently he started work at 6.00 a.m. A pot of tea was ready, and some thick toast, the fire burning brightly in the range, which was quite pleasant. He gave me a list of orders from Ma'am. I was to clean out and set three fires, take a tea-tray to Ma'am at exactly 8.00 a.m., take the ashes down to the dustbins and bring up four pails of coal. These I carried upstairs twice while the family moved around, getting ready to go to work and school, Ma'am fussing around them, wearing a dressing-gown.

After they were gone, I was told to have my breakfast, which consisted of two buttered rolls and lukewarm tea. There was work for every moment of the day. Ma'am only helped with bed-making, scolding me often, watching everything I did. By 9.00 p.m. I was so tired, I cried myself to sleep. How I missed the school childrens' chatter and fresh air, just waiting for the day I would receive my wages. Granny would help me to get pleasanter work than this.

On washing day, Gaffer lit the fire under the boiler in the wash-house, while I filled it with water from a tap. The washer woman refused to climb the stairs, so I carried down baskets of clothes, also a tray with cheese, rolls and cake, a large pot of tea with sugar and milk. When finished, she rattled the key on the iron gate and I ran down with her pay.

The heavy wet washing basket was more than I could lift, so I filled my apron with some of the clothes, left them outside the house door, then ran down again twice more till I had it all upstairs, where it was hung on screens or pulley. Asking about my own washing, I was told to wash my personal things in my room, and hang them on the piece of string put there for that purpose.

The wrappers and aprons went into the family wash. As my underwear was thick heavy school wear, it took all week to dry, they would hang forlornly from the string across the open window, the white vest grey with smoke from the chimneys.

On Sunday afternoon Ronald came into the kitchen with a book in his hand, asking me if I was any good at spelling, would I help him with an essay he was writing? I was pleased and quite flattered; someone had noticed me at last. The whole family just called me 'the girl' and then only to ask me to do something for them. Leaning over the table beside him, I pointed out his mistakes which were many, and felt his arm go round my waist. Blushing scarlet, I moved away.

He laughed, then asked me how many 'boys' I knew, telling me we could have 'fun'. I said I did not want 'fun', and he had better get out of the kitchen. Hearing someone coming, he went out quickly. I was now vaguely aware there was another kind of love than that for sisters, pets or even Granny.

Sunday afternoon I was free to clean my room, my clothes and myself. Carrying hot water up from the kitchen to my room, I washed myself all over, used the water to wash my clothes, than lay down to sleep. Just as I was falling asleep, the cistern next door made a lot of noise, the chain being pulled not once but many times. It must be Ronald up to his tricks so I paid no heed. He always rattled my door handle as he passed to the toilet.

Rising, I put on my coat and called out, that I would tell his father. (I knew his mother would not believe anything I could say about her 'blue-eyed' boy. He had come late in life after her three daughters, and was thoroughly spoiled.) I only had one week to go before my day off (and pay day), hoping I could keep Ronald at bay till then.

How I longed for fresh air and sunshine, opening my attic window as far as it would go, even wondering if I should jump out of it, to end this ceaseless drudgery. There were other pathetic lines of washing hanging outside these attics, a few white faces gazing out like mine. Looking over the window, seeing spiked railings surrounding every drying green, to fall there, and be impaled on these sharp spikes put all thoughts of jumping out of my head, it was too painful to imagine.

On Sunday afternoon the family went their various ways, leaving Ronald and his friend Steve alone in the house. Going up to my room, I met them coming out of it, each swinging a sanitary towel from their hands by the loops. Burning shame and confusion sent me racing to lock myself in the family bathroom. The boys knocked loudly, ordering me to open it, laughing and jeering. I shouted back that I would stay there till his father came home, and I would tell him.

They coaxed, wheedled, saying it was only a bit of fun; the last girl had liked 'it'. Gaffer would not believe me, anyway. They also hinted they would give me a shilling if I let them into my bedroom. It seemed ages before the family came in. Hearing Gaffer's voice, I unbolted the door, walked out and ran up to my room. To my dismay, I found they had broken the bolt (a very flimsy one) on my door. Without more ado, I marched down to the kitchen.

It was Gaffer's pleasure to make tea on Sunday, he just filled the huge teapot and told them to help themselves. He was sitting at the kitchen table, his Sunday papers spread out in front of him. He nodded in the direction of the teapot, I filled a cup, then told him the bolt on my bedroom door was broken. An hour later, after mending the fires, I asked him again. He looked at it, said it would need a new bolt, he would get one tomorrow.

That evening I pushed the rickety wicker chair against the door, put the basin and jug on it, as I knew they were all going out again to some special service in the chapel. The light was fading as I lay on my bed. I heard a rasping noise. The chair was moving, pushed by the door slowly opening. I leaped out of bed, picked up the heavy iron poker, shouting, 'Get out, get out!' Both boys now stood inside the door, sniggering at my short nightdress. They began to close in, one came round the bed, the other jumped on it saying, 'Hit me, hit me!'

Backing against the wall, I lifted the poker above my head. They became serious; a cold tight feeling clawed at my stomach, though every nerve was alert. Steve jumped off the bed, knocking me to the floor. Their hands were everywhere, attempting to pull up my nightdress. I went berserk, and still hanging on to the poker, I swung it at Steve, hitting him on the shoulder. He backed off, holding his arm, but Ronald was holding me down on the floor, I prodded him in the stomach with the poker, and he recoiled, giving me the chance to get on my feet.

He ran to the chair, lifted the jug and basin off, then held the chair in front of him, mocking me, daring me to hit him. I jumped off the bed and with all the strength I had swung the poker, smashing it into the flimsy chair, which broke up in his hands. These young men did not know I had had years of experience in avoiding blows, thanks to Beatrice. Keeping an eye on Steve, who was holding the door open, ready to run, Ronald now picked up a bit of the chair, and looked over to Steve, in that moment I swung the poker again, and felt it connect with flesh. Ronald's hands flew to his face, clutching his nose. Blood streamed out between his fingers, and ran down his white shirt.

Steve yelled, 'Come on, Ron,' and pulled the moaning boy out by his arm. I ran after them, not wishing to be cornered in my tiny room, should they retaliate. Four astonished, upturned faces gazed at the scene. Ma'am was the first to find her voice, shouting abuse at me, saying she would have me jailed for assaulting her son. She did not hold Ronald close, as she was wearing a very light-coloured expensive suit. Gaffer told her to take him to the sink and put cold water on his nose, and a cloth at the back of his neck. The oldest daughter and her young man stood quietly watching, glancing at her I saw her smiling faintly, with a new interest in her eyes.

Gaffer turned to Steve, inspected the bruise on his shoulder, saying, 'You are not really hurt, get off home, and keep your silly mouth shut!' The mark on his shirt was only rust from the poker. Donning his jacket rather sheepishly, Steve disappeared. Turning to me, Gaffer said, 'See you in the morning,' but when he put out his hand to take the poker, I refused to part with it, and ran back into my room. Once inside, I tried to block the door, then realised Ronald would be unlikely to annoy me that night.

Sitting on the bed, I made plans to get out of that house, quite certain they would not believe it was their son's fault. Ronald's injuries had looked serious, maybe I had broken his nose. (At this thought I felt smug.) Waiting for whatever punishment was in store for me was unthinkable, flight was the only solution. That I would lose three week's wages for such punishing drudgery made me really angry. Dressing myself fully, I packed my school-bag with the still wet underwear I had just washed, rolling it up in the nightdress, put the bag under the pillow, and wore the horrible wrapper over everything.

Next day was Monday and 'washday'. When Gaffer knocked on the door next morning, I straightened the blankets, spreading them over my coat and bag, before going nervously downstairs. As I drank tea and ate hot toast, Gaffer asked me what had happened the evening before. Telling him everything, he said he would speak to Ronald, and would put a new bolt on my bedroom door that evening, also telling me that Ronald's nose had stopped bleeding, but he had a bad bruise on his face.

Again we carried down the empty coal-pails, Gaffer lit the fire under the boiler, which I filled with water. He went out of the close, where his grey van stood, and only then did I move quickly. Leaving the pails unfilled, I ran upstairs, threw off the wrapper, apron and dust-cap, and picked up my coat and bag, pulling on my coat as I ran down these long stairs, hopefully for the last time. Turning left, I sped out of the close, gasping in the fresh air, and feeling the warmth of the early morning sun. Recently having asked Gaffer how I would find my way to Motherwell, I tried to remember what he had told me.

I walked quickly down Buchanan Street, passed Queen Street Station and emerged into George Square. A few tramcars were being boarded by workmen, each destination displayed above the driver's platform. Uddingston was the one I looked for, and was supposed to change there for Motherwell. Waiting till it moved away, I set out to follow the tramlines, having no money. Coming to Parkhead Cross, the lines diverged, and I waited till another tram came, the same thing happened at Tollcross.

Fearing to see Gaffer's grey van, I kept close to the shops.

Thin, ragged, tired-looking small boys emerged from the tenements, trailing up and down, delivering newspapers. My sympathy went out to them, I had just had some experience of that! School children began to collect at tramstops. Greatly daring, I got on the tram with them, managing to ride three stops before the conductress ordered me off. To my story of having lost my fare, she said, 'Tell that to your Granny!' Walking quickly, I was soon out of the city. A great surge of happiness flowed through me as I reached the wide road at Mount Vernon. I felt very conspicuous, as all the children were now in school.

Reaching a park, I sat on a seat, and wondered when the McBride family had found me gone. I hoped the lazy daughters would have to carry (and fill) the coal-pails, and the washing baskets. Watching every van, dreading Gaffer would come after me; knowing I had no money, he would be sure to follow me. A man, walking his dog, said 'You're late for school.' So I ran till I was out of his sight. Walking steadily for a long time, I reached Uddingston.

Many trams came. When I saw a Motherwell one, I watched which set of tram lines it went on, and followed them for a few miles. The lines kept shining, I had to stop looking at them, as they seemed to move and merge in front of my eyes. Never will I forget them, seeming to stretch never-ending before me. Reaching Bothwell, I must have followed the wrong lines, not recognising the destination names. Turning back, I entered a school, using the toilet, washed my hands, and drank from the school well. Returning to where I had turned off, I waited, and to my relief and joy I recognised the dear, familiar names of my childhood – Hamilton, Motherwell, Wishaw.

Following the right tram lines, I passed a woman sweeping out her shop, and asked her if she had any broken biscuits. The water had refreshed me, but hunger gnawed at my stomach. She shook her brush at me, told me I was like as not, playing truant, and to get back to school! Walking more slowly, very tired, I felt safer with every step which put distance between me and the McBride family.

Reaching Hamilton, I lost my way once more, having to ask where I would get a tram to Motherwell, I was directed to go down Quarry Street, cross over at the picture house, and arriving there, I was sorely tempted to get on the tram.

My legs were heavy, my head ached, but hunger drove me on, till I reached the Clyde Bridge. Entering the gate of the Clyde Park, I sat down beside the pond, where once we had sat as children in a little rowing boat, the three of us, so happy! Climbing the brae, I passed Dalziel School, and eventually coming to the library, I knew I was only five minutes from Granny's house. Here there were no tram lines to follow, but they still seemed to shimmer in front of my eyes. Now so weary, I cold scarcely walk, I passed the Baths, went down Farm Street and entered Granny's house. Her door was never locked in daylight; turning the handle, I managed to close the door behind me, and walked unsteadily into the kitchen. The sun shining hazily on the well-remembered brass hangings and flower pots. Granny's eyes grew round with surprise, her lips moved, but all melted away as relief, hunger and exhaustion caught up with me, and I sank unconscious at her feet.

When I recovered, I found Granny had put a pillow under my head, and a cold wet cloth on my forehead. Putting my arms round her, and weeping, I pleaded with her not to let the police take me to jail, should they come for me. Pouring out the whole story, she was both shocked and very angry with Father. Even in my distress, I could see poor Granny was twisted, bent and crippled with rheumatism, not having seen her since the fateful day in 1919 when she had visited us in Rothesay, and she climbed into our bed for warmth.

After some food, my spirits soared, and soon we were talking happily together. It was so long since I had had a conversation with anyone, I just could not stop. Granny helped me wash my aching feet and legs, then sent me to bed, amazed that I had walked all the way from the centre of Glasgow to Motherwell. It was dark when I wakened, the gas light was turned down, Granny and Uncle Johnny were speaking in very low voices. When I sat up, they turned the light on full. Granny gave me a cup of hot cocoa, and both started to question me.

They wanted to know where Father was, but I did not know. They had received the trunk sent by him from Dunoon, and a letter to say he would collect it when he had found suitable accommodation. He did not mention what had happened to any of us, poor Granny was utterly bewildered! She knew that Gertie was in Girvan, but what had happened to Gina made her very sad, 'our little angel' she repeated over and over again.

Now the conversation took a more immediate turn, and they questioned everything leading up to my running away. Granny seemed very anxious to know exactly what the two boys did to me in the bedroom, scarcely believing I could fight off two of them and I was not to be afraid to tell the whole truth. She sent Uncle Johnny out of the room, thinking I was too shy. She seemed quite worried about me, but told me to go to sleep again, not to get up that day. Indeed, I was glad to just lie there warm and relaxed, though extremely tired.

Granny's doctor and a nurse came in, examined me thoroughly, told Granny some technical term, which meant I was still a virgin, only then did Granny seem relieved. The doctor thought I was too thin, and told me to stay in bed at least for another day.

Uncle Johnny came in from work that evening, he hurried through his meal, changed his shirt, then told me he was going to see that I got my three weeks' wages. I was frightened, not knowing if the McBride's had reported me to the police. It was my word against theirs, and my experience of that was bitter – no grown-ups ever admitted it was their fault, or let anyone else believe your story.

Granny told my uncle not to say I had been examined by the doctor, but to accuse the boys of attempted rape, and if they did not pay my wages, he would report this to the police. I rose after he left, and nursed Kiki, now old and fat, but a gentle reminder of happier days. Finding myself surprisingly stronger after two days in bed, I now helped Granny to clean the kitchen. About 9.00 p.m. Uncle Johnny came in, whistling merrily. We waited with some apprehension to hear his news.

Ronald had a 'beauty' of a black eye, his nose was swollen, and he had not gone to school. Mrs McBride had been quite nasty at first, but changed her tune when Uncle Johnny said he intended to report the boys. Gaffer said, as no great harm had been done to the boys, he would see they behaved in future. I was a good worker, and they wanted me to come back. They were very surprised to hear I had walked the miles to Motherwell.

Apparently the whole house had been thrown into confusion

when they arose to find no fires lit, no breakfast, and the washerwoman bellowing upstairs for the clothes. Ronald and his sisters had to fetch and carry, and Gaffer said it had taught Ronald a lesson which I was grateful to hear. Gaffer handed over one pound, saying he hoped I would come back as he had now paid me an extra week's wages, and replaced the lock of my bedroom door. Uncle Johnny said he would let me know, I would have to make my own decision. He knew I would never return to work there again, but did not say so to them.

When he handed me the pound note I was elated, the first money I had ever been paid for hard work. Handing it to Granny, I said it would keep me till I got another, hopefully, better job, but with a 'Please Granny, can I have a shilling? I never, never want to be without money again, to have to walk miles for lack of a penny, to look hungrily in shop windows, full of cakes and pies, that made the ache in my stomach almost unendurable.' I got my shilling, spent one whole penny on sweets, and rattled the other eleven pennies in my pocket, counting and re-counting them so often that both Granny and Uncle Johnny told me I could not be happier if I had been given the Crown Jewels.

Aunt Mary made one of her regular, but very short visits. I told her I dearly wanted to become a missionary, like her daughter. She said the training was expensive, and without certain qualifications, I would not have a chance. I spent the next week spring-cleaning Granny's house, loving every minute. We would sit down in the middle of the morning, and in the afternoons drinking tea and eating hot scones.

How we talked. She had not heard from Kirsty for a long time, she had moved to one of the larger council estates, many of these being built to improve on pre-war housing. They had electric light, hot water systems and a bathroom. Sheer luxury to the people who were accustomed to an outside toilet, a tin bath, and paraffin lamps. The rents were three times higher, but wages were rising, and there was more money about. An old friend of Granny's had taken her to see such a house. She told her that the first time she pressed the light switch, she thought she had set the house on fire and ran outside.

This came to mind thirty years later when we bought our first television set. My husband's mother, who lived with us looked quite taken aback when it was switched on. When she saw the announcer, she walked quickly out of the room, returning shortly, having changed her dress, combed her hair and applied perfume to her wrists. On inquiring why she had changed, she said the gentleman in the box looked well dressed, and she wanted to appear as well dressed to him as he was to her. No one ever really did quite convince her that he could not see her!

Giving up all hope of becoming a missionary, I applied to the local hospital to become a nurse. My hopes in that direction were dashed just as completely. At the resulting interview I was told to apply again when I was 16 years old, then if I passed certain tests, I was expected to pay a yearly premium of ten pounds, and my parents to provide off-duty clothes and pocket money. In my case an utterly hopeless situation.

My fourteenth birthday came round. Granny and I remembered that it was ten years to the day since that first fateful telegram arrived, informing us that Father was missing. Whatever the future held for me could be no worse than the last few years, the nightmare of life with Beatrice and Father's broken promises. There was one hope that nothing would diminish, it filled my heart with a great determination, that somehow, somewhere, I would find my mother.

The Last Battle

The sheets billowed, swirling round me as I strove to peg them securely to the clothes line in the boisterous wind. Humming happily to myself I surveyed my own clothes, fresh and clean, though not quote free of the smoky grime from the chimneys in Glasgow. I had now been staying with Granny for a week since I walked from Glasgow. Although I could have obtained domestic work, I abhorred the thought of working for another family like the McBrides, though Granny could not afford to keep me.

A friend of Granny's came to my rescue. Her name was Miss Pearson. Her niece was about to leave a nice job as a Nanny. Her employers were moving to England. Bunty Pearson (her niece) was engaged to a Motherwell lad, and she did not want to live so far away from him. Mrs Herbert (her employer) asked her to find a girl who could speak well, and when she took me for an interview, the lady said I could start in two days; Friday, to be exact. Bunty would be leaving on Saturday, which gave her some time to show me her duties. I was overjoyed at the prospect of getting away as far as possible from Beatrice, and kitchen drudgery; to me that was domestic slavery!

Turning towards the house with the now empty clothes basket, I saw Granny at the window shaking her head from side to side. Although certain I had pegged everything securely, I glanced backwards to see if anything had come loose. When I looked again, Granny's face had disappeared from the window. Slightly puzzled, I bounced into the house, dropped the basket, and entered the kitchen.

Too late! The awful truth hit me like a blow! The expensive fox-fur, familiar kid gloves and Moroccan leather hand-bag lay on the table. Turning to run, the door slammed in my face, and Beatrice stood before me, barring my escape. I knew now why Granny had been shaking her head, she was trying to warn me till Beatrice forced her away from the window.

Gazing at my stepmother, the old familiar knot of fear coiled in the pit of my stomach, sheer terror made me feel sick! I stood absolutely still, as Beatrice pushed her face almost into mine, her eyes dark pools of intense hatred! 'I want your Father's address,' she hissed, rather than spoke. 'I won't leave here without it. He owes me money. You know where he is, he would tell *you*, and I'll get it out of one of you, even if I have to beat it out of you.'

I could not speak. Granny said, 'She does not know George's address. She has not seen or heard from him since they left Dunoon.' Beatrice turned on her, snarling, 'Shut up, you old fool, you both know where that rotten, cheating Father of hers is staying.' Pouncing on Granny, Beatrice pulled her walking stick from her trembling hand, and was about to bring the heavy stick down on her poor defenceless head. I cried out, 'Don't hit her.' Beatrice glared at me, 'So you can speak,' she said, 'You'd better tell me where he is, he tells *you* everything, you wicked brat.'

Again she raised the heavy stick to hit Granny. I leapt to grab hold of it, shouting to Granny to get outside! She tottered to the kitchen door. Beatrice wrenched the stick from me, and ran to stand with her back against the door. Granny faced her, 'Get out of my way, this is my house!' Beatrice laughed in her face. 'Not till I know where that rotten son of yours is hiding.' Desperately I looked round for something to distract her attention, knowing the outside door was open. If I could just get Beatrice away from the inside kitchen door, Granny would reach safety. Two cats, Kiki and Stripey, were curled up on the bed, eyeing us warily. Pouncing on Stripey, a ginger tomcat with extremely sharp claws, I threw him straight into Beatrice's face, spitting, hissing and scratching!

She staggered backwards, and I pushed Granny out, shut the door, and stood with my back against it. Her face contorted, her eyes wild and blood-shot, Beatrice threw herself on me, punching kicking and swearing. Expecting no mercy, I cried out, 'I will tell you all I know if you stop hitting me.' Breathing heavily, still barring the door, she waited, leaning on the stick.

I told her Father had brought me to Glasgow the day after she left Dunoon. He put me in a Servant's Registry office to get work. I had not seen or heard of him since, nearly six weeks ago. He had labelled and sent off two trunks, one to Granny's house, the other to be picked up at the Railway Office in Glasgow's Central Station. I also told her I had worked for three weeks in Glasgow, but had left that job.

Beatrice's face was full of disbelief. 'Rotten little liar, all lies, he has put you up to this. I'll kill you if you don't tell me where he is.' I pleaded and cried, but she ran at me with the stick, pressing me against the wall. Feeling my chest would burst, I tried to slip to the floor, but Beatrice pulled me up by the hair. I tried wriggling sideways, dodging some of the heavy blows, but could not match her strength or weight. My scalp felt it was being torn off. Seizing a chair, I pushed it into her with every ounce of strength I possessed. She let go of my hair, and I ran for the door, burst through and reached the outside door.

Even as I stepped out, her heavy hand gripped my clothes at the back of my neck, jerking me backwards. Choking for breath, I hung grimly on to the strong iron handle of the outside door. I caught a fleeting glimpse of Granny, supported by two women. Something crashed down on my knuckles and I let go the handle. Suddenly losing all control, I threw myself at Beatrice. What this awful woman had made my sisters and I suffer at her hands roused me to a strength of fury I did not know I possessed!

She retreated before my attack, lifted the kettle sitting on the gas-ring behind her, and threw it at me. Hot water spurted over my feet and legs, steam scorched my face, and I screamed in pain and sheer uncontrollable terror. I was hardly aware of a hard, strong arm lifting me bodily out of the doorway. Beatrice spat in the face of another man, then tried to claw and scratch his face. He lifted his heavy steel-tipped working boot, his foot pressing down on hers. Her fine kid shoes were no protection. She yelled, spat again, a torrent of abuse was directed at both men and me.

A neighbour brought out of a pail of water, the man threw the contents in Beatrice's face. 'That will wash your filthy mouth out, and it's a bar of soap you'll swallow next! Beatrice crumpled to the door-step, all the fight out of her. The two workmen had been passing when they heard my screams, they now turned to Granny, asking her if they should run her into the "nick" (Police Station).

A knot of people had now surrounded Granny. She told them to bring Beatrice into the house. I followed, holding on to Granny.

Beatrice tried to dry herself in front of the fire, her rouge, mascara and lipstick had run down her face in streaks, staining the collar of her expensive silk blouse. Her suit had a great wet patch down the front. Granny told her to get ready, the men would put her on a train for Glasgow.

She scorned the remark, saying she would not be seen with such common "trash". Tossing her fox-fur over her shoulders, she pulled on her gloves, straightened her velour hat, and marched out. As she reached the door she turned on me, saying 'I'll get you for this!' I cried out, 'I won't be here, I'm going to my Mother.' She sneered. '*She* won't want you.'

I picked up my coat, calling to Granny, 'I don't trust her, I'm going to the Station to see Beatrice gets on the train.' Granny said. 'You're not fit to go anywhere,' but I paid no heed. Running out, I saw Beatrice turn the corner, the two men were not in sight. I took a short-cut over the foot bridge, which led to the Station by another road. Crouching behind a fence overlooking the platform, I searched the faces of the people waiting for the next train. Beatrice was not among them. Panic seized me, had she evaded the men, and returned to vent her ill-temper on Granny?

The train drew in, clouds of smoke blotted out the figures for a few minutes, the platform was empty when the guard blew his whistle, just then Beatrice hurried out of the waiting room. I could see her face was freshly painted, hair tidied, and her wet patches covered over by her handbag and fur. Limping slightly, she entered a carriage, the guard holding open the door for her. It slammed shut, the guard waved his red flag, and the train moved slowly out of the station.

'Oh God, don't let her come back again,' I moaned. Now pain enveloped me; up to that moment I had ignored it, now every part of me ached, feet and legs seemed on fire, my head hurt, and a new pain grew in my heart with Beatrice's last words. '*She won't want you.*'

Granny sent her neighbours to find me and bring me home. They drew me to my feet, I cried out in pain. A car stopped, voices said, 'Hospital.' 'Oh no, no hospital, please, take me to Granny.'

Summoning all my courage, I stepped by myself into the car, determined to look stronger than I felt. Granny was waiting at her door, tears streaming down her dear, sweet face. 'Puir lassie, my poor bairn, what an evil woman that is.' She asked the women to bathe off the heavy woollen black stockings. (These had actually prevented more serious scalding). I had borrowed them from Granny, as my own were washed and still hanging on the line outside.

I felt I had been through hours of torture, and was surprised that only an hour had passed since Beatrice's arrival. Blisters had formed on my feet and legs, Granny made me sip a little brandy while she directed the women to put cold wet cloths on my burns. I had to lie on my side, my back and shoulders hurt too much, and I fell asleep on the couch from sheer exhaustion.

Uncle Johnny was having his evening meal when I wakened. I tried not to get too wide-awake as the pain increased. Uncle Johnny was saying I could not possibly go to Glasgow in that state, that I should go to Hospital, 'She looks half-dead!' Now I became fully awake, and called 'Granny'. She bent over me, her face full of concern. 'Granny do not send me to Hospital. I've been as badly hurt before, and got better. I must go to Glasgow on Friday, Beatrice is not going to stop me, I won't let her, she has done her worst, now I will get better.'

Granny asked me why I had told Beatrice I was going to my Mother, and I said I did not want her to find out where I would be working. If I was not in Granny's house it would keep her from coming to 'get' me. 'Anyway, I *am* gong to find my Mother. Please Granny, find out her address and sent it to me, that is, if the lady will have me now.'

After a restless night, I rose early, bathed and patted the most painful areas, putting fresh cold water on the clothes. Every weal stretched, stinging and smarting, but a fierce determination spurred me on. I put the irons to heat at the fire, pulled my clothes from the pulley, and was about to iron them when Uncle Johnny came through, dressed for work. He scolded me for rising so early, but I said I must get ready to go to Glasgow tomorrow. Lifting the heavy iron, my legs folded under me. Uncle Johnny caught me, and the iron in one movement, as I slumped to the floor.

When I came to, I cried bitterly from sheer frustration, as much as from physical pain. Granny, sitting up in bed, told Uncle Johnny to lift me in beside her, and to mix an Abdine powder, dissolved in warm water, a great stand-by of her's when she felt poorly. Miss Pearson came in later, and was shocked by my appearance, doubting very much if I would get the job tomorrow. Bunty had told me to say I was sixteen years old, and if asked for a reference from my last employer, to say I had been looking after my Grandmother since I left school. Mrs Herbert had insisted on the new girl being able to speak properly, as she did not wish her children to pick up a Glasgow 'twang'.

Uniform would be discussed when I arrived, Bunty offered to sell me hers, but maybe I would never need it! I grimaced at my reflection in the mirror next morning. white face, yellowish blue-black bruises on my cheeks, forehead and jaw. The swelling on my jaw had gone down, though eating was still painful. Patting cream and powder over the worst parts disguised them a little. Every movement I made was extremely painful, the burns on my feet and legs stung, raw flesh showing through the broken blisters.

I drew my new lisle stockings gingerly over my feet, hoping the blisters would not leak and stain them. Granny had sent me to the hairdresser earlier to have my hair trimmed. Father had always cut our hair since it was shortened, one of the skills he had picked up as a prisoner-of-war. We used to wince when he ran the hair-clippers up our necks, sometimes they pulled the small hairs out. The hairdresser did the same, but much more gently. I had been fascinated by the way the hot tongs were used to give some customers a 'Marcel wave'. This cost a whole 1/- against my 3d trim. The result looked very smart. All the women I had known had 'buns'. When the hair escaped from the numerous hair-pins, especially in windy weather, it looked very untidy!

Now I was ready to leave, and said a rather shaky 'Goodbye' to Granny. If I got the job, I knew I would not see her for a while. She insisted I buy a return ticket, 'No more walking from Glasgow!' I smiled wryly, feeling lucky to be able just to get on and off the train and tram. Uncle Johnny took me to the Station, bought me a small box of chocolates, wished me luck, but said he would not be surprised to see me back that day!

Alighting from the train in Central Station, my eyes searched the crowd waiting for trains, ever on the alert for a sight of Beatrice. I would not feel free of her till I was out of Scotland. At 10.00 a.m. I arrived at the house where I had had my first interview. An elderly lady answered the door, and asked me what I wanted! I said nervously I was the new Nanny. Looking surprised, she told me to come in, closed the door and left me standing in the narrow hall.

Bunty appeared, dressed in a blue uniform, spotless white apron, cuffs, collar and belt, topped by a large stiff square worn round and over her hair. She asked me where my luggage was, said I looked ill, to which I replied that I had no other luggage, and that I had been travel-sick.

She led me into the same room where I had had my first interview. Ayette, the little girl, was drinking orange juice, her Mother nursing the tiny baby. She smiled, then stared, asking me if I had been in an accident. I could not find words to answer this question, trying to hide my badly-bruised hands behind my back. Again she smiled, asked me to sit down and we would have tea, 'You look as if you could do with a cup.'

She nodded to Bunty to take the flushed and sleepy infant from her, and Ayette went with them out of the room. Mrs Herbert must have seen my bruised hands (Beatrice had hit them with a rolling pin) when I accepted a cup of tea, refusing a biscuit, as my jaw was still painful. She did not ask any more questions, but when I had gratefully drunk the hot sweet tea, she led me to the nursery-cum-bedroom.

My bed was in one corner with a screen in front of it, a small bed for Ayette and the baby's cot across from it. She explained that they were rather short of space, living here in her Aunts' flat, but I would have a nice room of my own when they moved to England. Bunty and Ayette came in, and Mrs Herbert asked her to fetch her spare uniform for me to try on. I sat on the bed behind the screen, but before I took off my blouse I asked Bunty to wait outside the screen, she laughed at my modesty, and I had to undress in front of her.

No sooner had I uncovered the weals and bruises on my shoulders and back when Bunty cried out, 'Look, she's been thrashed, who did that to you?' Hearing Bunty cry out, Mrs Herbert looked round the screen, and appeared to be absolutely horrified. 'You poor girl, we'd better have the Doctor into see you.' My head ached, my legs were on fire, I was in pain, and stopped trying to pretend I was not. I took off my stockings to find some relief, I would be sent home anyway.

Mrs Herbert asked Bunty to run a warm bath for me, told me just to pour water over myself and gave me a lovely soft towel to pat myself dry. I murmured that I was sorry to have caused so much bother. Soon I was sitting on the edge of the bed, wearing a most unusual, pretty pink dressing-gown. Bunty brought me a large cup of hot cocoa. Mrs Herbert and Ayette came in. Mrs Herbert proceeded to examine me thoroughly, listing all the bruises, scratches and burns. I told her everything about me that hurt, especially my scalp, I could not bear to touch my head.

Examining everything in my old school satchel she tut-tutted at the meagre contents. An old darned jersey, one pair of heavy school knickers, a very washed-in vest, a penny tooth-brush and a broken comb, all rolled up in an old flannel nightdress. I had meant to wash my only pair of stockings at night to be dry in the morning, and only had the clothes I stood up in, the school blouse, skirt and coat, all too small for me now, plus my old canvas shoes. She was quite angry, exclaiming she would get in touch with the proper authorities to bring the person to court who had inflicted these horrific injuries on a defenceless girl and allowed her to leave home so poorly equipped for work. At this statement, I became very agitated, pleading and crying, so much so that Bunty was told to take Ayette away, as I was upsetting the child.

I refused to say who had beaten me, told them I did not know my Father's address. It would be useless, the Welfare people would not be able to find him. I did not want my Granny to be troubled, she was too old and frail, and had done her best for me. She had been a widow for many years and had nothing but her pension. The Doctor's arrival put an end to further conversation.

He examined me thoroughly, prodding here and there, asking if this or that place hurt. Smiling, he said there were no broken bones anyway, and he would leave me a prescription for tablets, which I was to take three times a day, apply bandages to my burns, and ointment to the weals. He had a long conversation with Mrs Herbert in the next room, during which I dressed myself completely, packed my satchel and waited, quite certain I would have to go home.

I examined the pretty, pink dressing-gown, with its design of birds with multi-coloured feathers, quilted and lined with silk. Someday, I promised myself, I would have one like that too! The Doctor left, and Mrs Herbert exclaimed when she saw I was fully dressed and ready to go out. 'Why, Nanny, do you not want to stay?' I stammered that I did not think she would want me now, and apologised again for being a nuisance. 'I can't make you stay if you don't want to, but I would like you to try for a week, especially as I have these prescriptions for the ointments and tablets the

Doctor says you must have. Now, let us try on the uniform again, you are so different from Nanny in size and shape.'

With a great feeling of relief, I protested no more. How they laughed when I put on the uniform, the dress could have gone round me twice, the belt slipped over my skinny hips, the cuffs would have fallen off my wrists had my knuckles not been so badly swollen. My waist was $17\frac{1}{2}$ inches, my bust 30 inches, Bunty said I looked like a school-kid, and looking at her curvaceous bosom, I wondered if she would tell Mrs Herbert I was only 14 years old. However, she did not say any more, much to my relief.

I was informed my wages would be 7/6 weekly, to be paid monthly, 30/-, when we were in England, as this was only a trial period. I would need proper shoes, and fine black stockings. Bunty would sell me her navy-blue coat for half-price, this would be deducted from my first monthly wage, and Wednesday was my half-day holiday, from 2.00 p.m. till 8.00 p.m.

Determined to do my best to keep the job, I hid the pain as much as possible. Bunty had shown me how to bathe the baby. I could have cried when I lifted him and sweated profusely. He was so tiny, his head fell to one side, and I learned to support it all the time. Bunty was amazed that I had never handled such a tiny baby. The best part of the day was when I took the children for their daily walk in a nearby park, my head would ache less, and my body eased a little.

Although I remember previous homes I had lived in, I cannot conjure up a picture of that flat, or the faces of the two aunts, or remember the food. The routine outside the nursery made no impression, my whole mind was centred on fighting pain, my body cried out for rest and healing warmth. All I longed to do was hide in a dark corner and nurse my pain, but there was little time to indulge in these thoughts. I did not realise how demanding children could be.

The day started at 6.30 a.m. Baby Roger was bathed and dressed, usually howling like a 'banshee' for his first feed of the day. I would gratefully hand him over to his Mother to feed him, then washed and dressed Ayette. We all had breakfast in the nursery at 8 a.m., after which I had to change Roger, wash all the childrens' clothes and clean up the nursery, making my own bed up too. I then dressed the children and we wheeled the pram in the park for another hour.

Lunch at noon, and at 1.00 p.m. Ayette and baby were put to bed for their afternoon rest. I ironed any clothes that were dry, Ayette and Roger had innumerable little dresses and aprons, my own aprons, collar etc, brushed and dusted the pram, ready to take to the park in the afternoon. At 4.00 p.m. we had a cup of tea. Ayette had juice, which I made fresh every day from oranges. After that I played with Ayette till dinner at 5.00 p.m., which one of the aunts brought to the nursery.

The food was sufficient, again I cannot remember, my jaw still too painful to eat with comfort. 6.30 p.m., and Roger was bathed, then Ayette. When both were settled for the night, I took a bath and crept thankfully into bed at about 8 p.m. It says much for the kindness of Mrs Herbert, she must have lifted, fed and changed the little boy, and put Ayette on her potty about 10 p.m. while I slept.

The pills the Doctor had prescribed for me had a strange, numbing effect. All right in bed, but during the day I worked like some mechanical object. I stopped using them through the day, and felt more aware, especially of my aches and pains. The only place I could indulge in a good cry was in the bathroom, when cleaning it out. The bending and stretching involved in this operation was so painful I just let the tears fall, and was sorely tempted to break down altogether, telling myself *not* to give in, I *must* keep this job.

Walking in the park later, trying to answer Ayette's many questions kept my mind off my aching head and body. Once I had to negotiate a steep incline on the path. I could not find the strength to push the heavy pram, and had to walk back the way we came, much to Ayette's surprise. She was a sweet-natured child, very like her pretty mother.

Later I heard that the family had to flee from Shanghai. Trouble had flared up, there were riots in the streets, shop windows smashed, looting and destruction was rife, houses were set on fire and police arrested people without discrimination. Mrs Herbert was six months pregnant, her husband brought her and Ayette to the elderly aunts in Glasgow. They would be safe there while he attended to his business in Shanghai and London.

The little boy, Roger, was born in Glasgow. He was now six weeks old. Mrs Herbert did not wish to burden her aunts longer than was necessary, and she herself needed more space for the children. A furnished house had been rented in Darlington, with eight rooms and a large garden. The children needed to get out more, two short walks during the day meant too little fresh air and sunshine, they would see more of their father too.

I was now at the end of my first week, feeling very anxious as to my suitability. I seemed to make so many mistakes, but Mrs Herbert showed me pleasantly the proper way to do things, but I was still very apprehensive as to whether she would keep me on. I had not gone out on my half-day, asking if I could just lie in bed. She was very concerned, told me to stay in bed and she would see to it that I was not disturbed till next morning.

Now I waited, as she put three half-crowns in an envelope. 'Well, Nanny, you look much better now, I hope you will stay with us.' Looking down at Ayette, she said, 'Would you like Nanny to stay?' Ayette gripped my hand, saying, 'Don't go away, Nanny.' I managed to smile, though tears of relief were not far away, saying, 'I will be happy to stay and to go anywhere with you.' Her Mother laughed, 'Even to China, Nanny?'

The days that followed were busy, packing and sorting. She kept putting the odd article aside, asking me if I liked it. She then produced a case, which could lock, told me it was mine, and to fill it with the selection of silk knickers, underskirts, camisoles, and two pretty nightdresses, saying it was time she had some of the new 'French' knickers that had come into fashion, and that I needed more luggage than I came with. There would be two other maids in England, and they would notice everything I had, she even told me I could keep the pink dressing-gown! My spirits rose immediately and I felt very happy.

I had imaged Mr Herbert would be young and handsome, his wife was so young and pretty, she spoke so lovingly to the children about 'Daddy'. To my surprise he was neither, but dark, stocky and slightly bald! After an excited meeting with Ayette, he turned to look at me, his expression pleasant, his bright beady eyes twinkling. 'So you are the new Nanny?' Ayette piped up, 'Daddy, Nanny's been sick, but she is better now.' I was taken aback, thinking I had cleverly concealed the worst of my pain. Children are more perceptive than we give them credit for, I was to learn.

The Accident

A few days later we were travelling to England in a large, black Ford car. Telling Mrs Herbert I would be travel-sick, she gave me a tiny wicker box of pills, two of which I was to take an hour before we left. Sitting in the rear seat, with Roger's travel-basket between Ayette and myself, I rejoiced inwardly as the car travelled south, leaving Scotland behind. I would write to Granny, send her my new address, and ask her again to find out my Mother's address. I had an instinctive feeling she could if she wanted to, there must be neighbours and relatives of the Stirrat family still in the area.

As we approached the Borders, a motor-cyclist careered out of a side road, obviously out of control. Mr Herbert shouted, 'Hold down the baby.' The car slewed sideways, into a hedge, with a blur of blue jacket and a tremendous crunching bang. The seat rose under me, throwing my body over the cot. I just managed to catch Ayette as she catapulted out of her seat, both children screaming with fright. Mrs Herbert looked ready to faint, but her husband pulled her out over the driver's seat. The door on my side was buckled. Lifting Ayette over to her Father, I caught up the baby in his basket and clambered over, Mr Herbert saying, 'For God's sake, hurry!'

Mrs Herbert was running with Ayette, and I was almost pushed away, the basket pressed into my arms, being told to, 'Run, for God's sake, run!' There was a strong smell of petrol, a pool was forming under the wheels of the motor-cycle. Mr Herbert was afraid it would ignite and set car and luggage on fire. We stopped about 30 yards away, and looking back could see the fumes shimmering in a blue haze above the car and the crumpled motor-cycle. Cars stopped, men got out, helping Mr Herbert to drag the inert body of the young man away from the petrol.

A car stopped beside us, and Mr Herbert asked the driver to take us to the hotel nearby, as he would have to stay by the accident till the police and ambulance men arrived. Mrs Herbert had regained her colour, now soothing a frightened and tearful Ayette, and lifting the baby, we were soon in the Ecclefechan Hotel. A room was put at our disposal, we were given a welcome cup of tea by a sympathetic landlady.

We freshened ourselves up, Mrs Herbert lay down after feeding Roger, so Ayette and I went outside. It was a beautiful day, the walk calmed us both, though Ayette talked excitedly about the 'big bang' and the 'naughty' man who had run into us. We found a narrow country lane, the banks lined with fragrant hedgerows, poppies and pinks in abundance. Ducks slept on the banking, birds chirped and suddenly it came to me: I had no headache! Whether it was the effect of the accident or the fact I was away from Scotland, I was now free of pain!

I ran, whooped and skipped from sheer joy! Ayette's eyes were round with amazement. How could you explain to a three year old? All about me seemed to bring back the memory of long ago, the smell of the countryside, an echo of the happy days at Craigberach Farm.

Returning to the Hotel, Ayette clutching a bunch of wild flowers, we were shown into the dining-room. Her Father had joined his wife, and to her anxious inquiries, replied that the young man, a lad of seventeen, had a broken arm, severe concussion, and bruises. He would mend in time, which was more than could be said for his cycle, *that* was beyond repair! Our car had to be towed to a garage to be repaired, another was hired to take us and our luggage to Darlington. I know I enjoyed my dinner, beautifully set and served, it seemed to make no difference that I was in uniform, which made me feel I was one of the family. All were relieved that we had escaped injury, or even worse!

Entering Darlington, we exclaimed at the sight of the brightly painted trolley-cars, the pretty houses and wide streets. Now we turned into a tree-lined avenue, up a long drive, gravel crunching under the wheels. A sign on the gate said 'Orchard Holme'. A beautiful grey stone house came into view, with many windows and chimneys. Ivy trailed over white painted verandahs, red geraniums in tubs, beds of brightly coloured flowers all around, making a welcoming picture.

We stopped at the door, where a plump, smiling woman stood beside a young housemaid, dressed in frilly cap and apron over a black dress. Cook introduced herself, and Ruby was the daily housemaid. Ruby stared at me, did not smile, and I had no chance to speak, as Ayette pulled me away, wanting to explore. Her Mother said to let her run, as she had been sitting for a long time.

In the garden a swing took her attention. I looked all about me as I pushed the swing to and fro. The trees were laden with half-formed fruits, apples and pears, the plum trees heavy with blossom. The orchard covered a large area, hence the name of the house. Soon Ayette was on the move again, anxious to see inside her 'new' home. I was curious to see my room. Ruby was waiting to show her around, making it very plain that I was to receive no 'attention' from her, asking me to pick up my own case and a large box, she herself carrying a much smaller one.

We walked up a wide stair-case, on the landing the sun shone through a tall stained-glass window, and a few more steps led to a long corridor. The last door opened to reveal an all-white nursery, with pretty frilled curtains swaying, gently in the soft breeze. This contained Roger's cot, and a small bed for Ayette. Nursery furniture lined the walls and on the polished wooden floor lay some sheepskin rugs. Ayette immediately wrapped one round herself, pretending to be a big, bad bear.

My room led off the nursery, and I was delighted to see it was painted all-white with the same pretty curtains. A small dressing table, a single bed and huge cupboards were all it contained, plus a white wicker-work chair. I smiled when I saw the cupboards, my few things would be lost in them, but I liked the feel of the thick carpet under my feet.

Now Ayette saw the table and chairs outside on the verandah and demanded we sit out there for her juice. Later we toured the house with her Mother. It was very well furnished, and well-kept. As we came back to the nursery Mrs Herbert put her hand on my arm, saying I looked different, had a 'glow' about me, to which I replied that my 'headache' had gone, with the aches and pains, and only the burns on my feet and legs were visible, and *they* were healing well. She patted my hand saying, 'You will be safe here.' That night I said, 'Thank you God.' I did not think I could believe in God, since I left the convent, if God could allow people like my stepmother to live, he was not very kind!

Next morning Ruby brought up the breakfast tray, where Ayette was already waiting, seated on a chair on the verandah. Only Ayette's orange squeezer and toast was on the tray, my usual breakfast of toast, egg and tea was missing. Thinking that maybe there was to be a change in routine, I asked Ruby if I was to have my meal downstairs. 'Don't know about that,' she said, 'but I ain't paid to dance attendance on servants.'

Nothing could hurt me now, and I cheerfully told her I would fetch my own breakfast, but she would have to watch the children as Mrs Herbert would not allow them to be left alone at any time, and was very firm about that! Running down to the kitchen, I met Mrs Herbert on the stair, and had to explain why I had left the children unattended. We turned and when I entered the room, Ruby was looking through my clothes in my room. Mrs Herbert told me to go to Cook and bring up my breakfast, and closed the door behind me. Cook was nice, asked me what I'd like, a boiled egg, or bacon and egg. I chose the boiled egg, because Ayette loved to dip little fingers of toast in the yolk.

Returning to the nursery, I met Ruby on the stairs, head down, she ran past me without speaking. Mrs Herbert must have scolded her, though she said nothing to me, and at lunch-time Ruby brought both our lunches, even setting the dishes on the table. I smiled and spoke normally, after all, she was the only young girl apart from Bunty I had spoken to since I left school just two short months ago.

During our subsequent meals, she told me about herself, and I grew to like these little chats. She worked every day from 8.00 a.m. to 4.00 p.m., except Sunday, lived with a married sister in town. Her parents had a small farmhouse in Wales, which could barely support them, so their large family of girls all had to go into domestic service. Ruby said she could not stay with her employers night and day, like I did. She had a steady boyfriend who took her out on his motor-cycle every night and often all day on Sunday, depending on the weather.

I led her to believe I was sixteen, had a boyfriend, saying the first name I could think of, David Stirling. Looking at my flat chest, she said I did not look sixteen, I was a bit skinny. How I envied her well rounded bust, but she was eighteen, had lots of boyfriends and went dancing. The Charleston was the rage, and she could dance the Black Bottom, she just lived for Saturday nights. She also smoked, and offered to teach me when Cook was not about.

A month later, Mrs Herbert weaned the baby from breast to bottle, which meant I could now take complete charge of him. Changing his nappies, (these were thick terry towelling with squares of muslin to protect his tender skin) I asked her when the untidy loose skin between his legs would disappear. She laughed merrily, 'Goodness, Nanny, have you not seen a naked boy? Had you no brothers or cousins?' Replying I only had sisters, afraid to say more lest I gave away too much about my life with them.

She went on to explain that the tiny 'penis' would grow with him, the loose skin was his 'testicles', they would also grow with him. When he was a man, he would make babies with his wife, it was called 'making love', and can be a very beautiful experience, though making love was only part, a very important part, never-the-less, of a happy marriage. I said I could not understand why our private parts were so important, I felt it was 'dirty' in a way. 'You are quite right, Nanny, it will feel dirty if a man forces you to make love against your will, but when you are older you will find a man's intentions quite easy to discover.' 'How will I know,' I asked, 'if it is love or just a bit of fun on his part?' Mrs Herbert looked at me earnestly, 'Your instinct will guide you, if you really love each other, you will find great happiness in each other's company.'

Pondering over this conversation, I decided I would just try to think of David Stirling, though whether he even remembered me would surprise me, school days now seemed so far away. Walking every day in the Park, I noticed other nurses and nurse maids, dressed like myself. Most were elderly, severe-looking, and showed no interest in me, but the young girls would talk to Ayette, inviting her to play with their charges. We would compare 'babies' and they loved to wink and giggle at the young men who strolled through the park on their way to a large College building on the other side.

These young mens' favourite approach was to call out, 'Hello baby, how's Nurse?' At first I blushed furiously, hating myself for doing so, as it seemed to amuse them. Then I realised they said the same to the other young nurses. One afternoon, a smartly dressed fellow in grey 'Oxford Bags' and 'Fairisle' pullover stopped me by putting his hand on the pram handle. 'You're new, you sound Scottish,' he said, and proceeded to tell me he had relatives in Edinburgh, and had spent many holidays there. I asked him to remove his hand, which he did, but walked by my side, jingling money in his pocket, watching my face intently. As we neared the gates, he said in a low voice (not to let Ayette hear) that he would wait for me here on my half-holiday, he knew a place where we could have a cuddle and a bit of fun!

Anger flared up, 'I will not meet you, I don't need your kind of fun, anyway, I have a boyfriend'. He seemed taken aback, flushed angrily, then laughed, 'Prickly as a Scotch thistle, you are!' He walked away, whistling, though I sensed the whistling was to cover up for the rebuff I had given him. I felt confused, flattered and disappointed. It was the first time I had been asked to meet someone. If only he had asked whether 'I' would like to meet him! His high-handed way of expecting me to be there had angered me. From then on I looked for him in the Park, but he would turn his back on me while chatting up girls.

Now I would sit in front of my mirror, examining myself closely. Was I really pretty? Father had killed any vanity I may have had, saying often I was the plain Jane of the family. The mirror reflected pink and white skin, no doubt due to my Spartan diet of porridge and vegetables when at school, even white teeth, also due to Father's insistence that we brush our teeth after every meal with salt and water, one toothbrush between us. It was a 'status' thing, working-class children would not know what a tooth-brush was meant for!

My face was now a little rounder, I had very bright blue eyes like Father's, and auburn hair which I had had cut into a 'bob'. This style was the result of women working in factories at munitions. Long hair was dangerous: if it escaped from the many hair-pins it could become entangled in machinery. The idea had caught on, no young girls had long hair, unless their parents resisted.

Plucking up courage I asked Cook if she thought I was pretty. 'Nanny, you don't need to ask me, you be as pretty as a picture. Ruby don't take to you because she's real jealous of your clear skin.' Poor Ruby, she was plagued with blackheads and sallow skin. Lank brown hair and pale grey eyes did nothing to make her attractive, yet she maintained she could have any boy she wanted! Cook tried to put 'some meat on my bones', she thought I was too thin, neither of them knew anything about the treatment I had received at my stepmother's hands. Only the scars on my feet and legs were all that was visible, and I always kept them covered.

Playing in the garden with the children, I felt like a child, savouring a little of my lost childhood. The past was a closed book, or so I thought.

The Past Returns

Mr and Mrs Herbert worked long into the night, writing in ledgers. One evening, when Cook had retired to her room, I was asked to fetch a glass of water. The kitchen was in darkness, I stretched my hand out to find the candle and matches which were left on a ledge just inside the door. As my hand rested on the ledge, something warm and furry ran over it.

'A Rat!' Terror gripped me, blackness descended, an evil menacing force seemd to be clawing me into the depths. I fought madly against the inhuman hands that were dragging at my straining body, desperately struggling to reach a tiny pin-point of light. This light receded and appeared and disappeared. I was about to give up, to fall into a bottomless pit when the clawing ceased, I could hear a dreadful screeching sound coming nearer (it was myself). Suddenly the light grew brighter, blinding me. Human hands held me, Mr Herbert held me tightly, his wife crying, 'Nanny, Nanny.'

My body sagged, my hands and arms, rigidly extended towards the light, now dropped to my side, finger nails spurting a little blood. I tried to stand, my legs felt like putty, and I was shaking and trembling. Cook, watching me, drew me into her bosom, muttering that she wished she could get her hands on the 'devil' who could so frighten a child out of her 'wits'. What had I given away during my panic-stricken ordeal? Lying in bed, the words 'out of her wits' worried me, the memory of the terror in Gina's eyes before the blank stare took over still haunted me.

Suddenly I was alarmed, what if the Doctor was called to see me? He could put me away, as he seemed to have put Gina away, apparently out of this world! Quickly, I drew on my pretty robe, willing myself to be calm, I *must* look normal! To my tapping on the sitting room door, both voices said 'Come in.' Mr and Mrs Herbert were very surprised to see me. 'Are you all right Nanny? You should have stayed in bed!' Blurting out, 'Please don't send for the Doctor, I am all right now. It was just because I was once bitten by a rat, and I was frightened in the dark!'

Cook came in, saying the poor 'mouse' must have got the fright of its life! Mr Herbert wanted to know who or what I was fighting, 'It seemed as though someone or something was trying to shut you in the dark,' my screams of 'let me out, let me out' had disturbed them. I did not want to talk about it, repeating over and over that it would not happen again. Cook fetched tea and biscuits, leaving me to sit with my employers.

Mr Herbert said I spoke well, where had I attended school? I answered that happily enough, and when the tea was finished, I carried the tray back to Cook. She was putting curling-pins in her hair, and said she was glad to see I was all right though 'You did give us a turn, I can tell 'ee!' This event made me think of Granny. I had only written once, when I arrived in Darlington, and had changed my mind about giving her my address, lest Beatrice should find out where I now lived.

Now I longed to hear about her, Gertie, (or even Gina) and Father. Soon it would be Christmas, I would send Granny a wee present, cards were too expensive in those days. They were made of lace and trimmed with ribbon, pasted on cardboard, only the well-to-do could afford them. However, a change took place in the household, which kept me so busy I forgot to write.

The Chinese Collection

November brought a great many crates marked FRAGILE to the house. They were piled up in the hall, we were very curious about their contents. Mr Herbert came home, called us into the library and said his wife was about to open a shop, to sell her 'Chinese Collection'. He hoped we would give her our help and support. There would be a bonus for us if the sales made a profit.

He put on a heavy canvas apron, and proceeded to dismantle the library-cum-diningroom. He himself took down the heavy curtains, blinds and pictures, which we dusted and packed in boxes, labelled and numbered. The gardener and two men removed the heavy dining table and chairs to the hall. Ruby and I were asked to empty the bookshelves, Mrs Herbert looked after the children. Ayette, running round getting in everyone's way, was excited and happy. The great carpet was swept, lifted and rolled up, it took three of us to carry it upstairs to a spare room, where we had already packed nearly 1,000 books.

Next day, Ruby, Cook and the washer-woman scrubbed and polished till the room shone. We began to unpack the boxes, gasping in awe as each article was revealed. All shapes and sizes of beautiful vases, decorated in rich blues and gold. Porcelain tea-sets, light and fragile as egg-shells, embroidered screens, pictures, curtains, cushion covers and table linen, hand embroidered. Jewellery, ornaments, bells, lanterns, quilted jackets and bed-mats. Chinese dolls and tiny figurines. Thick carpets and wood carvings, pretty little boxes and tea-trays.

Most impressive was a huge brass gong. This rested on a wooden frame, into which was carved dragons, snakes, idols and flowers. Two hammers, one quite small, tipped with green baize, the other so heavy I could scarce lift it with two hands, hung on a hook behind the brass plate, also heavily carved. It took the gardener, his two helpers and Mr Herbert to carry it up to the landing!

Here the light, shining through the stained glass window sparked off a wonderful kaleidoscope of colour. An air of mysticism seemed to hover round it, especially at night, it still seemed to glow in darkness. Nearly 8 ft high, it had come from a Chinese Temple, and been used to summon the people to prayer. In the event of attack it would sound the alarm, and people in out-lying villages would run for safety to the temple. Ayette was allowed to hit the gong with the small hammer, the resulting boom made her drop it hurriedly, but she soon picked it up to make another 'big bang', her Mother eventually had to take it from her, and hang it out of reach. I heard the Herberts working well into the night, I had offered to help after the children were in bed, but they said some of the stuff was so fragile, they would rather not give me the responsibility.

Cook, Ruby and I had often commented on Mrs Herbert's almost fanatical cleanliness. Even Ruby had a cupboard to keep her uniform in. Mrs Herbert did not permit her to take it home. She often came to work in pretty short-sleeved dresses and artificial silk stockings, these were kept in the cupboard till she was ready to leave, and had to change into them. Cook said. 'They had lived so long among them dirty heathens in China, she did not suppose they washed themselves from birth to death!'

Next morning, we were called in to see the 'Chinese Collection' on display. As the door opened, bells tinkled clearly and sweetly, we gazed in wonder, the whole room presented a riot of colour. The ceiling was festooned with coloured lanterns, kites and bird-cages. Painted screens were arranged in front of the windows. Silk cushions lay on thick richly embroidered rugs, the delicate China placed safely in sets along the bookshelves, along with vases, ornaments etc. Every corner was filled but one, near the fireplace. Here a desk and chair, with paper, string, boxes, tissue-paper, pen and ink was arranged neatly. Pamphlets and printed cards were placed on the table in the hall. The cards read as follows:

THE CHINESE COLLECTION
OPEN EVERY DAY EXCEPT MONDAY
FROM 10 a.m. TO 6 p.m.
ALL WELCOME, PARTIES CATERED FOR.
PHONE DARLINGTON 258

Monday was Cook's day off, although Ruby did not come in on Sunday. Mr Herbert was often home at week-ends. The notices appeared in the Daily and weekly papers, as Mrs Herbert wanted to catch the Christmas shoppers. Ruby and myself were asked to stay in view near the Chinese room, and to keep an eye on visitors' children. A notice was placed above the door of that room saying, 'NO CHILDREN'. I was not to allow Ayette in either, but she could play in the hall, and hand out cards to waiting customers.

Both Cook and Ruby said 'Mistress' to Mrs Herbert, but I could not, Beatrice had flown into such a fury when Father came in late, taunting him about his 'Mistress'. We assumed she must be a very wicked woman, and I could not associate that name with my kind employer. She herself did not appear to notice, though the other servants did!

The 'Chinese Collection' proved very popular, bringing in a constant flow of well-to-do clients by cab, car, taxi and mini-bus.

Now I had almost complete charge of the children. Roger was now 8 months old, a bundle of energy. He wanted to see everything and my arms ached, carrying him around, but I was too happy to grumble.

Ayette enjoyed giving visitors the cards and lists of goods, and would show her toys to any children who came with their parents.

The Burglary

Late one afternoon a prosperous-looking couple came in. The gentleman stayed inside the front door, while the lady asked me if she could use the bathroom. I said she could only use the W.C. outside the kitchen, but she shook her head wearily, saying she had had a long journey and needed to freshen up. I called to Cook to take over, and preceded her to the downstairs bathroom.

When I returned Ayette was telling the man her Daddy was 'away' and no, she did not have a nice big dog. I called her over and gave her a card to give to him, but I did not like the way he smiled and winked at me. His wife had been fully ten minutes in the bathroom, I was relieved when she came out. Just then Mrs Herbert ushered a group out of the Chinese room, and the two went inside with her.

As there were no more clients waiting, we all went out into the garden, although it was getting dark. We looked over the garden gate, and spotted a small Austin Seven car in a dark colour sitting under the trees, and invisible from the house. A funny place to park a car, I thought, most cars came up the drive.

The couple seemed to take a long time in the Chinese Room, but when they left Mrs Herbert was very pleased. They had bought the most expensive items, and had requested that they be packed in fairly small boxes for easy lifting. They were so charmed with the beautiful merchandise that they had purchased more than they had ready money for and would have to visit the bank in the morning. They would call to collect the goods as early as possible, as they had a long journey before them.

When the children were in bed, Cook helped Mrs Herbert and myself to wrap each dainty piece in tissue, then tied up each parcel securely, in their boxes. Mrs Herbert only turned the key in the lock of the shop at night. We did not fear intruders, as Mr Herbert had brought a locksmith in to secure all the windows.

Being a light sleeper, perhaps because I had to listen for the children should they wake in the night, I sat up suddenly, certain I heard a bell ringing. Mrs Herbert had a small bell by her bedside which she would use to summon any of us. I peeped into the nursery, the night-light spluttered in its little saucer as I opened the door, but all was quiet there. I tiptoed to the bannister, and saw two figures emerge from the Chinese Room, each laden with parcels.

I ran into Mrs Herbert's room, shook her, saying, 'We've got burglars!' She said, 'Nanny, bang the gong, shut the nursery door first, and I'll phone the police'. She had a phone by her bed, as Mr Herbert often had to take business calls at strange hours. Pulses racing, I reached the gong, lifted the biggest hammer carefully and swung it with all my strength to hit the great brass plate.

Bedlam broke loose, the crash reverberated through the house, dogs barked, the children screamed. Cook rushed out of the kitchen, waving a carving knife and shouting, 'Murder, murder, let me get at the varmints!' Mrs Herbert ran downstairs carrying a gun, I carried the small hammer. The two figures disappeared into the bathroom. Well, they were trapped in there, we would keep guard till the police arrived.

It was very quite in the bathroom, too quiet, just then Ayette came to the top of the stairs, she was whimpering with fright. As I lifted her up, I heard the crunch of gravel under the feet of the intruders. I shouted to Mrs Herbert, 'They are getting away!' She fled to open the front door, but could not see anything. Just then the police car arrived, the other car was just starting up.

The police did a U turn and chased after the small car. Roger had fallen asleep after his rude awakening, but Ayette made me stay with her till she too fell asleep. She said I was very 'naughty' to bang the big 'drum' when she was sleeping. Policemen were speaking to Mrs Herbert, looking over the bannister she saw me and called up that everything was all right now, 'The police caught them, just get back to bed, Nanny.'

It occured to me I had not been frightened, as I would have been had Beatrice stormed into the house, but of course *I* was not the target. In the morning police discovered the screws in the bathroom window had been removed by someone *inside* the house. Cook,

Ruby and myself were questioned for some time. Cook became angry, saying we were all under suspicion, and she would leave the house if she was questioned any more. Mrs Herbert looked worried, she had sent for her husband.

Ayette and I told them the 'lady' had been a long time in the bathroom. The window was made secure by 4 inch screws right through the wood frames, alowing a gap of 2 inches at the top for ventilation. Sure enough, when the lady's bag was searched in the police station, it contained two strong screwdrivers, a pair of pliers and two long screws.

All the goods had been recovered, and were none the worse. The couple were well known to the London police for stealing. When Mr Herbert came home, he was most upset, and thanked Cook and me for our help. I was glad to hear there were no bullets in the gun, it was kept by the bedside in his room to frighten off intruders.

Cook was given a week-end off work, and her fare paid to visit her hometown. She, poor soul, had been married only a few months when her husband was killed in the war in 1914. She could not bear to live in the house they had bought and furnished together with pride, so she rented it out and went back into service as a cook. He had now been dead for twelve years, but she often cried when speaking of him. How I hated the word 'WAR'!

When I was offered my fare home, I was startled into answering vehemently, 'No, no I don't want to go home!' They gave me a Nursing Watch instead, which fastened to my apron or coat lapel. I was very proud of it, as only the senior nurses wore them. My own silver watch, won at school, with my initials engraved on it, had been ground into fragments under the heel of Beatrice's shoe in one of her tempers. They said we had been very brave. 'Brave, me brave, I was terrified, but I'd have carved them up before they got me!' said Cook.

New locks were put on all the windows downstairs, especially the small ones. The police were around the area for a time, but soon we were back to normal. Christmas was not far off. Ayette attended a small kindergarten class for children under school-age. Christmas was a simple affair, a small tree adorned the dining table. Cook excelled herself, working at the stove for hours.

On Christmas Day, we all sat down. Cook and myself, the baby in his high chair, and a very excited Ayette. What a change from our usual nursery meals of thin soup and sandwiches at midday!

We could eat as much as we wanted, of roast beef, Yorkshire pudding, chicken and stuffing. Sauces and sausages, vegetables and bread rolls, followed by plum pudding, mince pies, trifle and Christmas cake.

Ruby had been given the day off, to have Christmas with her family, so Cook and myself cleared the table and washed up, the parents looking after the children till we finished. Returning to the sitting-room, we were given a glass of port wine, and an envelope with two months wages, one of which was the promised bonus. Mr Herbert thanked us for our help and support in making the 'shop' a success, and hoped we would continue to do so.

It seemed a little strange to me that the children were given no presents, their daily routine was not disturbed, except for sitting at the dinner-table, even that fitted into their usual lunch time. When I had mentioned 'presents' to Mrs Herbert, she said she would prefer not to get them excited. They were too young to know what Christmas really meant!

Ruby arrived back next day, and chatted to Cook about the wonderful time she had had, not getting to bed till 5 a.m. She had visited three houses, and (looking at me) been kissed many times under the mistletoe, and given twenty presents. She said we were a right miserable lot, could not understand why I did not want to 'enjoy' myself, which gave me rather a jolt, and I felt restless and unhappy for a few days.

I had sent a Christmas card to Granny, together with my address and a 2/6 postal order, asking her not to let Beatrice know where I was. A few days after Christmas I received a letter from Father. He had visited his mother at Christmas, read my letter, and was annoyed that I had not written sooner.

His daughters were not very attentive to his needs, and he had to look after himself. Gertie had given up working, did not feel very well, she was just being lazy. There was no mention of the beating I had received from Beatrice, though he must have heard about it from Granny and Uncle Johnny. No mention of Gina either. As I seemed to have kept this job, I must be doing quite well. Gertie was of no use to him, as she had no money. He hoped I would now be able to reimburse (his own word) him for the money he had spent on our education. £2 a month would be acceptable, meantime. I should look for better-paid employment if a rise was not forthcoming.

He had 'rooms' in Montrose House in Glasgow, I was to send the money to him there. He even signed the letter, 'your poor old Father'. Mrs Herbert noticed how worried I appeared to be. She knew I had received a letter, the first for eight months. I burst into tears, and handed her the letter to read.

She told me to write to him, explaining that I was paid the proper rate for a 'trainee' nursemaid, that I needed every penny to keep myself in clothes, and other necessities. She herself enclosed a note, saying I was in a dreadful state when she employed me, my clothes were a dlsgrace, I would have been better equipped had I come from the poorhouse! She believed he had a good position, and could have provided the necessities for my comfort and well-being. That she had a Doctor's certificate to prove the extent of my injuries, and lack of adequate clothing, which, if he persisted in his demand for my wages, she would not hesitate to show to the proper authorities.

Fearful of Father's reactions to these letters, I slipped £2 into the envelope before sticking it down. Goodbye to my bonus! He did not reply, but I am certain the letter from Mrs Herbert rankled when next I wrote to him concerning my future. Gertie wrote the following week, saying Granny had been ill with bronchitis, it had been very wet and cold. She herself had been quite ill, her nerves were bad, but she had good news to tell me. Beatrice was in prison!

She had taken a position as housekeeper to a widower with two children. She had thrashed the boys to such an extent they needed hospital treatment. Their Father had charged her with grievous bodily harm to both children, and she had received a sentence of three years in prison. Though Gertie pitied the children, she was happier than she had ever been, it was a great relief to know that Beatrice was behind bars.

When Father had visited them, he did not mention it, though he must have known, as the case was printed in the newspapers. No, she had not found out our Mother's address but would make an effort when she felt better. She was pleased that I was happy in my work, said the 2/6 postal order came in handy, that Uncle Johnny was getting married, so she would have to stay with Granny for a while.

Spring came quickly, the trees blossomed and birds wakened me with the 'dawn chorus'. Roger was learning to walk, Ayette at school. Mr Herbert helped me, by taking Roger for an hour or two, telling me to run along, the little rascal was too heavy for me. Indeed my back ached. I would join Ruby and Cook in the kitchen, helping to fold the sheets to put through the mangle, or trying to reduce the huge pile of ironing that seemed never-ending. I ironed everything belonging to the children, nursery or myself, but Ruby ironed sheets, pillowslips, shirts and everything else. Mrs Herbert was extremely particular in this respect.

On a windy day in April, Roger threw Ayette's kite over the verandah. It caught the wind and sailed to the top of a tall cypress tree, where the string tangled with the branches. Both children started to cry, so I took them down to Cook, asked her to look after them, while I fetched a ladder. It was much higher than I expected, and when I looked down, the ground seemed very far away. I was enjoying myself immensely, and crawled onto the top-most branch, which bent under my weight. I managed to catch the dangling string and tried to work the kite loose.

Afraid to pull too hard lest it should tear, I decided to get down the tree again and get a pole to dislodge it. Climbing up the second time was much more difficult with the long 'stretcher ' (clothes pole) in front of me. Ayette clapped her hands when I finally released the string. I told them to go away, as I would tie the kite to the pole and drop it on the grass, which made it much easier for me to climb down. Mrs Herbert was quite cross with me, saying if I had broken a leg, or even my neck, she would have been held responsible, and one of the gardener's boys could have rescued the kite!

She was curious to know why I was so afraid of the dark, yet had no fear of danger, as witnessed by her in the car-crash, the burglary, and now the tree. I really was afraid of the dark, refusing to stay out late on my half-holiday. I only took off my uniform for a few hours and looked at the shops, picking up some ideas to copy, I bought tiny pieces of pretty material to make 'modesty vests'. The fashion for very deep V necks in dresses and coats made these necessary, pinned or sewn into the bottom half of the V necks.

Mrs Herbert dressed very smartly, and had given me one or two dresses. Camisoles were out, brassieres came in, whale-bone corsets had disappeared and the new stretch elastic girdle had taken their place. Dresses were narrow, straight and hip-tight, reaching just to the knees. Snake bangles were worn, sometimes three of them on the upper arm, beads to match dangled below the waist. Fringing adorned many frocks, made with silk, chiffon and voile.

I liked the new 'Charleston' style with its pocket-handkerchief hemlines, the corners floated round the knees when dancing. Ruby showed me her 'fancy' garters, ruched pink satin, trimmed with ribbon and rosebuds, which Ken had bought for her birthday and insisted on putting on above her knees, with much mirth and saucy remarks from her sister and brother-inlaw. She aspired to become a 'flapper' but did not look like the models in the shop windows.

Summer passed in a warm haze, we had picnics and trips to the coast, Roger doing his utmost to escape from our restraining hands. He was a beautiful child, golden curls and chubby limbs, but he could be very mischievous, and I had to watch him constantly. Mrs Herbert did not often come with us to the beach, she would or could not leave the 'shop'. Sometimes Cook would come if she had time, but usually it was only Mr Herbert. He would stroll along the beach, read his newspaper, and help to amuse the children. He appeared to adore them, and his wife, I secretly hoped that if ever I had children, they would have such a loving father. He was quite careful of me also, if any of the young men tried to speak to me, attracted no doubt by the uniform, he would tell them to take themselves elsewhere.

Autumn came, Ayette started school, but developed a nasty cough which became so persistent the Doctor was called, and he diagnosed tonsillitis. She was admitted to hospital, her parents concerned and anxious, visiting her as often as they were permitted. I had sole charge of Roger, who became more of a handful as he could now run about. Ruby detested him (he made more work for her) and Cook said if he was hers, she would spank his bottom.

David Stirling

When Ayette had recovered a little from the operation, she asked for me, wanting her favourite bed-time story made up by me, adventures in the life of the 'naughty kitten'. Mrs Herbert agreed to put Roger to bed, and Mr Herbert ran me in his car to hospital. As we walked through a long corridor, I could see a group of men at the far end, one of whom seemed vaguely familiar, although all wore white coats.

Sitting beside a pale and tearful little girl, who clung to my hands, I started nervously on a story. Her Father, sensing my shyness, strolled round the beds, speaking to the other tiny patients. Half-way through 'Kitty's' latest adventure, the group of men entered the ward. My heart leaped with joy. It *was* David Stirling! He too was startled, recognition lit up his eyes, the well-remembered smile, so like Martha's, flashed across his thin face.

He turned to answer the senior Doctor's questions, and he moved away with him. I had great difficulty concentrating on my story, Ayette pouted and nipped my hand. As the group left the ward, David stepped over to me, and pressed a piece of paper into my hand. It read, 'See you at the library tomorrow about 3.00 p.m.' I was thrilled, hugged Ayette excessively, and promised I would come back tomorrow, secretly hoping to see David again.

Now I had a dilemma, Ayette's parents would visit her in the afternoon, Roger would be on his afternoon sleep, when I had to iron and clean up. It would be impossible to be at the library at 3.00 p.m. Deciding to ask Mrs Herbert for her advice, I told her all about David, and that he wanted to meet me. She told me to write him a short note, give him my address, and ask him to call any time after 8.00 p.m. She would leave it for him at

Reception, if she did not see him.

I stuck the flap down carefully, wrote 'David Stirling' in large letters, and waited, hoping he would come. He duly arrived that evening, and was shown into the sitting room. Mr and Mrs Herbert went into the Chinese room and left us alone. He was not in the least shy, but I was nervous, sitting on the edge of my chair, not feeling at ease, I said I would get my coat, and we could walk and talk, there was so much to talk about.

When I returned, Mrs Herbert was talking to him, turning to me she said, 'This man is out on his feet, he has been on duty since 5.00 a.m. Take off your coat and sit with him, Cook will bring some tea.' With a huge sigh of relief, David sank into an easy chair, closed his eyes for a moment, his legs stretched out to the warmth of the fire. In a moment he recovered, exclaimed how I had grown, how well and happy I looked.

As he lay back again, I went into the kitchen to help Cook set the supper tray. She teased me about the 'handsome' young doctor, said I was a 'dark horse' not telling about him. After tea and biscuits with my employers, David left, saying he had to be at 'prayers' by 9.30 p.m. I walked to the gate with him, and asked to meet him outside, told him I would have Wednesday afternoon off and would he meet me at 3.00 p.m. at the library? He said he would try to be there, but could not promise, as he had lectures to attend, and he was to sit his 'final' exams that year.

Thankfully, Ayette came out of hospital, so I would be able to get out on Wednesday afternoon. Excited and happy, I told Ruby I was to meet him. I had given no thought to what I should wear, till Ruby surprised me by saying, 'You are surely not going to meet him in that get-up?' meaning my uniform. She told me to buy a pair of artificial silk stockings, and she would lend me her best dress and make-up.

The powder, lipstick and mascara had all been purchased in Woolworths at 3d each, so I declined the make-up and bought my own, fearing I would get blackheads from her powder puff. Came the day, I put Roger to sleep and slipped into the kitchen. Ruby helped me to put on the bright-red lipstick, powder and mascara, painted a 'beauty' spot on my cheek, and coaxed a 'kiss' curl on to my forehead. The scarlet dress was quite daring, just touching my knees, the same knees looking naked under the transparent stockings, held up by my old black garters! The stockings had cost

$11\frac{1}{2}$ d, and Ruby said the cheapest way to buy them was to pay 2/6 for three pairs of the same colour. They laddered every time you wore them, which seemed very extravagant to me!

Cook tut-tutted when she saw me emerge from her room, 'dressed up like a tart' and I was afraid to meet Mrs Herbert, stepping quietly on the gravel should she look out. Entering the library, my heart leaped to see David sitting there pouring over a large book. He did not look up till I sat down opposite him. He frowned, his lips set in a thin line, it was plain to see he was not pleased to see me. He hurried me out of the library, into a small tea room, choosing a table in a secluded corner. I murmured that a table in the window would be nicer (I did so want to be seen in my new finery), but he merely nodded to the waitress, ordering two cups of Russian tea, fashionable among the young people at the time.

As I sipped from the tall glass, and squeezed the lemon slice with the long spoon provided, I was unable to break the awkward silence between us. Suddenly, the familiar smile broke through, lightening the atmosphere like sun through cloud. 'What's this?' he said, 'nothing to say, Mary, you are usually such a chatterbox!' He spoke of his mother, she had sold everything, giving him every penny to pay his way through medical school. He hoped to qualify as a missionary doctor. If he passed his final exam this year, he would be sent to Africa, for field training next year. All too soon, he glanced at his watch, said he had to attend a lecture at 4.00 p.m. and with a quick 'God bless' he strode off, leaving me outside the tea room feeling cheated, deflated and disappointed. He had not even suggested I should meet him again.

As I crossed the road, some young men gave out wolf-whistles. Realising the daring dress must have attracted them, I hurried home, taking a different route, not wanting to meet Ruby on her way home. Cook saw me come in, I brushed past her, and washed my face, then took off the dress, leaving it on Cook's bed. I ran upstairs, donned my uniform, and combed the 'kiss' curl away. That would be the last time I would dress up for a man, I vowed.

Ayette soon discovered that I was home, we went down to the kitchen together, both her mother and Cook were surprised at my early return. I pretended it was great to have seen David, but he had lectures and exams, which left him with very little time for himself, and he was not sure if he could meet me every

Wednesday. Ruby wanted to hear everything we said or did, but in her opinion he was a poor kind of lad who could only spend less than an hour once a week with his girl. *She* was out *every* night with Ken.

When Wednesday came round again I decided to visit the library, the only difference I made was to remove the white square cap on my head. I loved to feel the wind blowing through my hair, it was captive under my cap for $6\frac{1}{2}$ days of the week, only taking it off when the children were in bed. David was not there. Disappointed, I turned to leave, when he appeared suddenly at my side, with the most welcoming smile, which left me in no doubt that he really *was* pleased to see me.

We did not go into the cafe. Completely honest, he said he could not afford to treat me, his budget was very strained, nor would he accept my offer to pay. Walking in the park, curiosity got the better of me, and I asked why he liked my company today, yet did not seem to want it last week. He stopped, put his hands on my shoulders and made me face him, looking straight into my eyes. 'Mary, I was ashamed to be seen with you, that dress and paint on your face, so unlike the really nice girl I had just met, please don't dress like that!'

Laughing now, I told him they were borrowed clothes, and only worn to impress him. He had watched me enter the library, and meant to walk away if I had been dressed as I was the previous week.

We sat on the bench, and I talked my heart out, he was the only person who knew everything about me, squeezing my hand gently at mention of the darker moments in my life. He took me home, said he would meet me next week, and strode off with quick 'God bless you'. I ran up the drive, heaven was in my heart and the strains of 'Moonlight and Roses', the latest record, came through the open windows. That tune was to remind me of David for many years.

How the week dragged, it seemed to me Wednesday would never come, but it did, and brought me great disappointment. He was not in the library. I sat in the tea room in a window seat, watching the door of the library, but after an hour, I walked home slowly, trudging through the piles of autumn leaves and the sadness of their falling matched my drooping spirit.

However, on Friday evening he called for me, and as the children were asleep, I asked Mrs Herbert if she would mind if I went out for an hour with him. She hesitated, then said, 'Nanny, I think he is a very decent young man, but you are too fond of him. I don't like you going out at night.' The suggestion that I was too fond of David made my cheeks burn with embarrassment. I mumbled that I would only go as far as the gate. David was quite happy to agree, I had hoped he would say we could take a walk. He apologised for not turning up on Wednesday, but an important lecture had lasted all afternoon. What he had really come for, was to tell me he had been offered a field posting in Africa, and would take the post up early in the New Year.

He was elated, but I felt sad. To lose him so soon would break my heart. I put my arms about his neck and was about to kiss him, he drew back, startled. 'No, Mary, don't, we can never be more than friends. My work for God is the only love I can have.' I dropped my arms, the sadness in my face must have touched him. He clasped my two hands in his hands, I sensed that he was tempted to kiss me, but I drew away. I did not want to lose his friendship by tempting him against his will, and said so, in a small voice. We would remain friends, he would meet me till he went away, he promised.

Next day Ayette and I had a walk through the shops, now lit-up for Christmas. Ayette gazed in wonder at the shimmering tinsel and Christmas decorations. Most streets and houses were still gas-lit. We watched the lamp-lighters passing from one lamp to another with their long poles. In the house we still had gas light and paraffin lamps. David met me every week, sometimes we sat in the tea room if it was too cold or wet to walk. On the last week, just before Christmas, he said he was finished with his exams, he would get the results posted to him at his mother's address. He intended to spend all the time he had left in her company, and she had sent him money for his fare home.

He seemed pleased with the fountain pen I gave him, in return he had a small parcel for me, asking me not to open it till Christmas Day. We walked very slowly home, both knowing we would never see each other again. At the gate I turned and said, 'Goodbye, David. Write to me when you can.'

Suddenly, there on the icy pavement, with the white-frosted branches above us, he knelt down, clasped his hands, looked up to the sky and prayed. I was taken aback, felt self-conscious as one or two people were about, but he did not appear to see them. 'Dear Lord, bless, comfort and keep this dear girl safe in your arms. Teach her to love You, as I love You. Amen.'

He rose, pressed his lips lightly on my forehead and walked away. Strangely, I was not too sad, knowing he was a dear friend seemed more worth-while than another kind of relationship. If God brought us together again, we would know we were meant for each other, so I comforted myself.

Opening his present to me, I found it was an autograph book. 'To my dear friend, Mary, from David.' On the first page he had beautifully drawn the following text, surrounded with doves and leaves:

"TO LIVE IS NOTHING, UNLESS TO LIVE,
BE TO KNOW HIM BY WHOM WE LIVE"

This was all I had to remember him by, I wrapped the book up again, locked it in my case, not wishing Ruby to see it.

Christmas passed happily enough, but on Wednesday, I sat in the tea room at the table we had occupied on our last meeting. Lingering over my tea, lost in thoughts of David, I was unaware of the young man who kept smiling to me across the room. He rose, carrying his glass of tea, and laid it on my table. He sat down very close to me, and I was about to edge away when his hand closed firmly on my knee under the table-cloth. Annoyed, I turned to stare him in the face, rising at the same time. The face that was too near me was pimply and red, light-blue eyes, but it was his smile that appalled me. His teeth were prominent, dark brown, one missing.

I picked up my coat, walked to the counter, paid my bill, and emerged into the gloom of a January afternoon. Looking behind me, I saw the man had also paid his bill, and followed me out. About to cross the road, an arm went tightly round my waist, his voice said, 'Don't be shy, my pretty miss.' He kissed me full on the mouth, the awful stench of bad breath filled me with disgust. Slapping his face as hard as I could, I ran into a draper's shop. I was a strong girl, and I knew the blow must have hurt him.

Waiting for some customers to leave the shop, I stayed close to them. There was no sign of my unwanted companion, and I ran all the way to the house, reflecting that if David had kissed me like that, how wonderful it would have been. I never did go near the tea room again.

It was now Easter 1929, soon it would be my seventeenth birthday. Mrs Herbert announced she was selling up, and had a great 'Sale of Chinese Goods' notice put in the window. All was sold, even the huge gong, how empty the staircase seemed without it. We put everything into the dining room again, arranging it as it was before. Once again we were called into that room, Mr Herbert saying he had important news to give us. They were returning to Shanghai at the end of April. We were asked to go with them, but Ruby and Cook declined. Ruby would not leave Ken, and Cook would return to her own home.

I was absolutely thrilled, what an adventure that would be! I felt I could not bear to part with the children. To get a passport for me would require my birth certificate. As it had been, as far as I knew, long lost, Mr Herbert wrote to the registrar in Wishaw. That my true age would now be revealed did not worry me, I would not be sacked for that reason. When Mrs Herbert knew I was only fourteen when I came to her, she said she suspected I was not long out of school, but I was in such a dreadful state she had not the heart to send me away, and she added that I had been a real treasure.

However, as I was under eighteen I would have to have my parents' consent. I wrote to Father at once, not foreseeing any objection, as he had been quick enough to get rid of me. His reply, when it came, was like a blow. He would not give his permission for me to travel to a foreign country. He needed me to make a home for *him* to look after *him*. Did I forget he was a disabled prisoner-of-war? I was to let him know the time of my arrival at Central Station, and he would meet me.

Mrs Herbert was as dismayed as I was. Her 'Ayah' (nurse) in Shanghai was getting old, but had been with her husband's family for two generations. She had expected me to take over in time. She would have to employ a local girl to assist the Ayah, the children would not understand her language nor she theirs.

She wrote to Father, almost begging him to let me go, but he did not deign to reply. To this day I believe she thought it was my father who had beaten me. I was unhappy and apprehensive at the thought of living with Father. He expected much more from me than I could give, there would be no way I could please him. Mrs Herbert wanted all my uniforms washed, starched and ironed, she would need them for the new girl. She made me promise I would come next year when I was eighteen, writing her Chinese address in my autograph book. When Mr Herbert was on one of his business trips, he would arrange to meet me and take me to Shanghai himself.

She then paid me five pounds for the uniforms, more than their value, and proceeded to unpick the waistband of my thick navy skirt. Inserting the folded note she sewed it up again, telling me on no account to give it to Father, or any one else, it would ensure that I would be able to visit my mother when the time came. Taking me into her bedroom, I was to try on and pick any garment I wanted from the pile on her bed. She was packing her own trunks, and did not need these garments.

There was one dress that I knew I wanted. Mrs Herbert had bought it in London. It was made of layers of transparent chiffon with handkerchief ends, which floated round her knees. A matching scarf could be tied round her head, in a circle, or in a bow on her upper arm. She had worn it on two or three occasions, and had looked a dream coming down the staircase, the lights from the windows and brass gong shining right through the flimsy material of soft colours, ranging from coffee to palest cream. A large 'rose' of the same material tucked into the low neck was very appealing. Long silk gloves, cream stockings and satin court shoes made a really stunning outfit.

Breathlessly, I asked her why she was giving it away, she looked so lovely with her brown eyes and dark hair when she wore it. Ruefully, she said she really did love the dress, but since Roger's birth she had lost her trim waist, and it was too tight. I also chose some lovely underwear, two velvet and gaberdine skirts, two frilly 'tissue paper' blouses as her husband called them. Departing in great delight with a huge armful of clothes, I spent the entire evening after 8.00 p.m. trying them on. They fitted beautifully, except for length, and I could shorten the skirts.

Married women had not yet adapted to the 'flapper' style, and wore skirts below the knees. Older women wore theirs down to their ankles, as they all did before 1914. The other change at that time saw lace-up whalebone corsets disappear among the younger generation. Gertie and I had had to pull Beatrice's laces as tight as we could to give her the appearance of having a slim waist.

Now 'stays' appeared, these had a broad metal fastener with a row of metal loops, which snapped on to studs, the body made of strong cotton material was shaped and lightly boned. One could just imagine ladies snapping them open after a large meal. What a relief to be able to do so; no need to wait till you undressed to loosen the laces of the old whale-bone corsets. No wonder ladies looked haughty and straight-backed, the metal fastener was rigid from naval to cleavage, if you bent your body, even to look down, the end of it dug into you!

Two years later, the stretch-elastic corselette came into fashion, and long-suffering womanhood was free at last. Unpicking the hem of my navy skirt, I put my savings of six 10/– notes inside and carefully stitched it up, as I had seen Mrs herbert do. How rich I felt, almost six months' pay, and I did not have to use it immediately, as I had been given my ticket home and a month's wages.

Ruby presented me with a tiny bottle of perfume, Cook hugged me as though I was about to die, weeping on my shoulder, saying if I was in 'trouble' I was to go to her house, she gave me a packet of stockings, and a made-up parcel of sandwiches and cake. It was agreed that I should get the early train to Scotland, Mr and Mrs Herbert thought the children would be too upset if I said goodbye to them. Mr Herbert would run me to the station before they woke. Cook and Ruby waved me off. Was it really three years since I had seen them standing there, waiting for us? It seemed only yesterday!

My heart was heavy, leaving my pretty room, the fine well-run home, the pleasant people, for what? I shuddered to think. Cook and Ruby were to clean up, close the house and return the keys that same day. The house would stand empty and deserted as though we had never existed; the happy laughter of the children, the singing of the birds, all part of one of the happiest periods of my life!

The Journey Home

As Mr Herbert put me into the train he merely said, 'Till next year, Nanny.' I found a seat near the window, but felt sad, the elderly couple sitting opposite spoke to me, but I was in no mood to carry on a conversation. The country side flew past in a blur of rain streaming down the sooty windows. The train stopped at Newcastle, the couple got out, and I paid a penny for a tin mug of tea, from a man with a barrow who stopped outside the window. The letters L.N.E.R. were printed on the mug, with a request to hand it out at the next station.

Eating my sandwiches and cake, I began to feel better, and took an interest in the passengers now entering my carriage. Two young men, dressed up to the 'nines' (as Ruby would say) and two pretty girls who appeared to be with them now filled the compartment, spreading their belongings over the empty seats. The men wore striped blazers with badges and grey flannel trousers. One sported a straw 'boater' which he placed carefully on the luggage rack. The girls wore tight, hip-skimming dresses with very deep neck lines, painted faces made up like dolls, and smoked from long cigarette holders.

The men offered cigarettes at intervals, lighting them up for the girls, with much hand-holding and giggles. I was offered a cigarette too, but declined. I had tried to smoke when Ruby had shown me how, but I was quite sick, and had no wish to repeat the experiment. Once they discovered I was Scottish, they became quite familiar, asking me if all the lads in Scotland wore kilts, and they bet I knew what they wore under them! Did all the family sleep in one box bed, or did most of them sleep in the heather? Embarrassed, and angry, I asked one if he had ever visited Scotland, and where had he heard all that rubbish? 'A mate of mine, he comes from Glasgow, he says Scots girls are a push-over, we would not mind rolling you in the heather.'

The girls laughed with them, mocked my Scottish accent, and dared the men to have a go with 'Miss Prim'. To my alarm, they walked out of the compartment to look for a toilet. Both men stood up, then seated themselves, one by my side, the other opposite, talking and joking. I gripped my purse tightly in my coat pocket. They appeared to discuss something closely, then turned round pushing their faces into mine. Then I realised they smelled of perfume, putting my hand in my other pocket I found it empty. It had contained the tiny bottle of perfume, the small box of face powder and a Chinese embroidered handkerchief, a present from Mrs Herbert.

Wiping his 'powdered' face with my pretty hanky, he blew his nose vigorously on it, then up-ended both the perfume bottle and the powder box on to the floor. 'Rotten beasts, why don't you do that to your friends.' I shouted, rage and frustration bringing tears to my eyes. They threw the boxes and hanky on to the rack above, told me to stretch up for them. Naively I did so, as I stood up, their hands went up my skirts, trying to unfasten my suspenders.

Kicking out I started to scream, and then the ticket-collector came in. 'Are they bothering you, Miss? Get your luggage and I'll put you in another carriage.'

Passing the first man, I knocked up the 'tray' purse that held his money and ticket, sending his loose change spilling on the sooty floor. To the other I said, 'You should only travel half-fare, you're just school children!' Retrieving my now soiled handkerchief, I followed the guard along the corridor, where he deposited me with a young couple who had two children, and were also bound for Glasgow.

As I settled down, I recalled a film I had seen as a child at a matinee. A herd of deer were running from a pack of wolves. The cunning wolves cut out a young, defenceless deer bringing it down to savagely kill it. How like wolves some men were! Girls without protection were easy prey. I wanted to use the toilet, and asked the mother of the young children if she would go with me, as I felt dizzy. It was as well she did, the two 'rotters' were standing in the corridor.

We had to pass them, and one whispered, 'School children? We'll show you!' I would not let the lady leave me, and hung on to her arm when we had to pass them again.

Above my head, I saw the cord which would stop the train if pulled, and said, 'You touch me, and I'll pull the cord.'

Once in the compartment, I felt safe, the children handed me sweets, and I held the little girl on my knee. Twice during the journey, one or other would look in, but I looked away. I think they disembarked at Berwick, I saw the white boater hat pass the window, and breathed a sigh of relief.

By the time the train steamed into Glasgow, I was ready to be pleasant to Father, perhaps he *did* need me after all! Walking towards the ticket barrier, I saw Father, the years disappeared, he was just as I last saw him, on the day he put me in the Servant Registry Office, three years ago. The jaunty air, smart city suit, bowler hat and grey spats over well-polished shoes. His gold 'hunter' watchchain spread across his ample waistcoat, the 'fob' a large golden-coloured Cairngorm stone in a filigree setting. Now polished to a glass-like smoothness, he fondled it with his chamois-leather gloved hand, the right one of which had gaps which accentuate the missing fingers. How the watch had escaped destruction during the years was a miracle. Handed down to him when he was twenty-one years old, his initials, G.M., were the same as his father's and *his* father's before him.

He was smiling broadly as I came near, the neat moustache, the bright blue eyes darting here and there. He took my case, exclaiming that I had become a fine strapping 'dochter' (daughter); he liked to stress his Scottishness. He thought I would not be pleased to come home, judging by my last letter, but I assured him I was quite happy and pleased to come back. I knew him too well to anger him, it would do me no good. We proceeded in exactly the same direction as we had that fateful morning, a little tremor of alarm grew as we walked up Buchanan Street, then subsided, as we passed the dreaded Registry Office.

Crossing Sauchiehall Street, we passed North Frederick Street, then reached Montrose Street. The rooming house was a relic of wealthier ownership, now dreary and dilapidated, still with the shadow of its former glory in its high Oriel windows, and the name 'Montrose House' engraved in the glass panel above the heavy studded door.

Father talked all the way, giving me a glowing account of how the Duke of Montrose had lived there, which excused any short-comings it may have had. There were plenty. Inside a wide, but dim hall, he opened the door to his 'rooms'. These consisted of a square room and a tiny box room, which held a single bed, and nothing else. Light was reflected through a pane of glass above the narrow door. Father said it was his bed, but that he would sleep on the sofa. I said I would much rather sleep on the sofa, but he told me he often came in late at night, sometimes with a friend, I would be in the way. A hard-faced woman, with yellow hair and heavily rouged cheeks was introduced as the landlady. Father explained I was his daughter and that I would be staying for a few weeks. She sniffed, saying she only took in gentlemen, did not like women about the place, and hoped I would get somewhere else to stay as soon as possible. When she went out Father told me not to listen to the 'silly old bag', saying 'We will go when it suits us!

Desperate to use the toilet, Father showed me to a door across the landing, telling me to turn the key in the lock inside. As I pulled open the door, a stout, middle-aged man emerged still buttoning his trousers. He winked at Father, 'Never knew you had a daughter like that, quite a tasty bit, eh?' The toilet smelled of urine and stale tobacco smoke, everything about it reeked of decay. I said to Father it was not very nice, or even clean, but he just said if it was good enough for him, it was good enough for me.

Over a meagre meal of tea, bread and cheap shop jam, he astounded me by saying he had found a 'decent' job for me in a nearby bookshop, and I was to start first thing on Monday morning. He had apparently given the manager (a Mr Wilson) a glowing account of my progress at school. Wages were 10/– weekly, and would increase if I showed an aptitude for the work. Father dismissed the wage as merely temporary, with my education I would be manageress in no time at all!

The hours would be from 8.00 a.m. to 6.00 p.m., with a 30-minute break for lunch. How was I to cook, shop and eat in such a short space of time? Father said I would have to work that out for myself. He ate in the office canteen at lunch-time and had dinner with friends most evenings. I would find plenty to do, besides cook, the rooms needed a good clean-up and he had a drawer full of socks ready for darning, buttons were missing from most of his shirts, and it was time I did something really useful!

When I mentioned I wanted to visit Granny next day he said that could wait, she had Gertie to look after her now. On Sunday morning I rose early, boiled two eggs in the kettle on a gas ring, while father made toast at the gas fire. He warned me not to run out of pennies for the meter, asked me to turn out my purse, seemed annoyed that I only had thirty shillings, wondered why I had not saved more in three years. I was to pay half the rent of 5/- weekly, keep the gas meter supplied with pennies, and pay for any laundry I required. There were no washing facilities. A cracked wash basin, a large jug, a soap dish, and Father's shaving soap, razor and mug lay on a marble slate on a small rickety table, a slop pail underneath.

Heating a kettle of water, I cleared up the few dishes using the basin we washed ourselves in, my spirits sinking lower and lower, missing my lovely white bedroom, linen sheets and the sweet-scented bath which I had every night, feeling dirty already. We walked down to the shop at the corner where he seemed to be well known, and charmed the two women behind the counter. From there we went along to Renfield Street and turned into Bath Street. The bookshop's entrance was below the level of the street, a few wide steps leading down to the main door, the basement area had litter blowing about it which depressed me even more.

Returning home, Father looked through my case, bringing out the autograph book, saying I seemed to have spent a lot of money on 'fripperies'. (I did not let him know they were nearly all Mrs Herbert's clothes.) Reading the autograph and David's signature, he said he hoped I had not had anything to do with that 'disease-ridden' family!

He read his papers, then went out about 4.00 p.m. to meet his friend, saying he would not be back till late, I was not to wait up.

I scrubbed out the pantry, throwing out jars of stale jam, almost empty, and hard, mouldy cheese, relining the shelves with newspapers and reflected that I would clean, darn and do whatever I was told this Sunday, keep the place clean so I would not have anything to do next Sunday when I would be ready to visit Granny.

Wanting to wash my hair, I had to fetch water from the bathroom and left my room door open, while filling the kettle. Entering my room, I found the stout, middle-aged man standing with his back to the fire. I left the door wide open and asked him if he wanted something. Taking 6d out of his pocket, he asked if I had any coppers for the gas meter, his fire had gone out. I knew I had none, but fetched my purse to let him see. Putting the kettle on the gas ring, I told him I was about to wash my hair and would he please go.

'Why can't you just sit down and be nice to me? I could just do with a pretty girl, I really fancy you.'

As he spoke he came over to me, but I backed over to the open door, and said very loudly, 'My Father will be here at any moment.'

A door opened, the landlady crossed the hall, and the man stepped quickly out, saying, 'See you later, sweetie.'

I locked the door, two or three times that night I heard the handle turning. Putting out all the candles I sat by the fire, hoping he would think I had gone to bed. The dark bedroom, the meagre furnishings, the lack of warmth and brightness was so typical of the bare existence of my childhood, my skin began to crawl, sensing Beatrice's presence was not far away. Actually she was not, Duke Street Prison was only half a mile away, where she still serving her sentence of three years for beating the children of her employer.

Tuesday afternoon came round, I ironed, washed and dusted once again, trying to wash my own clothes without being able to dry them properly. Father came home annoyed I had no meal ready for him. I explained *all* the shops were closed, even the corner shop. He told me I should have known all the shops closed on Tuesday afternoon, I was useless, having learned nothing in the last three years, running after messy brats. He made tea, ate bread and cheese, then stormed out telling me to pull my socks up!

At work, I had been interested in the amount and variety of books, opening up a whole new world. Girls and boys of my own age bought and exchanged books rapidly, I would stare at the young women, how did they get time to read? Girls were supposed to be occupied with domestic chores, all that reading would not cook a dinner! There were three male shop assistants, an office girl and the manager, besides myself. One young man took me round the shelves, gave me a list of books to find, and left me. It took me ages, and the manager was quite cross, 'Thought you knew all the books by heart.'

I hated Father, he must have said I knew all the authors and titles of their books. Making tea, dusting shelves, running errands, by 6.00 p.m. I was dusty, tired and hungry, having eaten only a bun at lunch-time with a sip of milk. I had worn my pretty blouse and skirt, but these were completely covered by a large black overall.

The rest of the week was even more difficult, the young men started to tease me, one especially. He would send me to fetch a book from the highest shelf, and as I came down his hand slipped up my leg. I kicked out, missed him, he laughed and pulled me from the ladder into a dark corner, squeezing me hard against him. Struggling fiercely I said, 'I'll scream,' he stopped, let me go, said I was a stupid bitch, but he would 'get' me yet.

When I carried tea to the office, the office girl warned me about Jack's goings-on, 'He only sends you up the ladder to look up your skirt, tell him to get up there himself.'

I dreaded the lunch break, three of the staff were out for half-an-hour, Jack and myself at counter, the manager in his office, where he ate his lunch. I stayed close to the counter, where Jack usually succeeded in pinching my bottom, or squeezing my waist. He kept asking me to meet him outside the shop, but I detested his whispered innuendos, and avoided his company as much as I could. He would wait for me outside the shop when it closed, but I waited for the office girl who had warned me about him.

Friday came, I would get my pay. We each were given a small enveloped. I pushed it into my pocket, and sped back to the rooms. Imagine my horror, when I opened the packet, the sum of 3/3 was all it contained. I showed it to Father who said that it was right, 9d for an insurance stamp, 1/– for tea, sugar and milk (the cup of tea morning and afternoon) and 5/– 'lie-time'. He explained that all new employees only received half-wages for the first week, to ensure they returned to work, and would only receive it when they left, but not if they were dismissed.

On Saturday evening I arrived home to find Father had gone away for the weekend, leaving me a note with some instructions on how to spend my time next day, and a pile of shirts to be washed and ironed. No point in paying laundry bills when I had 'nothing' else to do. Lifting the kettle, I peeped out to see if the coast was clear, and ran into the bathroom to fill it. Turning to come out, the stout man barred my way, 'Well, well, my pretty miss, give us a kiss.'

I dodged, ran to the room, and tried to close the door, but he put a foot in the doorway and stepped inside, closing it behind him.

'I'll scream if you don't get out,' I shouted. He said everyone went out on Saturday night, and we had the place to ourselves, if I screamed he said he would shut me up!' Come on, lassie, let's be friends,' and putting his arm round my waist he walked me over to the sofa.

Panic gripped me, I looked round for a weapon, anything. Still holding the kettle I threw it at him, but he only laughed and said, 'Got you, my beauty,' and tried to kiss me, his wet slobbering lips trying to find my mouth. Suddenly the door flew open, the landlady stood there. She swore at the man, 'Up to your old tricks again, Bertie?' (he must have been her husband) 'get out of here.' Turning on me, she berated me as though it were my fault, told me to get out as fast as I could, she would see my Father about this, and flounced out.

I needed no excuse now. I turned the key in the lock, packed everything in five minutes, told Father in a hastily written note that the landlady had ordered me out, and I would not come back. Locking the door from the outside, I pushed the key under it. All my loose money had gone, but I had the 3/3 still in my wage packet. Soon I was running down to George Square, away from another intolerable situation which was not of my making.

Journey's End?

This time I was quite jubilant, I had my fare, knew the right trams to take. Climbing to the top deck, I found the only vacant seat. It was crowded with men of all ages, smoking and smelling of drink. A besotted creature leered at me, tried to pull me onto his knees, amid loud guffaws from the others. I turned, descending the stairs, glad of my heavy coat, as I had to stand on the outside platform, there were no empty seats inside.

Once in the Motherwell tram, I became full of happy anticipation. Soon I would see my dear Granny and Gertie. As usual, the door was open, the door that was never closed, and I ran in, surprising Gertie, Granny and the dark young man seated round the fire. Granny looked smaller, so frail and ethereal, I was careful not to hug her too tightly. Gertie was so thin and pale, compared to myself, except for a huge bump on her stomach. She laughed at my expression, 'Yes Minnie, I'm expecting a baby soon.'

She now introduced me to the dark-haired young man. He had nice eyes and a pleasant smile. 'How wonderful,' I cried, 'Why did you not tell me sooner? Let's celebrate!' I was so delighted to be there, to feel the sense of belonging, to be myself. Gertie said she did not have much in the house to 'celebrate' with. Ravenously hungry, I asked where I could buy a fish supper. Willie, her husband offered to get one for me, I gave him my last 2/6 and happily said, 'Spend it all, we will *all* have a fish supper !'

He came back with a bottle of lemonade, three fish suppers (6d each) and two packets of Woodbine, with a box of matches, and had a penny over! I felt I'd never tasted a better meal. They were so pleased to see me looking so strong and healthy. Granny remembered the awful state I was in when I left her that day to go to Glasgow. We talked far into the night, I told Gertie everything about me, how David Stirling had turned up, she said I was lucky, she would love to have met him as she was one of a number of girls who had a 'crush' on him.

During a lull in the conversation I asked if they had found our Mother' s address. To my great surprise, Gertie had not only got Mother' s address, but had visited her in Ireland. She seemed reluctant to discuss this, to me, wonderful news, said it was time we were all in bed, and we would talk about it next day.

Before falling into a wonderful, dreamless sleep, I knew now I was going to visit my Mother, and in the morning told them I would take the first boat, for two reasons, the first that Father would come for me, the second that maybe someone, even Mother, may want to put me off . It was decided I should sail on Monday at noon, arriving at Belfast about 6.00 p.m. We would send a telegram to Mother just before I left Motherwell next morning.

I wore my navy skirt that day, and taking the scissors into the toilet, I unpicked the hem, took out my precious 10/- notes and pinned it up again. The fare was 10/- single and I would have enough to keep me till I obtained employment of some kind. Gertie just answered all my questions with, 'You will see for yourself, Minnie, but don't expect too much!' Too happy to sense all was not to Gertie's liking, I had no doubts at all, we would be together, my darling Mama and me, the hope that had sustained me through long dark days of misery. Gertie had only stayed with her for three days. She seemed bitter, Mother's new family had a happy comfortable life, it should have been ours!

Next morning the telegram was duly sent, Gertie and Willie took me to Broomielaw, I paid all their fares, treated them to breakfast in a tearoom, blessing Mrs Herbert for her wisdom, remembering how I had walked penniless from Glasgow. Now we waited beside the great ship of white and gold, the screaming sea-gulls, the huge cranes, the ship's hooters, the calls of porters and hubbub of passengers waiting to embark. The red and black funnels belched clouds of smoke, and with great joy I boarded her, waving to Gertie and her husband.

I had a very tender kiss for Granny when I left, would I ever see her again? As the ship passed the Bute coastline, dark memories intruded, but just for an instant, my heart was too full of joyous anticipation! As we reached the open sea, the clouds descended, hiding the hills, the waves grew higher and the ship rolled heavily. As it heaved, so did my stomach.

I found a sheltered corner beside the funnel on the top deck. Rain drops spattered on the hot sides. An elderly seaman brought me a pail, told me to use it if I was sick. He appeared a short time later with a big mug of hot cocoa, refusing the penny I offered him. I half dozed and half froze, very few passengers were up on deck, but the great warmth in my heart made the journey so worthwhile.

Amazingly, still thinking we had a long way to go, I heard a voice telling the passengers we would dock in Belfast in half-an-hour. Dragging my case I reached the toilets, where I washed my face, tidied my hair, and pinched my cheeks to restore some colour into them! I did not want to arrive looking like a ghost! In happy tremulous expectation I stood at the rail, straining my eyes for a sight of my Mother.

Amid a great clanking of chains a gangway was lowered, once more I was standing thankfully on terra firma, my feet firmly on the ground. People milled all round, passengers waiting to board, I searched all the faces, not seeing anyone like the slim pretty woman I remembered from her wedding picture. Soon the quayside was almost deserted, had the telegram not arrived in time?

Walking about, I saw a stout and very large woman, dressed in black, seated on a bench with a large basket at her feet. She beckoned me over, and I stood before her, staring, a vague faint memory stirred. It *was* her smile, and the lovely violet-blue eyes, could this really be my beloved Mother?

She spoke, saying 'You'll be Mary. You are taller than Gertie. What a rush I've had, to be sure! We just have time to catch the bus home. Here, love, pick up that basket.' She looked even larger when she stood up, I had to shake myself, this could not be the lovely Mama I had cherished the memory of all these years.

There was no great welcome, no word of endearment, Gertie's words came back to me. 'Don't expect too much.' However, after the initial shock, I listened to her with interest, she seemed to know the other passengers all by their first names! Twenty minutes later, we arrived in Hollywood, a very pretty town, with many spires and hills all round, clothed in the deepest, loveliest green grass, truly the 'Emerald' Isle. Roses everywhere, their sweet perfume pervading the still summer air, people talking and laughing in little groups.

We had to walk some distance to the house, (said Mother) we were well into the country-side by the time we reached home, which was a tall square house surrounded by a great deal of garden space. Just as we were about to stop at the low white painted gate, Mother caught my arm. 'The children think you are my niece, call me Aunty, I will explain later.' I stopped and stared at her in sheer disbelief. Seeing the shock in my face, she squeezed my shoulders, saying, 'We will have a cosy chat tonight when the children are asleep.'

Two boys and a girl gazed shyly at me, then ran into the kitchen to see what Mother had brought them from the shops in Belfast. Then Hughie Aird stepped forward, stretching out his arms, and held me close. He murmured, 'Lassie, dear lassie, it's good to see you.' Emotion filled my heart, I cried on his shoulders. Dear Hughie! He had not changed so much as Mother, a little more stooped, the hair grey, the same kindly man. I had almost forgotten him, just remembering Mama.

The children were now properly introduced, the oldest lad was Hughie, which meant he was the baby Mama had after she left us. It was something of a jolt to hear he was named Hugh Aird. I had never, in my childish innocence associated him with Mama's baby. The girl's name was Annie, fair like her father, then Alan, with his mother's beautiful eyes.

The youngest girl was at a party, she was named Elizabeth (Betty for short). By this time Mother had spread a long table with masses of food, or so it seemed to me, not realizing what hungry appetites young boys have. Ayette had only had the tiniest portions of everything, I thought, wistfully. After the meal of floury potatoes, Irish stew and vegetables we wandered out into the huge garden, and I felt I was walking into another world.

A clutter of toys, cycles and prams in one shed, garden seats and gnomes outside the door, two cats and a dog just having been fed, now deeply engrossed in their dishes. Farther away from the house a turkey strutted with her young ones, hens and chickens, ducks and even a small pony, all had to be inspected.

The boys and the girl were feeding the animals, what a lively and happy atmosphere, so different from Father's dreary city life-style! Now I realized why Gertie was so bitter, this should have been our way-of-life, happy, carefree and with two loving parents.

As the evening drew to a close, we came back to the house, and I was able to look around. Cotton checked curtains hung by the narrow latticed windows, a huge range in the stone wall was flanked by the irons and steaming cloths, familiar childhood memories came crowding back with the smell of them. Now I was really home, though bemused with so much round me. Annie showed me where I would sleep, and I carried my case and coat upstairs. A square room held a double and a single bed, here the two girls and I were to sleep together.

The room, though plain, was clean and fresh, with large rag rugs on the floor, one at each bed. The boys slept next door, the parents downstairs. On the narrow landing I was pleasantly surprised to see a bathroom, that the bath was not long enough to lie down in reminded me of the bathtub at home. This bath was also made of zinc. There were many tall enamel jugs as water had to be carried from the boiler, all the children had a bath on Sunday mornings.

I asked Annie if I could have a bath now, and she ran downstairs to ask Mother, who said, 'Yes, there's plenty of hot water in the boiler.' How soft the water was, compared to the water in Darlington. The boys and Hugh had carried the water upstairs, while I unpacked my case, laying out my pink robe, now a little frayed and faded, and a pretty nightdress (Mrs Herbert's gift). Annie was very interested in all my clothes and wanted to know all about being a children's nurse, *she* would be one when she grew older, she was nine years old. Hughie would be nearly eleven, Alan was seven, and Betty would be four on her next birthday.

Annie ran downstairs, and I luxuriated in the warm soft water, the soap making pretty bubbles. I was so looking forward to our 'cosy chat', there was so much to talk about, so many questions that needed to be answered. Feeling fresh and clean, I put on my nightdress and robe, and with a towel round my damp hair, I came down to dry my hair before the fire.

The door was closed, and opening it, I nearly collapsed with shock, the floor swayed under my feet, an icy coldness sent every drop of blood from my face, had I seen a ghost? 'Gina' was sitting on Hughie's knee, the golden curls tumbling over her head, the great blue eyes staring at me, the same blue velvet dress with the lace collar she had worn the last Christmas we had had together with Mother and Hughie. The floor steadied, Mother's arms were around me, she led me to her chair.

As my eyes focused again, I could see there was a difference, this child was chubby and dimpled. Mother was speaking urgently. 'Mary, it's not Gina, it is Betty, Gina would be fifteen now. Gertie saw the resemblance too, but she was not so upset as you are. Betty, speak to Mary, let her see you are not a little ghost.' Betty slipped off Hughie's knee, came over to me, but I backed away in horror, and fled upstairs.

It was Hughie who found me hiding under the bedclothes, fighting the fear that burned into my brain. Gina had been born again, there was a big word for it, 'reincarnation'. It was weird, ghostly and dreadful. Hughie took me in his arms, telling me how he felt guilty about having to leave us that awful day, he had never forgiven himself, and seeing us now, learning of the awful life we had had with our stepmother, made Mother unhappy.

They had not known, or even guessed that we had been so cruelly treated. Rumours from Motherwell had reached them that Father had obtained a good position with the Civil Service, purchased a large and imposing house in Rothesay, and sent his three daughters to private school. His new wife was a real lady, who employed servants to work for her. It was not until Gertie's visit to them a year ago that they learned of Beatrice's hatred towards us, and how she made us suffer.

The two girls now entered the bedroom, looking curiously at me. I could not bear to look at Betty, and escaping from Hughie's comforting arms, I fled downstairs, out of the house, throwing myself on the wet grass. Beatrice's last cruel taunt burned in my brain, 'she won't want you.' I felt utterly defeated, the hope that had sustained me through my life with Beatrice was gone.

Oblivion beckoned, as I sank deeper into the depths of dark despair, trying desperately to obliterate this awful pain of rejection and sense of betrayal! I was unwanted and meant nothing to anyone. Cold numbed my body, I had no tears left to ease the dull weight of pain lying so heavily within my chest. All strength left me, flowing with my aching senses into the black abyss of self-pity.

Now I became aware of hands that were lifting me, I protested feebly, 'Let me die, I want to die.' Even as Gertie had cried out all the years ago, 'Let me die, let me die.' But death did not come, the darkness gave way to light, warmth and sound. Arms held me close, warm tears dropped on my up-turned face, the painful sobbing so close to me was not my sobbing. Slowly, with great wonder, I realized I was in Mama's arms. Hughie was murmuring words of comfort to her, and gradually the heaving of her bosom under my head subsided.

Mama's nearness overwhelmed me. I would not, dare not open my eyes lest the dream fade, it could only be a dream! Now she rocked me to and fro in her arms as though I were her little child again. She murmured, over and over again these words, 'My girls, my poor girls, what have we done to you?'

The long day's travelling, the final meeting and disappointments left me emotionally spent and exhausted. I drifted into sleep, floating on clouds, safe in Mama's arms, I was in Heaven!

I must have slept very late. When I awoke the house was very quiet, and the girls' bed was empty. Dressing myself, I ventured downstairs, feeling rather apprehensive. Hughie was sewing at the long table. He looked up, smiled warmly, and said he would make some fresh tea. I looked around, and he explained that Mother and Betty had gone to town, and the other children were at school.

At the mention of Betty's name, I blurted out, 'Why, Hughie, why does she, Mama, not want to own me? I can't live with that, my life is just ashes!' Drawing me closer to the warm fire, he said, 'We need to talk, but drink your tea first.' I cried out, 'No, Hughie, tell me now, I have to know.' The cup of tea grew cold as he talked.

'The reason for your Mother's request to call her Aunty was really necessary. All the customers we have are staunch Catholics, whose faith does not recognise divorce. If they knew Mother was a divorced woman, they would not only withdraw their custom, but would brand her new family as illegitimate, and she herself as living in sin. The children would be ostracised, and their whole livelihood would be threatened, that was why she did not want the children to know about us, or her previous marriage.'

Hughie now kneeled down and drew the well filled ash-pan from its usual place, 'Mary, what is this?' 'An ash-pan,' I replied, had I not emptied countless ash-pans for years! I spoke crossly, perplexed and annoyed that he had turned the conversation away from my immediate questions. He continued to disturb the ashes with a small poker and said, 'What do you see now?'

I made no answer, the ashes were smoking and made me cough. Again he asked me what I saw, but all I could see was a bit of red ash among the rest. 'Blow gently on that cinder, Mary, and see what happens.' I did so, the cinder glowed to a bright red, and picking up a spent match, Hughie laid it on the bright glow. It immediately burst into flame. Taking my two hands in his and looking earnestly into my eyes, he said, 'In every life a cinder glows, a breath of kindness, a wisp of hope and it will leap into flame, bringing strength and purpose into your life. No, Mary, your life does not lie in ashes, you have much to make the cinder glow. You have found your Mother, you know she loves you and always has. You have youth, health and beauty, experiences that will stand you in good stead should the need arise. Appreciate your own worth, be you own master!'

At that moment I grew up. There would be no more childish longings for home and Mama. I was free. Suddenly I experienced great peace of mind.

The next few days were happy ones. Mother taught me to sew on her old treadle machlne, the very one we had sat on as toddlers. She helped me to alter my skirts, (mostly Mrs Herbert's) remarking on the good quality of the material. We would enjoy walks in the surrounding countryside, and I was enthralled with the beauty of Ireland. The grass so green, the flowers so profuse, the soft air, the hills shimmering in their cloaks of silver mist. No wonder Mother loved living there, I knew now why Granny had missed it so much.

We spoke of Father, she said she could never have lived with him again, even if it had been possible. He was too ambitious, expecting her to keep up appearances on a small wage, even though her sewing money kept them better dressed than their friends and neighbours. She almost wished he had died, then we would all have been happy together. 'Hughie would have made you his and you know how fond he is of you.' We both sighed. She did not speak of him again.

I had no luck with my applications for employment in the area. My religion was against me, as I was not Catholic. People rich enough to employ a ' Nanny' for their children wanted a much older woman. There were so many unemployed girls in Ireland (often as many as ten daughters in one family) who would be glad to tend children for much less that I expected to be paid.

An advertisement in the Belfast News caught my attention.

AGENTS FOR ALL LINES.
TO AMERICA, CANADA, AUSTRALIA, NEW ZEALAND
DOMESTICS, SCOTS NANNIES, COOKS, FARMHANDS
REQUIRED IMMEDIATELY
SITUATIONS GUARANTEED
NO REPAYMENTS
BOYS TO AUSTRALIA AND CANADA FREE
GIRLS UNDER EIGHTEEN CHAPERONED £2
APPLY TO BELL' S SHIPPING AGENCY, SHORE STREET
BELFAST

The idea appealed to me, telling Mother and Hughie I would go to the agency that very day. They looked at each other, suggesting I should sleep on it, I could change my mind by tomorrow, also £2 was more than a week's wages.

Now I could be completely frank about the money stitched into my skirt. Hughie saw I was determined, and told me to get my coat, references and birth certificate. We soon found the Shipping Office, one street away from the dock, where I had arrived only a few days ago. The office was part of a long white painted shed, with very small windows. We entered a door, walked down a long passage, with doors on each side, then knocked on the one with 'INQUIRIES' painted on it.

A woman in navy uniform opened the door, smiled pleasantly at Hughie, then looked searchingly at me, before conducting us to another office, on the door of which the word 'EMIGRATION' was written in large letters. Sitting down at her desk, she asked if I could write, (much to my astonishment), my name, age and parentage. I was given a form to fill, told to sit beside Mr Aird who could assist me. Fortunately I had an excellent reference from Mrs Herbert, which seemed to please her. On the form it stated that one parent must sign approval if I was under eighteen. Hughie said Mother would sign, but she would have to do that in front of the Emigration Officer.

Given a choice of country, I chose New Zealand. The officer said I had very good references and with three years experience I would have no problems in finding a good position. She arranged an appointment for next day, when I would be medically examined, and if I passed, Mother would sign and I would hand over the fee of £2. The whole application was completed in three days. The Irish boat would take us to Southampton, there we would be transferred to the much larger ocean-going ship of the New Zealand Line, the S.S. 'Rapahoe'.

The day before I was due to leave we held a small family party. Hughie and Mama toasted me with home-made nettle-wine, both wishing me Good Luck! Annie presented me with a baby rabbit. I had to tell her it was too young to leave its mother, but she could look after it for me. She said, "I will call it Mary." Little Betty handed me a very pretty lace-trimmed handkerchief with a shamrock embroidered in one corner. I surmised that Mother had bought it for her to give to me.

Feeling guilty about avoiding the innocent child, I kissed her lightly, then wished I had not, the human contact threatening to break down my defences.

The boys gave me a note-book and pencil, begging me to write down everything that happened on board the big liner. *They* were going to sail to New Zealand when they were old enough!

I had bought each of them a packet of sweets, and the party ended in happy laughter.

After washing the dishes, I went upstairs to have a bath, wash my hair, and finish packing my case. Annie and Betty followed me. Once in the bedroom they stood in front of me, looking very serious. I said 'Surely you are not going to miss me so much' I was utterly taken aback when they answered, talking together, 'We want you to go away and not come back. We don't like you, you made Mama cry when you came here. She says she is glad that you are going away'

I was sorely tempted to tell them she was my Mother too, but I could only mutter: 'Oh well, I'll be gone to-morrow', Picking up the towel and soap, I ran into the bathroom, tears streaming down my face. When I returned to the bedroom they were both in bed, sitting up, watching me. 'Want my hanky back' said Betty, no doubt prompted by her older sister. Was she jealous? I wondered, but did not think they could possibly be jealous of me. I handed over the handkerchief without speaking, then proceeded to write two letters, one to Mrs Herbert in Shanghai and the other to Gertie, asking her to forward any letters that came for me once I had an address to send them to.

Sleepless and sad, I realized that there was no place for me in Mama's house. My visit had only opened old wounds and revived sad memories. I would never return to Ireland. The long years of yearning for Mama were over, and most of my questions had been answered. I was happy to have found her, but she was still a part of my unhappy childhood.

I would now look forward to a new life, far away from the family troubles which had caused my sisters and I such unnecessary suffering. The thought of my journey to-morrow made my spirits rise. What adventures lay before me? Both Mother and Hughie had told me that I was attractive, had a 'glow' about me, a freshness of outlook and a happy nature all of which would get me a husband soon. Although I laughed off these heady compliments, I had at last awakened to the fact that there was more to life than drudgery and penny-pinching!

Next morning, I rose to the sound of the old rooster crowing. Dawn was breaking, the rising sun sending pink streamers across the sky, heralding the new day, and filling me with a mounting surge of excitement and anticipation.

Not wishing to wake the children, I crept about on stockinged feet. Dressed, I carried my shoes, coat and case downstairs. To my surprise Mama and Hughie were up. Hughie toasting baps and Mama mixing cocoa in three tin mugs. We sipped the hot, sweet cocoa in silence. I dreaded the thought of saying goodbye. It was just ten days since I had arrived at this house. Ten days in which I had experienced many emotions. High hopes, deep despair, the calmness of acceptance and now great anticipation!

Hughie put down his mug. 'Come along, Mary, it's time to go, the bus will be here at any minute'. Lifting my case, he walked out and down the garden path.

I looked at Mama, she did not turn her head, staring into the fire. She muttered 'I hate goodbyes'. I knew in my heart she did not mean to be abrupt and cold. She could not, dare not, show any emotion lest we both break down. Hughie was calling, I ran out of the door, and did not look back.

The bus was crowded with factory girls and labourers. These girls, some as young as 12 years old, worked from 6.00 a.m. to 6.00 p.m. in linen factories and others.

The men, whose work was heavier, toiled from 6.00 a.m. to 4.00 p.m. Wages were very low, they looked tired and miserable.

The pier was crowded. Groups of parents and children had come to say goodbye to sons and daughters, brothers and sisters, leaving for a new life in a far-away land. There were many tears and white faces, but I was too excited to have much sympathy for them, and too impatient to start out on my own journey.

Now the stewardess called my name, and others, handing each of us a bright green armband. She wore a green band round her hat. We were to stay near her till the ship sailed. Other stewardesses were handing out different coloured bands to other groups. Our group consisted of 15 girls.

I took my case from Hughie's hand, gave him a peck on the cheek: 'Goodbye and thanks, Hughie', was all I could say and I ran up the gangway, almost the first passenger to get on board.

The Emigrants

Standing at the ships railing, I watched the other girls parting from their folk. One family interested me. The father was a big, powerful looking man, dressed in coarse breeches and leather gaiters, 'looks like a gamekeeper' I thought. His wife had a beautiful face, but she was fat and shapeless, like Mother, 'too many babies did that to a woman', she had said. The tallest of the girls hugged and kissed both her parents, the younger children crying loudly. Miss Wilson, the stewardess in charge of my group, came to them, and gently eased the sobbing girl away from their clinging arms, and led her up the gangway.

As she was wearing a green arm-band, I was not surprised when she was told to stand beside me. I felt sorry for her, and a little envious. Hughie had disappeared, no one was shedding tears for *me!* I would not return to Ireland again. My visit had only opened old wounds, and brought guilty memories to them both. 'Let them be happy' I thought, banishing my self-pity to the back of my mind.

Miss Wilson now herded our group together, gave us a short lecture on how we were expected to behave and how to keep ourselves and our clothes clean. There would be a daily inspection. We were to sleep four to a cabin. Breakfast would be served at 8.00 a.m. promptly. We must be seated in the dining-room five minutes before the gong sounded.

At first there were just a few passengers, but Miss Wilson said there would be at least 500 emigrants from Britain, though a portion of these would travel first class, and their quarters would be separated from ours. We travelled steerage, and our cabins were all below deck while they had much roomier cabins on deck.

The Irish girl had dried her tears, she smiled at me and said 'I would like to have the top bunk, please. It's a great fear I have of closed-in spaces.' We unpacked, combed our hair and spoke to the other two girls who were to share our cabin. Suddenly the sound of the gong startled us and, holding hands, the Irish girl and I ran to the dining-room. I counted about 70 people, mostly young like ourselves.

The Captain entered with another man, introduced him as the ship's Doctor. He hoped we would all arrive safe and well at our destinations. He said grace and left immediately, no doubt to welcome the first-class passengers aboard.

None of us had had much to eat before we left home, so we were very hungry, and welcomed the large bowl of porridge and a mug of milk. I was astonished to see piles of buttered bread placed at intervals on the tables. I stopped eating long before the others, having already enjoyed my porridge and milk, and watched in wonder as the piles of bread disappeared rapidly before me. I had never seen so much eaten in so short a time!

After breakfast, we went on deck. It was a lovely day, with a gentle breeze and the ship hardly seemed to be moving. We sat down on some lifebelts. The Irish girl said her name was Violet Delaney. She was 18 years old and was being sponsored by two sisters already in New Zealand. Their names were Daisy and Rose. 'Why are you named after flowers?' I asked. 'What if your mother had had a son?' Violet laughed, 'My mother said a boy would have to be given my father's good name of Patrick, but he would have been out of place in her garden of flowers and the Good Lord knew that!' Violet went on to say that was not the end of it. 'There are ten of us, all named after flowers; Lily, Rose, Pansy, Daisy, Heather, Marigold, Tulip, Bell (for Bluebell), Cynthia (for Hyacinth)' and herself. I kept her talking, anxious to avoid talking about my own sad life. Watching her as she spoke, her face changing, her expressions pronounced in her lilting Irish brogue, I found her utterly bewitching. Her's was the most beautiful face I had ever seen, completely innocent of make-up. Two delicious dimples came and went as she smiled, showing her pearly teeth in a Cupid's bow of pink lips. Large, deep blue eyes, heavily fringed with long curling lashes. Pink and white skin, as soft as a baby's, all framed by a wealth of rich brown curly hair. Violet continued: 'Mary, my sisters went out to New Zealand two years ago, both getting married within six months. They have done well and Daisy has opened a boarding house. Australia and New Zealand welcomed the emigrants, these countries were opening up, populations increasing by the boat load. Wages are higher than at home, if you could get work in the Ould Country you were lucky. I would have been married now, if I had not made up my mind to leave home, my sweetheart urgently wanted me to marry him!'

Her two younger sisters had married at 16 years old, snapped up by local lads, they too had been the bonniest girls in all County Kerry. Both had babies. Violet's eyes flashed in anger as she went on. 'They are stupid, they should have waited. Mother of God, can't they see what it's done to that dear Mother of mine? She had ten of us before she was 35 years old! I won't throw myself away like that, unless the size of their wage-packet was tempting enough. I'll certainly not marry just to give a man children, or what they call Love. No, Mary, I'll only marry for money, position and nice clothes, or my name isn't Violet Delaney!'

I gazed at her, 'Violet, you will find the waiting difficult with your looks, even now every man on board is trying to catch your eye.' This was true. We went over the ship together. The other two girls did not seem to want our company. Violet and I became firm friends, sharing each others views, and flirting outrageously with the crew and unattached men. We made a pact that we would stay close together, not to be left alone with a man at any time. Producing a 6 inch hat-pin, Violet said it worked wonders. Men turned pale when she threatened to jab it into them. As nearly all had recently suffered a small-pox inoculation, that memory was too fresh, some still nursing painful arms. She certainly knew how to deal with unwanted suitors.

Our first port of call was at Broomielaw in Glasgow. Here we took on board about 100 young men and a few families. Most of the men came from the Highlands and Islands of Scotland. These were mainly the sons of crofters or fishermen barely able to support themselves, even less their growing sons. As we got to know them, we found they were determined to work hard and make a fortune. They most certainly had no time to waste on chasing women or whisky. Some of them were exceptionally good-looking and their outlook as fresh as the mountain air they had breathed since birth.

However, before a week had passed, their will power had evaporated like the salt spray in the wind. One glance from Violet Delaney's wonderful eyes reduced them to willing slaves. I envied her a little, but as she turned them down, they attached themselves to me in the hope they could still get near her.

So far, there had not been much sickness on board. We reached Liverpool, taking on more and more emigrants. When the Irish boat docked at Southampton we had to disembark, and then board the "Rapahoe". She dwarfed the little Irish steamer, and the ferry boats that sailed to France. The noise was indescribable, so many people, so much confusion, children crying, baggage winched aboard by chains, all accompanied by the hoarse shouts of sweating, swearing men.

Once more on our way, we sailed through the English Channel, then into the swelling sea of the Atlantic Ocean. As the ship rose and fell so did our stomachs. On the first day out, there must have been a few hundred for meals, but by the third day this had dwindled to less than a hundred; the long tables almost deserted and the seats empty. We had a stormy crossing through the Bay of Biscay.

Miss Wilson helped us to get over our nausea with pills and drinks. When we recovered she asked us to help the young mothers with chidren. The crew issued bags for sickness, but the mothers, almost helpless themselves, could not prevent the children from bringing up all over the floors, and the crew were constantly mopping up. Some mothers were breast-feeding and were in a sorry state, their babies wailing for food, then throwing up all over their poor mothers.

This was something I could cope with. Organising as many girls and women as were on their feet, we carried the children on deck for a breath of fresh air. Afterwards we cleaned them up and fed them with warm milk and water. If they kept that down, we gave them thin soup, but we had to wait till dinner was served to get it. We attended to the mothers, bringing them the same thin soup, the first food they had had for two or three days.

Violet was quite useless with the babies and toddlers. This surprised me and I said, 'Violet, your Mother had babies all the time, did you not help her?' She said 'No, my young sisters fetched and carried for Mother. She seldom left the house, but cooked, washed and attended to the children. The smell of soap and soup will be with me every time I think of home. She wanted her girls to go out and enjoy themselves'. 'Make the most of your courting days, it's the happiest time you will ever have, and the shortest!' she told them.

Miss Wilson came to our cabin one day to let us know what our prospects could be in the new country. I was to be employed as a companion and nursemaid to a missionary's wife in a Mission House in the country. Mrs Emerson was in poor health and very homesick. The child, a girl, needed careful nursing. Mr Emerson, the missionary had asked for a Scots Nanny, hoping if his wife heard her native tongue her health would improve. He, himself, could not get leave for another year at least, when he had promised to take her to her parents in Edinburgh, for a long holiday.

A friend of his would meet me at Auckland Harbour and take me by car to the Mission. Violet, of course, would be met by her two sisters.

Now the weather became much warmer. We stopped at Port Said, the entrance to the Suez Canal. Here the ship had to be refuelled. Fresh water was taken on board, and fresh fruit was sold by natives sailing tiny crafts, so heavily laden I expected to see them overturn as the natives gesticulated, arms stretched out for payment. The first-class passengers bought most. We were fascinated by the appearance of these swarthy men, all wearing colourful clothes, with smiles of welcome showing rows of beautiful white teeth. The women at the water-side laughed and chattered noisily, all so very different from the sombre faces of the porters in Britain, bad-temperedly shouting, swearing and wrangling over the cargoes. Perhaps it had something to do with the weather. Here the sun shone all day, the skies cloudless.

Soon we sailed through the Canal, which was very interesting, the weather becoming really hot, once into the Red Sea. Here the water was so warm you could feel it through the steel walls. Inside the ship, the heat was almost unbearable.

We saw the sharks and native dhows. These tiny craft looked dangerously frail, as the fishermen pulled huge fish from the sea. We reached Aden in a few days, here it was so hot that the crew rigged up an awning, filled it with sea water and allowed twenty or thirty people at a time to bathe. When it was our turn, Violet and I wearing long slips, (we had no bathing suits) jumped into the pool. It felt really wonderful but it was too crowded. The men had their dip in another part of the ship. We could hear their shouts of delight and bawdy jokes (it was said they were quite naked). It must have been a great pleasure to the men from Britain, as they wore really heavy clothes. Most of them had discarded their heavy tweeds, except for trousers. They just could not envisage these seas, always the Northern Waters had been treacherously cold, and changeable.

Dances were held nearly every night, and were very popular with those who had enough energy to dance. It was just as hot in the evening. Music was supplied by a fiddler and two of the crew had mouth-organs. There was also a gramophone which kept running down, requiring to be wound up every five minutes. I learned to dance slow waltzes, Irish Jigs, and Scottish Reels. Many a stolen kiss, many a hug and cuddle we had, never losing sight of each other, much to the annoyance of Violets' love-sick swains. We flirted so much, and danced so late that Miss Wilson threatened to lock us in our cabin at 8.00 p.m. We hated being in the hot, airless cabin unless we were asleep. Violet especially had a feeling of claustrophobia.

I heard her crying one night, sobbing as if her heart should break. Between sobs she cried out 'It's sad I am to be leaving my mother and my father, my sisters, my home and my country. I love them all, will I ever see Ould Ireland again? Oh, Mary, I wish I had not come on this journey. I could have been safe at home, married to dear Brendon, he will be breaking his heart for me. How could I have left them all? Will I ever see them again?'

Comforting her as best I could, I said, 'Yes Violet, you will see them again. It took me eleven long years to find my mother but I did.' Now I told her the full story of my childhood. She forgot her tears and listened spell-bound. When I finished she exclaimed how thankful she should be for her free and happy childhood, never a care in the world, and she would remember her mother's parting words, not to take the first man she fancied, her beauty was both an asset and a disadvantage where men were concerned. She must respect herself then she would be respected, not just for her looks. We laughed at these words, vowed we would not get wed in a hurry, but looking at Violet I thought that would be very difficult. One glance from under those curling lashes would send many a man into a flat spin. I wondered if she would be determined enough to resist their advances.

The Cockroaches

In the evenings, cockroaches and beetles could be seen running about the dark corners of the ship. A few young boys would catch them in empty jars. Given the opportunity, they would drop one or two on the girls' laps, which sent them screaming to their parents. The boys would disappear and when confronted by irate parents, denied they were the culprits. This ended soon afterwards. The Captain, Doctor and some gentlmen, usually with their waves, dined in the Captain's quarters. This evening some boys crept into the galley. They spotted the soup tureen intended for the Captain's table. When Cook turned his back, they up-ended a tin of live cockroaches into the soup, replaced the lid and quickly disappeared.

The purser laid the tureen before the Captain, amid much talk and laughter. He lifted the lid and a struggling mass of desperate beetles fought to get out of the hot soup. A shocked silence was followed by an almighty roar from the Captain. Women screamed and chairs turned over in their haste to leave the table. The Captain's hand slammed down on the bell, used for summoning the waiters, but now to summon the crew. The red-faced Captain threatened to flog the entire ship's company till they found the culprits. From then on the galley was sealed off. He confronted the emigrants and announced no dessert would be served that day, or any other day, until the culprits were caught and punished.

As the days passed, the mothers became very angry, saying that innocent children were being punished. Small children had no appetite for the often greasy meat course, which made them feel sick again. Dessert was the high-light of the evening meal, usually consisting of ice-cream and tinned fruit, apple-pie with custard, trifle or rice pudding. A deputation of young mothers pleaded their cause, but the Captain was adamant. No dessert until the culprits were handed over!

Suspicion fell on the boys who had caught cockroaches earlier. A dozen of them were rounded up by angry parents and made to swear on the Bible. Two frightened boys confessed and were marched to the Captain's quarters.

The captain called everyone on deck to witness their punishment. With great solemnity he asked those present whether these two rascals should be hung from the top-most mast, or forced to walk the plank, and fall into the shark infested waters. Or perhaps they would prefer to be locked in irons, and thrown into the hold where the rats would satisfy themselves on their nice young juicy bodies. Maybe he would have them flogged till they had no skin left on their backs! They could choose their own form of punishment and he, the Captain, looked as though he would thoroughly enjoy watching the boys being punished.

The passengers, listening with mounting apprehension, began to murmur and were about to protest when the Captain told the boys to turn around and face the other way. They did not see the broad wink and wide grin the Captain gave the parents. Suddenly the boys dropped on their knees and pleaded 'Don't kill us, we won't do it again.' Captain pulled them up painfully by the ears and said 'What say you? What shall their punishment be?' Immediately everyone said 'Give them another chance, sir!' Still gripping the white-faced, trembling boys he said 'Repeat after me. I do solemnly swear to behave for the rest of the voyage, and to carry out the Captain's orders on pain of retrial.'

The boys having thus promised, he then proceeded to mete out a lesser punishment. Two sailors brought buckets with lids and the boys were ordered to each fill a bucket with cockroaches every day, bring the pails to a steward who would over-see them drop the contents into the sea. The Captain had intended to frighten them and had certainly succeeded, the boys ran to their mothers arms for safety, lest the Captain changed his mind. At first only the two boys hunted the beetles but soon the others boys joined in to help fill their buckets. They gave no more trouble and were fully occupied during the rest of the voyage.

After the trial, a very special dessert was served amid whoops of delight from young and old alike.

The Wedding

Couples were now pairing off, strolling round the deck arm-in-arm, and eventually two couples approached the Captain. He said, yes, he could marry them, but pointed out that it would be less work all round if both couples were married at the same time. This announcement created great excitement among the younger passengers. We borrowed ribbons and lace, cut up coloured paper for streamers and paper flowers for the brides.

After the ceremony, the grooms threw pennies, the children scrambled to pick them up. The ship's Cook had baked a huge wedding cake and the Captain distributed a tot of spirits to every male adult, and lemonade for the others.

The decks were cleared, lanterns hung on the masts and railings. The evening was balmy, with a soft breeze. It was almost dream-like, a tiny twinkling boat in a vast and empty ocean.

We danced till daylight. Violet, in her tight embroidered bodice and frilled skirt was the most sought after girl there. Many a sour look was directed at the married men by their wives, now taking the chance to hold the Irish beauty. Violet and I were dropping with exhaustion when we finally ran away, managed to reach our cabin, lock the door and subsided into giggles and laughter.

Now we were nearing the Equator, having sailed through the Arabian Sea to Colombo in Ceylon (Sri Lanka). A shoal of flying fish surrounded us, and we could not take our eyes off them as they leaped and dived, flashing silver and blue. In Colombo some natives came aboard, with hand-made carpets and ornaments which were quite beautiful. I bought a pair of ebony elephants with ivory tusks and toe-nails which I have to this day. Leaving Colombo we reached the Indian Sea, and were told we would not see land for many days, our next port of call being Freemantle in Western Australia. A long haul of some 3,000 miles.

One morning we woke to find there was a great deal of extra activity on the first-class deck. As we were now nearly on the Equator, this called for a special ceremony. The fore deck was roped off, an awning was filled with sea-water and as many as possible crowded near the rope to watch the proceedings.

One of the crew emerged, playing a flute, behind him came Old Father Neptune, complete with false wig and whiskery beard, carrying his trident. He also wore a small crown and huge sea-shells hung round his neck.

A group of men, laughingly protesting, were now pulled or pushed towards the awning pool. They only wore grass skirts and native beads. Each man was thrown into the water, came up spluttering to be tapped on the head by King Neptune, and handed a certificate to show he was now on the other side of the world. There was great hilarity, and not a little embarrasment as each man's skirt was dragged off quite openly to be put on the next man. This went on for the rest of the day, and some of the steerage passengers were rounded up to the shouts and laughter of their companions.

A few days later a shout went up 'Whales on the starboard side.' We all rushed over and saw a most amazing sight. At first the grey shining mass looked like a small island, then it turned over and moved closer to the ship. Another swam beside, under and over, the ship trembled as they displaced a vast amount of water. Suddenly there was this strange blowing sound, for all the world like the emptying of a giant balloon, then two great spouts of water rose about 10 feet in the air, mushrooming out like an umbrella, from the heads of the whales.

Later two albatross flew over the ship, circled and then settled on the top mast. Great beaks extended, looking for scraps, they gave me an eerie feeling. Their yellow eyes looked evil and menacing, their enormous wings shutting out the sunlight. We were relieved when they left us.

Now we were sailing down the Australian coast. The ship began to roll as we neared the Australian Bight. The wind was cooler, but the sun was as hot as ever.

We were now nearing Sydney. The emigrants who were due to disembark there began to pack their luggage and throw away a lot of rubbish and soiled underwear. The crew made us laugh, remarking dryly that all the lady fish wore knickers in that part of the ocean!

Arriving in Sydney, we passed a huge bridge under construction. Tall cranes, noisy engines and many men toiling in the heat of the day. Two-thirds of our emigrants left the ship. They looked so much healthier than when they came aboard; the wives were rested, the children chubby and rosy cheeked and the men bronzed and fit, pleased to have arrived safely at their destination. They looked confident and ready to tackle whatever lay ahead. There would be difficulties, maybe hard times and even poverty, but they looked forward to a new life of their own making.

We were soon on our way again, about to cross the Tasman Sea to New Zealand. As we sailed south the weather changed, and we had days of torrential rain. We were forced to stay either in our cabins or the saloon, and that was full of smoke. My own Father had smoked a pipe, but when a group of men smoked pipes we could hardly breathe in the atmosphere they created.

I missed the children's chatter, and felt a little sad at their departure, but Violet sighed with relief. 'Isn't it lovely to have the ship to ourselves, no messy children running after us.' I think she must have had too much of young children at home, and had taken a dislike to them.

Miss Wilson came to us in our cabins. She gave me a sheet of paper in an envelope, with a stamp and an address to post to her via the Shipping Line, only if I was having difficulty with my employer. Violet gave me her sister's address in Auckland, and I asked Miss Wilson for mine to give to her, promising to write as soon as we had settled in our new homes.

The heavy rain stopped and the sun shone on the city of Auckland as we sailed into the bay. The boat was manoeuvered into position at Princes Wharf. Once more we stood on firm ground, having come down the gangway to the accompaniment of wolf-whistles and cat-calls from both brown and white men working there. We certainly looked fresh and bonny, with our sunkissed cheeks and arms and glowing with health. Miss Wilson said she would be glad to hand us over to our employers, we were a big responsibility and too pretty for our own good, but she had really been very nice to us, and I rather dreaded losing her as our guardian.

At last we got out of the immigration and customs sheds and crossed the yard to the main gates. We were to wait here till we were collected. Violet looked around for her sisters, and became rather anxious when there was no sign of them, but Miss Wilson said she would stay with her till they came.

Phillip Jefferson

A sporty looking car, with an open top roared up to the gates and stopped abruptly in front of us. An extremely handsome man stepped out and spoke to Miss Wilson who called me over and introduced me to him as Mr Emerson's friend, Phillip Jefferson. Violet came up to me, and stood gazing at the stranger in admiration. His hat shaded his eyes, he had a fine profile, and was dressed in a white silk open-necked shirt, white cotton shorts, knee length white socks and expensive looking leather shoes.

He opened the door of the car and motioned me to take the front seat, but I became quite apprehensive and whispered to Miss Wilson, 'Can't you come with us? I don't want to be alone with him.' Violet found her voice, 'I'll go with you, my sisters will just have to wait.' Phillip Jefferson turned to me 'It will only be a for a few minutes, I am picking up the housekeeper from the Store.' Violet pouted, the man laughed, showing even white teeth. 'You would be wasted on a mission station, missy.' I noticed his gaze lingered on her lovely face. Lifting my case, he put it in the boot of the car, and once more opened the front door for me to get in. 'Is it alright if I sit in the back seat?' I did not look at him as I said this, but he closed the door and opened the rear one. Turning round I hugged Violet, and thanked Miss Wilson for taking good care of me. 'Just my job, Mary' but I detected a tear in her eye as we shook hands.

The car seat was quite hot, but as we moved away the breeze cooled the leather. A few minutes later we drew up at a very imposing store, the name FARMER'S painted in huge letters across the front of the building. A very large lady was waiting and puffed her way down the steps, carrying two large baskets. Phillip got out of the car, and took her baskets from her. She squeezed herself into the front seat, her smile as large as the rest of her. 'Good day, missy, I'm sure glad to see you, that child never gives up. My name is Rameha. I does the shopping with P.J. when he comes into town.' She did not seem to expect an answer, nor could I have found one. To be so close to a dark-skinned native woman and to hear her speak our language rather surprised me. P.J. (as he was known) now spoke to her. He had a deep melodious voice. I wondered if he was a singer.

As we drove on, I had a good view of the city of Auckland. It gave me the impression of being recently built, so different from the old buildings in our cities at home. There were many wooden sheds, with tin roofs and small shabby shops; but the streets were wide, especially Queen Street, the main thoroughfare. High-stepping horses pulled open carriages on which some very stiff-looking and elegant ladies held parasols above their heads. Just outside the city, a few tree-lined streets were lined with fine villas, each in their own section, with private swimming pools, landscaped gardens and wide verandas.

Leaving the bustling town behind us, we came to a much poorer area, the houses huddled and shabby. Here the children, mostly Maori, ran about the streets, some of them quite naked. Older Maoris sat about the doorways, in little groups, the men smoking, some women too, all smiles and chatter, and seemingly idle. The road now became rough, a dirt road edged with tall bushy grasses and trees. The wind blowing on my face prevented me from the travel sickness which such a bumpy ride usually engendered. As we bumped and twisted perilously near the edge of a deep ravine, I could see the tops of tall trees beneath the level of the road. The terrain flattened out as we came to fields on each side (known as paddocks). As far as the eye could see, these were filled with sheep and lambs, more numerous than daisies on an English lawn.

After a long run, we drew up at a filling station, which also served cool drinks. From the outside it just looked like the usual wooden shed with a tin roof, set in the middle of nowhere. I was glad to get out to stretch my legs, and Rameha led me inside the building. Here were pretty plants and gaily-coloured tablecloths on small tables, also lovely cool air from a fan above our heads. We had a large glass of orange. I noticed P.J. sitting with a jug of beer, outside on the veranda, talking to the owner who seemed to know him well. I asked Rameha to show me where the toilet could be. This was outside, very basic, and used by men and women alike!

The seat was a plank with a round hole, placed over a pail, inside a tiny hut; the usual piece of tin formed a very temporary roof. I was to see many of these in the wide open places, where drainage and water systems were still confined to towns.

Another long and now tiresome run brought us to a large settlement. Many Maoris were moving about, some on horseback. A large notice-board informed us that this was Jefferson Sheep Station. A larger house, also of wood, stood back from the road. Rameha said that was 'his' house, but we passed it, with the horn tooting, causing the workers to wave back to us. Another half-mile and we arrived at Kotori Mission House, the actual Mission building was across a small paddock. I was to discover that P.J. owned everything in sight except the Mission and Mission-house. These belonged to the State, having had missionaries sent here for the past hundred years.

As we stopped at the house, a young man came forward to greet us. This was Mr Emerson, the missionary. Rameha disappeared into the house, P.J. said 'Hope you'll stay' and roared off. John Emerson led me to where a woman lay on a couch on the verandah.

My first reaction was to hesitate, looking at Mrs Emerson brought back to me a vivid memory of Martha Stirling just before she died. John Emerson took my case, saying he would 'get some tea, and we ladies could get acquainted.' She smiled, saying, 'Call me Jean, and I'll call you Mary. Tell me how things are in Scotland. What a sight for sore eyes you are, so fresh, young and healthy, do talk to me, and Rameha will bring us tea, though John has to make it, one of my Edinburgh weaknesses.' She asked me so many questions, poured endless cups of tea in dainty cups and kept me talking for nearly an hour. John now came forward, took the tray from her and told her to rest. She seemed utterly exhausted.

He said 'Come with me, I will show you over the house later. You will want to see your own room'. He opened a door and I went in, seeing only a single iron bedstead, a basin and a jug, and nothing else. No curtains on the tiny window, no seats and a bare, rather dirty looking floor. John saw I was disappointed, saying his wife had been too ill to supervise the last nurse and servants. He pointed to very large old cupboard, produced a key and opened it to disclose mattress, sheets and bedding, all of which were soiled

and smelly. He explained the last nurse had left in a hurry, after a
row with the Maori servants. He had asked Rameha to put
everything in the cupboard as things can disappear. John told me to
lock the cupboard and room door, giving me two keys.

However, I was anxious to see my little charge, so hurriedly I
changed into my uniform and locking my bedroom door behind
me, I found my way to the verandah. Rameha was setting the table
and, sitting on John's knee was a thin-looking child, who
immediately wailed when she saw me. Jean lifted herself up. 'Oh
Mary, don't wear uniform, Edith does not like nurses, just wear a
dress. I am not able to give you orders, just do what you can, and
ask Rameha for anything you want.'

This was a great relief to me, already planning to scrub out my
room and wash everything in it. I took off my starched apron, belt,
cuffs and cap, folded them neatly in the package I had carried from
Britain and felt much happier as I returned to the verandah, where
dinner was waiting for me. Edith was in her high chair playing
with a small portion of gravy and potato.

I was hungry and enjoyed the huge slice of roast mutton, sweet
potatoes (Kumaras) and strange looking vegetables.

The child wailed. I lifted the untouched plate from her and tried
to spoon-feed her. She turned away, wailing louder than ever, such
a strange sound, and so mournful, unlike the normal cries of
children. She gazed at me so sadly, suddenly I felt great
compassion for her. I drew her into my arms, cuddling her close to
me, feeling her thin bones through her flimsy dress. She held on to
me, her skinny arms went round my neck, and her wailing stopped.
I felt by instinct it was companionship the child craved for. Her
mother too ill to hold her, her father away for long periods visiting
other Missions scattered far and wide. Rameha, rough and ready,
was doing only what was immediately necessary, then slipping off
to her own home as often as she could.

Soon I had little Edith as my constant companion. She was just
over 3 years old, I made her up pretty dishes of grated fresh fruit
and managed to make her a kind of soup with the strange looking
vegetables. This I fed to her and her mother, trying to nourish them
both. Edith improved rapidly, but her mother seemed to become
worse each day.

The Mission Hall was quite near. We saw many people, mostly
Maoris, coming and going. John played a small organ, preached to

them, listened to their troubles, married, buried and baptised them. The Mission had been built in 1845 and had survived massacre, tribal warfare and extreme hardship. The missionary's stipend only arrived once a year from the British Government. John had tried to teach the Maoris how to plant and water vegetables, but if he was up-country for any length of time, he found the plants dried up and withered, not having been tended.

There were few trees, one stood outside my window, on which the cicadas hummed all day, and these, allied to the constant bleating of thousands of sheep made one feel part of this very strange and spacious land.

It seemed P.J. had put the Mission on its feet, supplying them with donations of money, food and fuel. He had attended the Mission school as a young boy, was then sent to a private school and entered University to study law. He was even now gaining a reputation as a good lawyer. He was extremely wealthy, owned thousands of sheep, a number of woollen mills, and freezing factories. Jean Emerson told me all this and I asked why he had not married. At 25 years of age he must be the most eligible bachelor around. 'He has reasons, Mary, some day I'll tell you.'

Now I tackled my own room when Edith was sleeping. I asked Rameha to fill the ancient boiler for me, fetching wood to stoke the fire. Oil, paraffin and wood were the only fuels we had. Fortunately the weather was hot, and the bedding soon dried. After I had scrubbed everything clean, and made up my bed, I surveyed the bare, empty room and wondered where I could get a piece of carpet and curtain material. As though in answer to my thoughts, Rameha came bustling in, carrying a huge bundle. With a great flourish she pulled out and displayed a large woven mat, curtains and a sheepskin rug. Her wide smile embracing all. 'Missy, what else you need, you ask Rameha.' I could have hugged her. All were hand-made, (except the rug) in lovely colours. I put the mat on the bed, hung the curtains, and ran out to tell Mrs Emerson. She was pleased that I was so happy and told me to use anything in the house to make my room look more furnished.

P.J. came over every other day, sometimes to take Rameha shopping, fetching wood and paraffin to Jean Emerson. He was very attentive, bringing her a box of bon-bons and tit-bits for Edith, or a little toy. I was taken by surprise when he gave me two magazines, saying I would find them a change from too much Bible reading.

On one of his visits, Edith ran out to meet him, stumbled on the rough ground and howled. P.J. picked her up and carried her to me. Edith pulled off his hat and I found myself looking into a pair of startlingly blue eyes, so brilliant I could only stare back. The child whimpered, and I dropped my gaze, feeling an embarrassing blush rise to my face. P.J. retrieved his hat and stuck it on top of his shiny thick hair which curled down to his collar. I busied myself washing Edith's grazed knees, and took her over to her mother to be comforted. Jean lifted her hand, but let it fall again weakly. She whispered 'Come later, when Edith is in bed, I have something to ask you.' Edith was happier now, and we took a walk every afternoon round the paddock.

P.J. followed, then caught up with us. 'How would you and Edith like to come with me tomorrow? I have some business near Rotorua and I'm sure you would like to see more of our country.' I was very pleased, but said I would have to ask Mr Emerson to let Edith come with us. The doctor and nurse would be calling tomorrow, so he would be at home. P.J. smiled, his well-shaped mouth fascinated me, how would it feel to be kissed by him, I wondered!

Next morning I was ready, Edith very excited to be going in the motor-car. P.J. arrived promptly. I sat on the front seat this time with Edith on my knee, so close to P.J. I could feel the heat from his body. Just before he started the engine he looked at me, and the gaze from those brilliant blue eyes made my heart turn over. I felt a blush coming and quckly averted my eyes, aware he was staring at me. 'Not afraid to sit in the front seat with me now?' he teased. 'Usually the ladies are in there before me. You are different aren't you?' I did not know what to say, but blurted out, 'I had only just met you, your friends all know you.' I would like to have asked him why he was not married or engaged, but decided to enjoy this day without asking embarrassing questions. I sensed there was something in his background he did not want to talk about. I determined to ask John that very evening.

It was a perfect day, Edith slept on my knee most of the way, and was excited to have her orange drink in a strange place. P.J. went into the pools, the first one very hot, the next cooler, and so on to the last much cooler one, which made him shiver. The smell of sulphur hung over the area. He had given me his watch, wallet and ring to keep in my pocket; his clothes he left in an open type

changing room. Edith and I watched the other children jumping
and splashing in their own, shallower pool. It was amazing to think
that this heated water came from underneath the earth. It gave me a
feeling of insecurity, so many geyers and volcanoes spouting hot
ashes, mud and sulphur fumes. I had been reading a book of New
Zealand history. Apparently when tribes fought each other, the
dead of both sides were cooked in boiling mud, wrapped in large
leaves and eaten!

P.J. came out, dressed, and said 'Next time, Mary, you must come
in, I'm sure little Edith would have enjoyed it.' The child slept
nearly all the way home and P.J. asked me a great many questions
about myself. What could I say, but that my parents were divorced,
I had lived with Granny, but there was no work for me in Scotland.
I told him about my schooling and my previous Nanny's job, he
seemed quite interested, but said nothing about himself.

All too soon we returned to the Mission House. P.J. dropped us
at the gate and with a wave roared off in a cloud of dust. Edith ran
to her parents, laughing and talking. Her mother said, 'I'm so glad
she is getting out. She has missed too much, I hope she was a good
girl.' Later that evening she sent for me, 'Bring me my Bible, Mary, I
want to ask you if you will promise me something. Dr Low saw me
to-day, and says I must go into hospital right away for an
operation. I do not think I will get better. If I die will you promise to
take Edith home to my parents in Edinburgh? John will pay your
fare, and if you return, he will sponsor you. Please Mary, you look
after her so well, I know I can trust you, and I will die content if
you gave me your promise on the Bible.'

I promised at once, thinking her operation would cure her, and
there would be no need for me to make the journey. At the same
time I realised there would be no work for me if I did not have
Edith.

The morning after Jean had gone to hospital, I pushed Edith in
her little wheeled basket chair to the Mission Hall and found John
teaching a class of Maori children. He was a little surprised when I
told him I would like to talk with him. He said he would finish
soon, and would have an hour or two to spare. I made no mention
of the promise I had made to his wife, telling him I wanted to know
more about P.J.'s background. The Maori children gazed at me with
large brown eyes, they did not have much contact with white
women. The Maori word for Europeans was "pakeha". John took
Edith's hand and led us to the cemetery behind the Mission Hall.

There were many wooden crosses but four white marble tombstones in one corner stood out from the others. 'Read them, Mary, P.J. had them erected on his eighteenth birthday, when he came of age and inherited his father's fortune.'

TO THE MEMORY OF PHLLIP JEFFERSON.
DIED 15th MARCH 1904. AGED 53 YEARS.

TO THE MEMORY OF PHILLIPA JEFFERSON
DIED 15th MARCH 1904. AGED 19 YEARS

TO THE MEMORY OF HER HUSBAND, NEIL GRANT.
DIED 15th MARCH 1904, AGED 21 YEARS

Here was tragedy indeed, all had died on the same day, the same month, and the same year.

The other tombstone was set apart, and read:

TO THE MEMORY OF PHILLIP JEFFERSON'S WIFE,
CYNTHIA PEARSON
KILLED BY ACCIDENT ON 12th SEPTEMBER 1887

Edith fell asleep on my knee and John gave me the long, sad, story.

Unto The Third Generation

About the year 1865, a Dutch East India whale-boat sailed into Auckland Harbour to trade with the settlers. The captain, one Van de Jefferson was a hardened sailor nick-named 'Fiery' by the crew on account of his red hair, beard and temper. His eyes were a brilliant shade of blue, which had come from generations of his sea-faring ancestors, whose eyes had searched the limitless skies and seas, absorbing their colour and passing them on to their descendants. He had on board his son, who made no secret of the fact that he loathed the harshness of his life at sea. Young Phillip Jefferson had listened to tales of gold-miners, who could make a fortune in a few months in Queensland. The crew were permitted to go ashore a few at a time, as some of them would desert the ship for the mines, given the chance. As deserters were nearly all rounded up by the militia before they had gone far, and severely flogged when caught, young Phillip decided to ask his father's permission, saying he would be waiting in Auckland for the ship's return next year, hopefully with gold in his pocket. The old man ranted and raved, but finally gave his consent, and said Goodbye to his red-haired, blue-eyed son.

Young Jefferson was known as P.J. among his fellow miners. It was only a few months later that he quit the gold-fields, having made a small fortune in gold. He travelled back to Auckland, took lodgings with an English family and looked around for some means of employment. The owner of the house worked in the Land-Seers office, buying and selling land. He bought land from Maoris for a shilling an acre, and sold it to the settlers for ten shillings. It was not long before P.J. assisted him, and learning the tricks of the trade, bought land north of the Waikata river. He moved to Kotori Mission house, staying there for a few months till his own house was built, a sturdy wooden dwelling, with running water. There was a tribe of Maoris living nearby, a settlement of mud and grass huts. Chief N'Tui ruled over 500 men, women and children and claimed all the land around. Within a few years the settlement disappeared, the tribe being pushed further and further out to the banks of the Waikata River. P.J. bought them out for as little as a bag of flour, a blanket or an old horse, but worst of all, he plied them with whisky. When the elders of the tribe were confused with liquor, he got them to sign over more and more land. This he fenced off, paid the Maoris to clear the bush, and filled the paddocks with sheep. He utterly destroyed the ignorant 'bush men', working them hard for very little, and beating all who disobeyed him.

Athough he despised the men, he was often seen in the company of Maori girls. White women seemed to avoid him, as his violent reputation preceeded him at social functions. Athough now wealthy, there was a shortage of white women, and a surplus of wealthy men. Girls who came out from Britain were snapped up as wives, even though some of them could not write their own names. It was tabu (forbidden) to marry a Maori woman, or even to have an affair with one. One local Councillor had been deprived of his post and chased out of the area. Such were the conditions when chief N'Tui announced the wedding of his extremely beautiful daughter, the Princess Laelli, to the son of a neighbouring chief.

P.J. had long lusted after the princess. He knew she bathed in a small pool near the waterfall, which was out of sight of the Maori village. On the day of her wedding, she came to bathe with her young friends, who washed her hair, and rubbed fragrant oils over her slim body.

P.J. rode to a vantage point above the river, heard the laughter and singing, vowing he would have the 'bush girl' before she was married, it was now or never. Leading his horse to a hidden copse, he tied her up, and crept quietly to where the girls sat on the rocks, combing their long shining hair. At last two of the girls disappeared to gather flowers and berries and Laelli wandered out of the pool to follow them. P.J. saw his chance, pounced on the terrified girl and carried her a safe distance. He had stuffed his red spotted neckerchief into her mouth, and tied her hands to prevent her removing it, then flinging himself on top of her, he raped her.

Hearing voices coming nearer, he hitched up his trousers, and crept quietly away, mounted his horse, and galloped home, showing himself to all his work-men, trying to make them believe he had just come from his house. After his evening meal he sat out on the verandah and found himself listening for signs and sounds of the usual noisy celebrations of a Maori wedding.

Laella would not denounce him openly, she knew the tribe were almost dependant on the work he gave them. That they would avenge the violation of their Princes she had no doubt. 'Just let them try,' he mused 'he would have them turned out of their homes, and the men gaoled for sheep-stealing.' His word against theirs, the courts would judge in his favour, as the Maoris well knew.

The long empty silence made him uneasy and sleepless. When he rose there was no sound coming from the kitchen. Calling the housekeeper he found her gone, with all her family, and every Maori with her. A few paheka (white overseers) wandered about, at a loss to know what to do. He swore at them, and drove his truck to town, where he visited his freezer factories, and wool-sheds.

Entering his club, he ordered his usual drink, then became aware of an air of hostility among the usually jovial members. They turned aside when he addressed them, completely ignoring his presence. Leaving quickly, he ordered a meal in his favourite restaurant. The Italian cook brought it to him personally, explaining his Maori staff were attending an important palaver.

His banker conducted his business briskly then summoned a clerk to show him out, instead of his usual fawning parting when preceeding him to the front door.

The news of the outrage against the Princess, her tribe, and future husband's tribe had spread like bush-fire. Groups of both white men and natives stared balefully at him as he made his way to his truck, 'let them prove it was him!' he thought angrily. Once home he was relieved to find his housekeeper at work. He shouted 'Where were you this morning, I had no breakfast.' She stared at him with a look of such malevolence that he paled visibly. 'I was took sick.' He retorted with 'I suppose the whole lot of you took sick as well. If they are not back at work I'll have every one of their black hides flogged.'

He saw they had come back, and strode out to rebuke them. They scowled, fingering their knives and axes, as though they would like to attack him, he gave some orders to his foremen and left.

His thoughts now turned to his own position. He guessed it would be the sole topic of conversation at every dinner table in the county. Well, he would give them more to talk about, he would get married!

Next morning, dressed in a well-fitting riding outfit, he rode out on his prized chestnut mare to the house of his nearest neighbour, a wealthy landowner. Luke Pearson was as rich, as mean and as ambitious as himself. A man of the Church and a leader in politics, he was highly respected in the community.

He was a widower, and had an only child. Cynthia Pearson was a spoiled, haughty young woman, whose great love for horses had taken her to race meetings all over the country. She had won many trophies, and was well-known for her stable of fine horses.

It was rumoured that her father discouraged suitors, hoping to keep his daughter at home. He had lavished a fortune on her stables and horses, he also enjoyed escorting her to many social engagements.

Reaching the Pearson homestead he was ushered into a spacious drawing room, where he waited, somewhat impatiently for Pearson's appearance. P.J. did not like Pearson, but his daughter would be wealthy when he died, and she would bring prestige to his name. He had only met her at race meetings, and had admired her fine figure and proud bearing.

A clatter of hoofs stopped outside and the lady of the house entered. She looked very surprised to see him. 'Why, P.J., what brings you here at this hour of the morning?' He held out his hand saying, 'Could I speak with you privately?' Cynthia led him into the garden. He stood before her, his brilliant blue eyes gazing intensely into hers. 'My dear, will you allow me to visit you, with the intention of asking you to marry me?'

He knew she would have heard of his fall from grace, but she was a woman of the world, who like himself, believed a 'Bush woman' was no more than a necessary interlude, anyway, it was only gossip. She looked a little taken aback. 'I can only admire your spirit, asking me this when gossip is so rife about you. I must talk this over with my father.' She drifted towards the door, P.J. caught her in his arms 'Let me seal it with a kiss.' Their lips met, he was pleased, yet startled at the intensity of her passion. Her heightened colour, the smile playing on her lips encouraged him to hold her longer, but the door opened and her father looked out. Cynthia fled indoors. Pearson came to the point at once. 'Are you after my daughter, sir? She is a fine woman, and if I may say so, in view of your recent conduct, or misconduct, I do not think you are worthy enough to make her your wife.' P.J. felt his anger rising, but forced himself to say, 'I could not agree more with you, sir, but the young lady has not yet consented to marry me!'

'Well now, that is true' said Pearson, 'but may I suggest you listen to a certain condition I must make before you ask her?' Cynthia would leave you at the first sign of infidelity. I require an assurance that you will provide for her and any children you may have, by a sum of £50,000 for her use alone. The document to be drawn up and signed by you in the presence of my solicitors.' P.J. swallowed, the infernal pompous ass, how dare he! Controlling his temper, he forced himself to speak calmly. 'I think you should hear what Cynthia says before we discuss this matter further.'

At lunch they chatted about horses, sheep and politics, then Pearson visited the stables, leaving Cynthia and P.J. alone on the verandah. 'Your father strikes a hard bargain, do you know what he has asked from me!'

'Well P.J., am I not worth it? After all, he is only safeguarding my interests. If you agree to accept his condition, it won't be too great a loss, as my dowry will compensate you almost to the same extent. Well, do you agree?' 'Very well, I agree, will you marry me Cynthia?' When she nodded, he said, 'Let us get married as soon as possible. I am not a patient man.' Her father came to them, 'What news, my girl?' Seeing her smiling face, 'Is it yes? Then let me be the first to congratulate you.'

The wedding took place in a few weeks. The cream of Auckland society attended, the newspapers filling the front pages with the wedding pictures.

Time passed, Cynthia had stables built for her own horses, and owned a truck and horse-box of her own, keeping up the same life-style as she had previous to her marriage. P.J.s conduct was exemplary, as she frowned on heavy drinking and week-ends in town.

About six months after the wedding, the over-seer rode up to the house in great alarm. 'Boss, the whole tribe is on the march and they are heading this way.' P.J. ordered a horse to be brought to the door, helped Cynthia on to it and told the man to see her safely to the Mission House. He gathered his white workers and they, armed and ready, waited for the natives. Now a mournful dirge could be heard, getting louder by the minute, the stamping of bare feet and the deep growls of the men made P.J. realise this was not a war party but a 'tangi' (native funeral).

In front rode Chief N'Tui, on his white pony, dressed in full ceremonial dress, and carrying a long decorated spear. He was followed by four stalwart men carrying a raupo testle on which lay the body of Princess Laella. After the men came the women and children, wearing the white flowers of mourning. All came to a halt at a signal from the Chief, who now stood directly in front of the men on the steps of the verandah. P.J. asked, 'Why are you here? This is not your burial ground.'

The Chief signalled by raising the spear for silence. In the stillness his voice rang out loudly for all to hear.

'I, Chief N'Tui, descendant of many great chiefs, have spoken to the Gods of my people. They have taken the spirit of my daughter to join them in the great land beyond the clouds. They have pronounced sentence on you Phillip Jefferson, for the cruelties you have inflicted upon us, the true people of this land. We, the rightful owners shall own all this land again. You will know this before you die. The Gods also speak of vengeance for the death of my daughter. Every woman of your house shall die violently, your seed shall perish, and your name will be wiped off the face of this land. Thus speak the Gods!'

He turned away, but P.J. stepped forward, his intention to discover whether a child had been born. If stillborn, it would be in the mothers arms, as was the custom. Immediately many men stood between him, but not before he had glimpsed the dead wide open eyes of Laella.

The Chief plunged the spear into the ground at P.J.'s feet. His red spotted neckerchief hung from the hilt, on it was painted in bold letters the word ATU (retribution.) He now waved the procession on, and watched as the mile-long cortege passed, turned and went back the way they came. The lamentations grew louder then died away. As soon as the last mourners were out of sight P.J. withdrew the spear from the ground, broke it over his knee, then burned it with the tell-tale neckerchief.

When his workers returned to work next day, he pulled a young boy from his mother's side, demanding to know how the Princess had died, and if she had given birth to a child. He was a cruel and violent man who would vent his anger on any native who displeased him. He despised the tribes, and like other wealthy landowners completely ignored the Treaty of Waitangi. The boy's mother pleaded on her knees not to flog the boy, and he only let him go when she promised to find out the answers to his questions. Later she told him that from the day which should have been her wedding day, the Princess had locked herself in a tiny hut, not allowing anyone to see her shame. Food and water were left outside. Months passed, till one day they heard her cry out in pain, which lasted for many hours. When the cries ceased, her father forced the door open to find her lying dead. With the help of a woman, summoned from a different tribe, he himself dressed the body for burial. This woman had disappeared soon afterwards and no one knew where she had gone. Only the Chief knew the true circumstances of his daughter's death.

P.J. rode towards the high vantage point where he had watched the Princess bathing in the pool below. A row of posts, attached with wire netting, surrounded the steep drop to prevent sheep straying. He drew up sharply, painted on the centre post was a small brown face, indistinguishable except for two blobs of brilliant blue paint where the eyes should be. Underneath was painted in heavy letters, the words "Sky-Eye", the name given to half-caste children who had inherited the grey or blue eyes of their Paheka fathers. So there was a child, thought P.J., with eyes of his colouring, hopefully it was still-born. He decided to wipe the whole episode from his mind, daubed some dirt over the crude drawing, 'Superstitious savages,' he muttered. He had happier things to think about.

His wife was pregnant, and a few moths later gave birth to a daughter. Although disappointed that it was not a son, he named her Phillipa, which she herself was to shorten to Pippa. She had red hair, brilliant blue eyes and a fiery temper. All went well for two years and P.J. refused to think of N'Tui's revenge. He doted on his little daughter, often telling Cynthia she thought more of her horses than her child, but was pleased when she informed him that she was pregnant again and hoped it would be a son.

She was seven months pregnant, and had given up riding. The stable boy called to say Nimrod, the big stallion, seemed off-colour. She said, 'I'll take him to the vet, its only ten minutes away. Get him into the horse-box.' Nimrod was one of her favourite jumpers, she had entered him for a Gymkana in two days time. She drove the truck, with horse-box attached, along the country lane, hoping he would be well enough to take part in the event. Up a rather narrow drive, she stopped, and opened the box door, to lead Nimrod the rest of the way, leaving the doors open to air the hot interior. The horse was treated, 'not much wrong, just needed a couple of pills', said the Vet. 'He is in good shape.' She coaxed him into his box, then proceeded to back down the narrow lane. Reaching the road, she was about to accelerate when she thought she smelled burning. Finding nothing in the engine, she turned to the horse-box. Nimrod was whinnying loudly, she would have to quieten him, but when she opened the door, the smoke turned into flame. The great beast reared in terror as the door opened and fell out, Cynthia pulled him up by his bridle and held on while the terrorised horse leaped and twisted. Suddenly he bolted, the loose reins caught Cynthia's foot and she was dragged along the rough ground. The horse ran through some trees, the poor, limp body of Cynthia being hurled from tree to tree. He drew up panting, and men who had seen the whole thing came on her broken battered body, covered with blood. The horse-box was completely burned out, but they managed to save the truck.

In hospital they took her baby from her, he was quite dead, a beautiful little boy. P.J. was devastated, but if he thought that part of the prophesy had come true, he made no mention of it. The native workmen attended the funeral from a distance, as usual, but that night there were sounds of celebration in the settlements. They were celebrating a victory.

P.J. took little Pippa into his room at night, and hired a white couple to watch her during the day. Pippa preferred the Maori housekeeper, and played with her children. She grew up wild and carefree, and was sent to boarding school at the age of ten. She went from there to college in Auckland, and when she was eighteeen her father bought a little red Coupe for her. Her exploits were the talk of the town. Meanwhile P.J.'s sheep-station was expanding.

He employed a young man to assist him in the management of his estate. He was a steady industrious lad and soon became under-manager. Neil Grant was 18 years old when he left his native Orkney. He had learned book-keeping and knew all there was to know about the rearing of sheep. His father had been a shepherd all his life, and had taken his sons with him to the hillsides when they were not at school. Neil had been employed by another sheep-farmer when he arrived in New Zealand with his younger brother, Ross. The farmer left them to fend for themselves, and did not warn them of the dangers of living in a hot country.

One night it was so hot that young Ross stripped naked and fell asleep among the sheep. He awoke screaming in agony. A thousand sheep-tics had invaded his body, burrowing under his skin. No one was near, Neil was far away in another paddock, thinking his brother would be fast asleep in the bunk-house. It was two days before some Maoris found him delirious and in great pain, his body purple from blood-poisoning. Nothing could save him. Neil had the sad task of writing home after Ross was buried. He could not stay with such a careless employer and had come to the Jefferson station when he heard they needed a shepherd.

The first time he saw Pippa, she brought three friends with her, barely acknowledging him when P.J. introduced him to her. Right from the start he was fascinated by her beauty. The sun on her hair made it blaze in crimson glory, the wonderful blue eyes sparkled with fun. He would watch her from a distance, usually packing up the car for never-ending picnics, bathing and surfing at one of the many beautiful bathing spots around the coast.

Two years passed, this time Pippa came home alone, the little car filled with her belongings, announcing to her father that she had no intention of returning to college. She wanted to stay home. She was tired of college life.

Almost immediately she waylaid Neil, asking him about himself, and telling him how handsome he had grown in the past two years. She continued to meet him at every opportunity, showing great affection.

Soon he was head over heels in love, the cuddling and kissing turning to passion.

At first Neil resisted, his religious upbringing held him back, but he could not hold out against her insistence. Soon they were making love in the sheds or on the banks of the river. A month later she said she was pregnant, they must elope. Neil hated the thought of deceiving his employer but they quietly arranged to be married by the missionary in the tiny church. Pippa laid her posy of flowers on her mother's grave. They spent the rest of the day sunbathing and swimming in the lovely little bay at Takapuna, Auckland's nearest beach. Returning in the evening they confronted Pippa's father, holding each others hand. Neil said, 'I have just married your daughter, sir.' P.J.'s face turned an angry red as he spluttered, 'How dare you, you have nothing to offer my daughter. This marriage must be annulled immediately!' Pippa spoke, 'Papa, it is too late for that, I am carrying your grand-child. Please don't be angry with us. I love Neil very much.' Her father turned to Neil. 'Seems I will have to accept you as my son-in-law, but this hole-in-a-corner wedding isn't good enough for my only daughter. Get yourself a proper wedding dress, Pippa. We will send out invitations to all our friends, and arrange a wedding reception just like your mother had. She would not have liked you to get tied up like a bush woman.' Pippa answered, 'If she had been here, things might have been different.'

Thus it was, that two weeks later a huge reception was held in Auckland's largest hotel, attended by over 300 guests. P.J. announced quite openly that there was no need for a church service. The local missionary had 'tied them up good and proper.' Pippa looked radiant and lovely in her mother's wedding dress, which she had unearthed, finding it in good condition, and that it fitted her beautifully. She danced and drank so much that Neil became anxious. 'Come home, Pippa, you are tiring hourself out.' 'Oh Neil, I do so want to be happy tonight. It is probably the last party I will have for a while, after all it is *my* big day!'

Daylight came before the last of the guests departed. Pippa had to be carried upstairs, and was asleep before her head had touched the pillow. Neil lay awake, wondering how they could live on his wages. He did not want her to take money from her father. So far P.J. had paid for the clothes and reception, but that was his duty to his daughter and it must end there. She was his, Neil's, responsibility now and he would have to support her. So Neil decided, but P.J. went ahead, building a smart bungalow for them in the nearest paddock. Pippa spent a lot of time supposedly choosing furntiure, carpets, curtains and baby clothes. She would be away all day. Neil wondered if she was drinking and dining with her college friends. Even her father chided her, but she only laughed. 'I'll have to stay home when the baby comes. I want to get around while I can.'

Early one morning, about six months after the wedding, Neil was wakened by Pippa. 'Neil, the baby is coming, take me to hospital.' 'Its too early Pippa – are you sure?' 'Hurry Neil, it may be premature.' Neil knew enough to realise that could be a dangerous situation for both mother and baby, so helping her to dress, he called out one of the foremen to drive them to the hospital. He prayed it was a false alarm, but Pippa was groaning, seeming to get worse by the minute. Reaching the hospital, he left his white-faced wife with two efficient-looking nurses, one of whom told him to go home. First babies took longer to arrive, they would let him know when the baby came.

Six hours later Pippa's baby arrived. A fine healthy boy, 'both mother and baby are well' said the nurse. Neil was delighted to send the message to P.J.

Neil hurried to the hospital. Entering the ward, he was surprised to find Pippa in tears. She held out her arms to him and he held her tenderly. 'Tell me you will always love me, Neil, no matter what happens. We will have more babies, but just now I only want you.' 'Pippa, where is our son? When can I see him?' 'Neil, not now, promise me you won't see him to-day, I could not bear it.'

Neil became worried. 'Is there something wrong with him; I was told he was a fine, healthy boy; tell me Pippa, I have a right to know.' Pippa clung to him, 'Promise me, Neil, please, please promise you won't try to see him yet, not till I feel stronger.' The nurse motioned to him to go, his wife needed rest and quiet. He could have ten minutes in the evening.

Although he had promised his wife not to see the baby, the urge to do so was too strong. He stopped at the nursery and looked in. A young Maori nurse came to the door, and he asked if he could see baby Grant, adding that he was his father. The nurse looked quite startled, and seemed to hesitate, but Neil stepped into the room, and looked at the label tied to each cot. He read one out, 'Ha, got you!' He stared for a second, then turned to the nurse. 'Must have got the wrong one, where is the baby Grant!' An older nurse came forward, lifted the tiny bundle and uncovered the baby's face. 'This is the baby Grant, your wife's child.' Neil gasped, 'It can't be, we are both white. That is a Maori child, there must be a mistake.'

'No mistake, Mr Grant, I was there at his birth. He is not all native, look at his blue eyes.' Neil's strangled voice uttered, 'Is he premature?' The nurse said he was a full-term child. Neil walked slowly away, entered his car and drove to a quiet place. His tortured mind going over the last few months. What a fool he had been! She must have known when she left college that she was pregnant. She had used him, deceived him, making him believe she wanted him. No wonder she had rushed the wedding. Another thought struck him, if she had white lovers too and the chance of a white baby perhaps, they would have lived with a lie, and he may never have known. He would be the laughing stock of the country. A grim look settled on his face, his eyes wide and staring. He drove the car at an alarming speed into town. At the bank he drew out every penny he possessed, and asked the manager for a money-order for the amount, asking also for an envelope. He placed the money-order inside, wrote his mother's address on it, and left it to be posted urgently. Driving home, he could only see the brown face of Pippa's child in front of him. Arriving at the bungalow, he threw his wife's clothes into the piled-up baby's cot, emptied a can of parrafin over it, then threw a lighted match on top which sent a whoosh of flame leaping into the roof. On his way back to the hospital, a fire-engine hurtled past, but he did not even wince. He intended to shoot himself, but he must see Pippa, must know why and who.

P.J. had had a wonderful fishing trip, he had caught a 140 pounder Mako and several tuna. The weather was perfect. Life on his yacht, wonderful. He had celebrated his success with champagne and his party of pretty women and raunchy men. He had named the boat, "Pippa I" having bought it with the money he had received from his wife's legacy. Pearson still lived; he blamed P.J. for Cynthia's death, and refused to have any contact with him, but allowed Pippa to visit. He had also left her all his money and estate. She would be a wealthy woman. P.J. was sure Cynthia's death had been an accident, but Pearson had investigated the cause and believed someone had thrown a lighted cigarette end into the horse-box while it stood empty in the lane leading to the vets' house. Cynthia herself did not smoke.

Reaching the boat-house the message had come through from Neil 'Pippa had a fine healthy boy, both well.' P.J. visibly swelled with pride, he must see his lawyers straight away. They drew up a new will, with a clause that the name of Grant be dropped when he came of age. 'If my grandson has my land, he must have my name.' His lawyers advised caution in this matter, but made the inheritance indisputable and water-tight in favour of his grandson.

P.J. arrived at the hospital with a great bunch of flowers for Pippa. He gave them to a nurse, saying he would see his grandson first, and then he would see his daughter. Two nurses and a doctor barred his way, but P.J. pushed them aside. He lifted the white cover from the baby's form, exposing the tiny dark-brown body. P.J. recoiled 'What kind of bloody trick is this? This is not my daughter's child.' He strode out of the room, his rage mounting with every step. Behind him, the nurses hastily removed the cot and baby to another room for safety. P.J. thrust his face into Pippa's. 'Tell me,' he said hoarsely, 'it can't be yours, Pippa, not yours?' Pippa nodded, utterly terrified. 'Who was it?' he bellowed, 'I'll have him hung for rape'. 'No, no, we loved each other very much. He was the son of a Princess, and his grandfather was a great chief. There was something between us; he had eyes like yours and mine, he did not rape me.' 'Incest,' he roared,' that was your half brother.' He had just made the child his heir! The shocking reality maddened him, 'Never, never, I'll kill the bastard!' Pippa clung to him, 'No Papa, no, I love him.' Her words infuriated him so much he completely lost control of himself. 'You whore, you slut, I'll finish you both!' His iron-hard hands closed on ther throat. His manic grip tightened as he shook her like a sheep at the shearing. He threw her limp body to the floor, turned and ran towards the nursery foaming at the mouth. Porters and doctors came running to overpower the demented man. He fought like a raging bull, but they dragged him back to where Pippa lay, and they tied him in a chair. He saw Pippa, her lovely face purple and contorted, the tongue lolling sideways, the blue eyes bulging. He struggled desperately, mouthing obscenities against the Maoris.

This was the scene that met Neil Grant's eyes as he entered the ward. A scene so horrific he turned his head away. His wife lay dead, and she had died violently. It could only be P.J. who had done this. P.J. saw Neil and shouted 'Neil, kill the bastard, it's not yours. Kill it, kill it!'

Neil's distraught gaze rested on his wife's face. Kneeling down he stroked Pippa's hair. Turning slowly he accused P.J. 'you have killed your own daughter.' He drew his gun and fired at P.J., before shooting himself. Neil Grant died instantly, his blood mingling with that glorious red hair.

Dr Rewi appeared, one of the few Maori doctors in the country. He wheeled P.J. into an ante-room and closed the door behind him.

P.J. swore, 'Get me to surgery, this thing hurts like hell.' He was handed a sheet of paper 'You will have to sign here.' P.J. did not even glance at the paper (which was blank) but signed quickly, his crafty mind working on a new possibility. 'That bastard, with Grant's name, get rid of it, doctor, and I will make you a rich man, who is to know?' He was about to add 'It's only a bit of black shit anyway,' but this man was Maori. He stopped speaking and waited.

Dr. Rewi stood in front of P.J. and slowly removed his dark glasses, revealing eyes as blue as his own. 'Are you asking me to get rid of my own son? I am the father of your daughter's son. I am also your son, the Sky-eye. I did not rape your daughter as you did my mother, the Princess Laella. Pippa came to me willingly.'

P.J. was speechless, his pain forgotten as his past unfolded, and N'Tui's revenge became apparent. 'Now my mother has been avenged, you will die soon, and Mana (prestige) will be restored to our tribe. Your seed will perish with you. The elders have commanded me to be made sterile, and when the child is ready, I will undertake to operate on him myself. There can be no Jefferson blood in the land. That will be returned to us. This paper you have signed will be used to make me his guardian till he comes of age, only then will the Gods be satisfied.' P.J. stared, the awful truth hurt as much as the now agonising wound, blood spurted from his mouth. And so he died!

Dr Rewi replaced his dark glasses, called the elderly Maori nurse who had delivered Pippa, and instructed her to take the child home immediately, and to carry him in a covered shopping basket. Once the people heard of the three sudden deaths, the hospital would be besieged by reporters and spectators.

The word Atu (retribution) would be on everyone's lips. It was to spread from mouth to mouth, from tribe to tribe; from mudhut to mansion, from coast to coast; from mountain to river. The Maori nation exulted. They danced in the streets, chanting in their own language 'Our Gods are appeased. The spirits of our ancestors rejoice. Chief N'Tui is avenged. Mana has been restored.'

No Maoris attended the burial of the three coffins. Townspeople gathered to gaze, wonder and speculate. The Maoris held great feasts in every settlement throughout the land, to them it was a victory of the Gods. The spirit of their beautiful Princess Laella would now rest in peace.

John finished speaking and pointed out the inscription which P.J. had engraved on his grand-father's stone in Maori language.

"HE KURA TANGATA E KORE E ROKOHANGA"

Translated this read: "The treasured possessions of men are intangible."

My thoughts turned to Neil Grant. What of his mother who had lost two sons in this land on the other side of the world? A chill feeling crept over me. Suddenly I wanted to get away from the sight of these cold tombstones.

Violet's Visit

John Emerson told me he would stay in town for a few nights, to be at his wife's side before and after her operation. He asked me if I had a friend who would like to come for a week or two as I would be pretty much on my own with Edith. I immediately thought of Violet Delaney, she would cheer me up in this rather sombre atmosphere. Apart from P.J.'s visits, there were few white people. The Mission children ran in and out of the house, playing with Edith. Unfortunately, they lifted anything they could find. John explained that the Maoris believed that anything that was not kept under lock and key was theirs by right. They did not regard it as stealing. After finding my food stocks disappearing, I resolutely locked everything up and made the children play outdoors.

I wrote to Violet, and asked P.J. if he would post it for me. He glanced at the address and laughed 'I am passing this street every day, I will deliver it by hand, and perhaps get an answer for you there and then.'

Imagine my surprise and pleasure when his car drew up at the door, and who should step out but Violet. She hugged me 'Mary, you saved me just in time, I was on the point of running away. Holy Mother of God, and am I pleased to see you? I am never going back. Mr Jefferson says he can get me an office job.'

P.J. came forward, armed with food and vegetables. 'You girls can make my dinner to-night, but don't chatter too much or you will burn it.' Laughing at our pretence of hurt pride, never-the-less he seemed to be very much at ease with Violet. She was paler now, and much thinner. Her high cheek bones were more accentuated, but even lovelier.

We cooked and chattered, Edith clinging to my skirt, shy of the young woman whose Irish tongue sounded strange to her ears. Violet told me her sisters kept her indoors claiming it was for her own safety. She had to cook, clean and wash all day, then make up the books in the evening. She had written to firms for employment, but received no answers. She was as sure as God is in heaven, her letters were not posted!

On the day that P.J. arrived with my letter, she was alone in the house. 'It was a heaven-sent chance, Mary, and I took it. I left a note, packed everything I have and here I am, and I am never going back to be their skivvy. They are so miserable, too busy working to enjoy life. That's not for me at all, at all. I am going back to Ireland, you don't need money to be happy there, what with the singing and dancing and the friendly faces of my own folks. They are cold and hard of heart, my poor mother would not recognise her own daughters. I'll only work to save every penny till its my fare home I'll have!' I told her if Jean Emerson died, I could be sailing back with her. 'Glory be, that would be just great, that's the best news I've heard for a long time.' I did not think John Emerson would have been pleased to hear this remark.

Over the next few days, P.J. took the three of us to various well-known places of interest. Violet took great pains with her appearance and always looked fresh and radiant. It annoyed me that she monpolised P.J. She had no time for little Edith, or for housework, telling me to order Rameha to do more. When she was not shopping, she was making pretty blouses or stringing beads and flowers in her hair.

She made no secret of the fact that she wanted to be closer to P.J. 'What's the matter with the man? He seems to like the ladies yet he backs off when they get interested.'

I could have told her but wanted to talk to P.J. alone. Since the day John had told me of the dreadful happenings leading up to and including the day of his birth, we had not seen much of each other alone. Edith was not pleased either. P.J. seemed to be more attentive to Violet than to her, and she would not leave his side all the time he was with us, much to Violet's annoyance.

Violet was reading a romantic novel and was completely engrossed. She did not see P.J. arrive. Edith and I ran out to meet him. He looked around for Violet. I said she was too busy, and could he take Edith and I for a spin? A little reluctantly he opened the car door, watching the house at the same time. 'I want to talk to you alone P.J., please.' We stopped by the side of the river and sat on the grass, while Edith picked flowers.

'Well, Mary, what is it? You have been quieter than usual. Is it something to do with Violet?' 'No,' I answered, 'John has told me the story of the tombstones, would you rather not talk about it?'

He stared at me, only then did I see the pain in his eyes, the grim set of his mouth. 'Everyone knows, but no one speaks openly of what happened, yet the burden lies heavy on my shoulders. Mary, what must I do to find happiness? Everywhere I look I see accusing eyes. The curse of N'Tui haunts me. I dare not ask a white woman to marry me fearing Laella's revenge, that my wife will die violently, as my mother and grand-mother. No Maori woman would have me as a husband, either. Tradition is too strong. They only marry to have children, a barren woman is despised by her tribe.'

'But why have you not given the land back to the natives? You will have no peace until you do so. You would then be able to marry once the tribal demands have been met. What of your natural father?'

'He disappeared when I came of age. He too was unable to marry the Maori girl he loved. The Jefferson blue eyes were an affront and offensive to the tribe. That was why he wore dark glasses. He left the hospital soon after the tragedy, and only communicated through solicitors, to arrange for my schooling and upbringing.'

I think Violet would marry you, we both know she does not want to have children. If you changed your name to your legal father's name, the one on your birth certificate, surely that would appease the Maoris? She just can't understand why someone as handsome and wealthy as yourself can be so lonely. Neither could I till I heard the Missionary's story of your past. Will I tell her or will you? She will get it from Rameha, you should be the one to tell her.'

'I can't Mary, it's too awful. I will never be rid of the shadow. Two generations of hate and revenge surround me.' He touched my hand. 'Would you have married me, knowing the truth about me?'

'No, but not for that reason. I want to have children to love and be loved. I have known so little love, but I want to be your friend.'

He smiled, the pain left his eyes 'Here I am, thinking only of myself, come, let's ask Violet what she would like me to do. I do love her and hope we can be happy together. She is very beautiful and I don't want to lose her. You are my friend

Mary, and I value your advice.'

Two days later, Violet came to me at bed-time. She had spent the day with P.J., and he had told her everything. She seemed downcast, I asked her if she could marry him now. 'I just don't know, Mary, let us all talk together tomorrow. He will have to change his name before I could take his. I need the advice of the Holy Father.'

P.J. looked wonderful, his smile embraced all of us, but his eyes were only on Violet. We had taken a picnic basket to the beach, paddled, splashed and watched P.J. swim. He came out of the sea like a magnificent young God, his brown body glistening, the perfect muscles rippling. He was a keen sportsman, playing rugby and cricket with great enthusiasm.

Violet rose from the rug we had spread on the beach. She drew him down, 'Tell me, do you want to marry me? Tell me before I say any more.'

He held her close, 'Oh, Violet, if you only would. I would protect you and I do love you. Will you marry me?' She nodded assent.

'That's settled then.' Sitting apart from him now she surprised both of us with her next words. 'This very day you will put an announcement in the newspapers to the effect that you, Phillip Jefferson will from now on be known as Neil Grant, your legal father's name. I am going to call you Neil from this moment.'

P.J. was startled, but did not resist the idea. We packed up and on the way home called at the newspaper offices in the area, then stopped at the office of his solicitors to inform them of his change of name. They would need time to study the law, and how it would affect his business interests.

Another surprise awaited us. As we neared the Mission House, we saw a very elegant carriage standing there. Rameha was pointing us out to a very elderly gentleman. P.J. jumped out of the car, smiling to greet him. 'It is good to see you, great-grandfather, I trust you are well, but what brings you here? Won't you come in?'

The old man leaned over the side of his carriage. 'No, I am comfortable enough here, thank you. If the young ladies will excuse us, will you sit here with me? I have something very important to say to you.'

Violet, Edith and myself went indoors. Rameha told us the old gentleman was Pippa's grandfather, whose daughter Cynthia, had married the first Phillip Jefferson. He had vowed never to acknowledge the name of Jefferson, such was his hatred of his son-in-law.

When the carriage left, P.J. walked slowly over to us, looking quite bemused. We waited impatiently to hear what had been said between them.

'It appears my great-grandfather knows everything about me. He has followed my career, hoping I would take steps to give back my land to the Maoris. When he heard I was to change my name, he could wait no longer to inform me that if I renounced all claim to my inheritance, by returning the land, he would leave me all he has, which is twice what I have already. He wants me to come and live with him in his mansion.' Looking at Violet, 'Once married, it would be our home.'

Violet was quite over-awed. Next day she dressed in her most sombre costume, to visit Luke Pearson, and arrange to meet his lawyers. John Emerson came home for a short time to see Edith, and attend to his work. Jean was still very ill. She had survived the operation, but was making no real progress. There was very little hope as she was dying of cancer.

When Violet and Neil returned that evening they were in joyous mood. They had spent the entire day with Luke Pearson and his lawyers. Luke Pearson insisted that Neil should take all his private possessions over to his house and make it his home, the sooner the better, as he was an old man and wanted to see Neil settled in.

Neil called on his own solicitors and set the return of his land to the tribe in motion. A committee would be formed to build a new township within its boundaries. The tribe would have proper houses, stores and employment, and plans were put forward to build a magnificent meeting house in the centre, built by Maori craftsmen with a wide marae in the front to hold gatherings. (This is traditionally regarded as the spiritual centre of the tribal unit to whom it belongs.) The new town was to be known as Waikato, after the great river which flowed into the sea, and on whose banks the tribe had been forced to live for half a century.

Violet showed me her engagement ring. It was very valuable, and had belonged to Luke Pearson's mother.

The wedding was arranged to take place in two weeks. Luke Pearson paid for everything. We were to buy the best dresses, no money was to be spared. Invitations were sent out to the 300 guests. I would be best maid, Edith a flower-girl, and John Emerson best man if he was available. I asked Violet if she would invite her sisters, but she said 'They did nothing for me, and I can do without them now. I am going to be a great Lady, Neil will need me at his side. I will learn how to entertain, give dinner parties and travel with Neil to meet Ambassadors in other countries. Pearson House will be my home, and old Luke says he will help me to take the place in society his wife and daughter enjoyed'.

Violet's eyes were shining, she had a new determination, and had acquired a great respect for her own beauty, knowing she could now grace any social gathering.

She had also been given her own suite of rooms, and left orders for them to be re-decorated while she was on honeymoon. They would be away for a whole month on a chartered yacht. Once she said to me 'Mary, I am sure 'tis all a dream, and I'll wake up in my sister's house.'

I had chosen blue satin, and Edith a rose pink muslin dress trimmed with ribbons and rosebuds. How beautiful Violet looked, in a modern figure-hugging sheath of heavy satin, her face and figure swathed in veils!

Crowds collected at the Chapel (Violet refused to be married in Church), newspapermen besieged the couple. Luke Pearson, in morning suit, belied his years, and proudly led Violet to the altar. Neil looked so handsome in his pale grey morning suit, and so proud of his lovely bride.

The reception was held in the grounds of Pearson House. There were as many Maoris as white people; Neil had insisted that as he was part Maori himself it was only right. The dancing and singing were in full swing when John Emerson took Edith and myself to hospital. Jean wanted to see her daughter as a flower-girl, and Edith was eager to show off. Arriving there, John left me while he took Edith to her mother. I guessed it would be a very special moment for the three of them.

The quiet of the wards was in sharp contrast to the joyous reception we had just left. I was filled with foreboding, 'Was this the last time Edith would see her mother?'

John came to me, 'Jean would like to see you, I'll wait here.' Approaching the bed, Edith ran to me, and clasped my hand. She twirled on her toes, showing her Mama her pretty dress and sensing that the other patients were admiring her. I could scarcely hear Jean's voice, 'Take my rings, Mary, for Edith. Give them to my mother, she will give them to her when she gets married. Promise me again, you will take her home.' I promised. She closed her eyes, but she was smiling. A nurse came forward and asked us to leave.

We returned to the reception just as the happy couple were leaving. Rose-petals and confetti were showered on us all, Edith squeaking with ecstasy as she was covered with confetti.

John disappeared back to his wife. I had her two rings in my tiny embroidered bag. Violet hugged me, 'I am so happy, Mary', then threw me her bouquet, 'You're next' she laughed. Neil had gripped my shoulders and for the first and last time kissed me full on the lips. He said nothing at all as I joined the others in the mad, glad farewell. Neil Grant's kiss had set my pulses racing; the wonder of its strength and sweetness was to confront me often. 'Had I been a fool to put Violet in my place? What kind of future would face me when I gave Edith over to her grand-parents?'

Jean Emerson died that night. John came home about mid-day. Luke Peason had sent Edith and I home about midnight, and we lay in very late. He gathered Edith in his arms, 'Mama has gone to heaven, we must pray for her.' Edith was too young to understand and wanted him to play with her. Up to that moment I had not wanted to face the change that Jean's death would bring, but my dismay was negligible in the face of John's great sorrow. I helped him to arrange a very quiet funeral. Only a few friends were invited, but when we reached the little cemetery, it was surrounded by natives of all ages, carrying flowers. Edith asked 'Why are they putting the big box into the big hole?' I looked at John, he looked at me then said, 'Some day I will tell you, Edith, put your posy on the grave.' She did so, her father caught her hands, and prayed that she would never forget her mother. Edith pulled away, to join some children she knew. 'How could I tell her her mother was in Heaven, then say she was in the coffin.'

Soon we were preparing to leave. John had received a letter informing him that his services were required in Africa, and a post was offered which he could take up in a few weeks. He had applied for a transfer when he had known there was no hope of his wife's recovery. He could not bear to stay on in the Mission House, it held too many memories.

We were booked for passage on the "Gisbourne" in two weeks time. I would not see Neil or Violet again, which depressed me. John was arranging our passage, informing Mr & Mrs Gillespie, his wife's parents, of our expected arrival. He had contacted the Captain, who promised to see that we would have a cabin shared by two elderly Christian ladies. After all, I was only seventeen and it was quite a responsibility for such a young girl.

One week after the wedding, Luke Pearson acquired the Jefferson houses and gas station; the money going into the fund for the new town. He personally supervised the destruction of house, garage and out-houses. By this time all the stock had been sold also to help pay for the new town. A gang of Italian labourers cleared every stone and fence, till the ground was once more as bare as the day Phillip Jefferson had bought it fifty years ago. All the carts, trucks and lorries which bore his name had the name painted out, then were auctioned. Even before I left, bull-dozers, builders and labourers had started work on the land.

In years to come, Neil Grant was to lead the Young Maori Party into Parliament. For his services to both Europeans and Maoris, he was knighted Sir Neil Grant. Violet, as Lady Grant, took a great interest in his career. She was to be a leader of fashion in present day society. Luke Pearson lived long enough to see this happen. It was due to his considerable influence and wealth that Neil owed this success.

Sometimes I thought of this strange country. To me it seemed so beautiful, rich, and prosperous, with a wonderful climate. Only man spoiled it. The Europeans had built great cities, wide roads and industrial buildings, but had robbed the Maoris of their heritage, and reduced them to second-class citizens. They drank, smoked, fought and stole from the wealthy, claiming all as theirs. The young ones showed signs of revolt, which erupted in war. Although heavily outnumbered and beaten, their plight became known to the world, and in 1947 the country acquired equal powers for both the Maori and European population. At one time no Maori had a vote, and Maori women and children were not included in the census, as though they did not exist! Some part-Maoris, like Neil, were well educated, most having one white (and wealthy) parent. Schools and colleges were only built in large cities.

Return Journey

Arriving at the wharf in Auckland Harbour on the day of our departure, I was surprised to seek Luke Pearson's carriage sitting outside the gates. He beckoned me over, handed me an envelope containing £20 and pecked my cheek. 'I trust you will have a safe journey, and I will welcome you should you wish to return.' I was quite overwhelmed and gave the old man a hug. John had also given me money for my expenses and my return fare. Come the moment of parting, John held Edith tightly to him. I lifted her down and we started to walk up the gangway. I could not say anything, but John said 'I'll pray for you both, take care of my Edith.' As we sailed out of the harbour we watched him waving a very large white handkerchief, but he had managed to smile for Edith, for which I was pleased. She was excited and happy, but I felt I had lost something, yet not knowing what.

The two elderly ladies assigned to my cabin were very old-fashioned. They objected to the light burning after Edith was asleep, and I had just to get into bed and try to sleep. What a difference to the outward journey! The Miss Ogilvys let me know that they were not in the habit of sharing their sleeping quarters with a servant, and I was to make myself as inconspicuous as possible. I got into the habit of rising early, and taking Edith with me, we washed and dressed in the wash-room for the first sitting at the breakfast table. When, much later, these two ladies appeared for breakfast, Edith and I returned to the cabin, where I tidied the bunks, sorted out the washing, and looked out fresh clothes for the next day. On the third day out the weather worsened and Edith was sea-sick, much to the annoyance of the Miss Ogilvys. When she had lain all day, I carried her to the nurse, and the ship's doctor sounded her chest. He was very nice, told me to keep her warm, give her plenty to drink, and he or the nurse would come to see us in the cabin. The old ladies insisted I keep the door open to keep the air fresh. I could not leave Edith, and was forced to ask one of them if they would stay with her till I washed and had a meal. She refused, saying I was responsible for the child. I would have to ask the nurse. When the doctor eventually came, I had had nothing to eat all day, only dashing out to use the toilet. He was very kind, saying he would ask nurse to give me a break and would do something about my situation. Just as he was leaving, the two spinsters arrived. They complained loudly of having to share such close quarters with a sick child and a servant. The Doctor was as good as his word, and next day the ladies were offered another cabin. I was thankful to see them go. These good Christian women!

As the doctor did not wish to leave me alone, a kind and motherly women offered to share. Mrs Sim was so cheery in comparison to the crotchety sisters that I cheered up immediately and Edith soon recovered. We took walks on the decks every day. Edith did not mix with the other chilren, but stayed close to me during the voyage. When I walked with her, a young sailor would join us. He made Edith laugh, and pleaded with me to join him in the evening. I refused, saying I would not leave the child alone in the cabin, as Mrs. Sim stayed in the saloon playing cards till very late. Once he knocked on my cabin door, but I did not open it. I was not in the mood to make new friendships. Nurse came in every evening to let me have a wash and attend to the laundry after Edith was in bed. One evening I returned after twenty minutes, to find the cabin empty. I ran to the nurse, she had been called out to attend another sick child, but Edith had been sound asleep when she left her. Now, I panicked, I raced round the ship, alerting everyone I met to tell the Captain a little girl was lost. The crew spread out to search the ship. A loudspeaker warned everyone to look for a small girl in a white nightdress.

With no sign of her forthcoming, I started screaming hysterically. If she had fallen overboard I was ready to jump into the sea. A sailor and a nurse gripped me as I ran, telling me that all the ship was being searched. After what seemed a very long time, the Doctor arrived, carrying Edith. She struggled down from his arms and came to me. I picked her up and ran to my cabin. Mrs Sim was waiting at the door pleased to see that Edith was safe. I could not speak. I laid the child in the bunk, and crawled into my own, shivering, shaking and very frightened. Nurse followed with something in a glass, and I slept soundly till morning. When I wakened I felt weak and shaky, but determined I would dress Edith as usual. I asked Mrs Sim where they had found Edith. It appeared the Miss Ogilvys had looked in the cabin and seeing no one in charge, they had lifted the sleeping child and taken her to their cabin, to teach me a lesson!

The nurse was very upset. She knew I would only be away for a short time, but certainly never expected anyone to take the child. She said if they were so worried, they could have stayed with Edith till I returned.

I hoped I would not hear any more about the incident, but the doctor and nurse arranged a meeting in the dining hall. I was to be there with Edith which made me very nervous, but Mrs Sim said I would be alright. As I entered I saw the two Miss Ogilvys standing at one side of the room. There were about a dozen others, but the Captain, first mate, doctor and nurse were among them. One of the crew told me to sit down, which I did, placing Edith on my knee.

The Captain said 'You are all aware of a disturbance on board this ship yesterday. We are here to hear the perpetrators of this disturbance make a public apology to this young lady. She required medical attention owing to the stress of the disappearance of her charge. No one can lay the blame on her, as she had arranged for a nurse to sit with the sleeping child. The nurse was called out to attend another patient and during the time she left the cabin and the reappearance of Miss Morton, someone abducted the child. I would ask that person or persons to stand forward please.'

The two women, both red-faced, stepped forward. The captain turned to me. 'Are these the two people who were allotted to chaperone you by Mr John Emerson?' I could only nod, 'Then perhaps we will hear why they abducted the sleeping child.'

The two women turned on me. 'It's all your fault. When we saw the child alone we took her to our cabin for safety.'

The Captain asked, 'Could you not have left a note to say where you had taken her?' 'No sir, we had no paper.' 'Do you realise that abducting a child is a serious offence?' The sisters stood silent, 'Very well. You will now apologise to both these girls for the distress you have caused them.'

The elder sister spoke for them both. 'We are sorry if we have caused you trouble. We only did it to safeguard the child. We certainly did not expect you to turn out the ship like that!'

I was still too shattered to accept the apology, such as it was. 'I don't want your empty apologies, I may be a servant, but I could not sink as low as you!' Picking up Edith I returned to my cabin. From then on, people were much kinder, offering to look after Edith, but I refused to be parted from her, unless the nurse took over. She was very angry and told me she had given the sisters a real "blast". I had paid little heed to the places we docked at, my whole being centred on watching Edith. I could only think of the relief I would feel when she was safely with her grandparents.

We arrived at Tilbury dock on a dark, cold morning. Edith had no really warm clothes. Living in a warm country she did not need them. So I tied my cardigan round her shoulders, and a scarf over her head. We scrambled down the gangway; the young sailor, who had fancied me, carrying our cases. As he laid them at my feet, he smiled. 'Hope to see you again. I will be waiting.' I could now afford to laugh. 'You never know.'

I was wearing a silk scarf which Jean Emerson had been given by her mother and one which she would recognise. Her parents would be wearing yellow tea-roses in their button-holes.

Searching the crowd, I saw two people waving. They did not have yellow tea-roses, but wore a few artificial primroses. There were many who wore coloured signs so that they could be recognised, so I looked away and scanned the others. A voice called 'Edith, it's Granny,' and the two who had waved came to us. I said 'You are not wearing yellow tea-roses.'

'Now, isn't that just like John. Where would we find yellow tea-roses in December? But we recognise the scarf.' She tried to pick up Edith, but the child clung to me. I said, 'Give her time, she will be strange at first.' They looked very well-to-do, both rather short and plump, but seemed very pleasant.

We hurried to board the train for London where we changed to a train going to Edinburgh. While Edith slept on my knee, they asked me questions about her parents. Taking Jean's rings from my purse, I handed them over to Mrs Gillespie. She wept when I told her that it was the last thing she had asked me to do for her. Both of them were comforting each other, fighting back tears. Jean had been their only child. John had married her in Edinburgh, and they had left almost immediately for New Zealand. Jean had only been 19 years old then and was only 25 years old when she died. They should have been due home on furlough last year, but Jean was too ill to attempt such a long journey!

Mr Gillespie asked me what I intended to do now, a question that worried me often. Mrs Gillespie said I could stay with them for a few days, until Edith had settled down. I was grateful for the offer, as it solved my immediate problem.

At 12 noon, a very smart dining-car attendant announced dinner would be served in a few minutes. We rose, and followed him into a long Pullman carriage. Here the tables were laid with snow-white table-cloths and napkins. Each piece of cutlery had the letters L.N.E.R. engraved on them. They were very heavy, I would have to get a small spoon for Edith. She sat by my side and I spread the table-napkin over her knees. I felt much happier now, the burden of responsibility had been lifted from my shoulders and I knew I would really enjoy this meal of Brown Windsor soup, roast beef, potatoes, vegetables and Yorkshire pudding. My first meal back in Britain! The next course was trifle. Edith had only picked at the meat course but she finished the small portion of trifle quickly and asked for more.

Mr. Gillespie asked the attendant if she could have a second helping. He smiled and brought her a very large plateful. She could not finish it, so I spooned the rest onto my plate and ate it with relish. We laughed when the attendant came to collect the plates. He said 'you are a very little girl to have such a big appetite. I could not have eaten all that.'

We finished the meal with tea and biscuits, then returned to our carriage. The grandparents lay down for an afternoon nap, much to Edith's amusement. She was restless, so I led her along the corridor, as the train thundered on, lifting her up to see the snow lying on the hills. She had never seen snow before. 'The clouds have all fallen down on the hills', she said.

It was getting dark. When we returned to the carriage, we found the Gillespies were still sleeping. The carriage was now well lit. I pulled down the blinds, and with Edith cradled in my arms we lay down.

I stretched out on the seat, thankful and happy. These were nice people. Edith woud be loved and cherished, she would fill the great gap in their lives caused by Jean's early death. A tiny voice in my head warned me that I would not want to part with her, but I tried to stifle the thought.

Arriving at Waverly Station, a porter carried our luggage to a waiting taxi-cab. It stopped at a large, imposing house in the Portobello district. It was beautifully situated facing the Firth of Forth. Well-tended gardens sloped to the water's edge. The rooms inside were spacious and expensively furnished. How could Jean Gillespie have left this lovely home to live in the bare and very basic Mission House?

A week later I left Edith with her grandparents. It had not been easy, I had grown to love the wee girl, and her dependence on me was such that I almost resented the efforts the grand-parents made to woo her affection. We would all walk along the sea-front, and when her attention was distracted I would disappear, to let Edith get used to my absence. I wandered round the shops, which were so different from the shabby wooden stalls and shops in the villages of New Zealand. Only the cities there had proper shops and their prices and goods did not suit two-thirds of the population. Mrs Gillespie insisted on bathing Edith, and after two or three sessions of tantrums and tears, I was allowed to put her to bed. One day I said to Edith 'I want to visit my Granny, too, just like you'.

'I want to see your Granny, too'

'There is no room for you in my Granny's house, I'll have to go by myself.' She did not say any more, but as I put her to bed, she said 'Do you want very much to go to your Granny?'

'Yes Edith, I do, will you let me go?'

'Yes, Mary, but come back quick.' I kissed her, 'Goodnight wee lass, be good to your Granny and Grandpa.' Next morning I was gone before she awoke. Mr Gillespie drove me to the station in Princes Street. He said 'We are grateful to you for looking after Edith so well.' I asked him to drop me a note if and when he received a letter from John, giving him my Granny's address in Motherwell. I had given Violet the same address, I did not wish to lose touch with my New Zealand friends.

On the journey memories came flooding back, reminding me of Father, then Beatrice. At Queen St. Station in Glasgow, I searched the faces around me, fearful that I should see either of them among the passengers. Arriving in Motherwell, I was pleased to see Granny quite well. Gertie had a beautiful little girl. It gladdened my heart to see her so happy with her young husband. She had no news of Gina, or Beatrice. Father's visits were few and far between, he did not speak of them.

I had to sleep behind Granny in the box bed, and missed my own room. Every day I searched the newspapers for vacancies for nurse-maids. While waiting for something suitable to turn up, I took a daily job as a companion help to an invalid lady in Douglas Street, quite near Granny's house, which was just as well as I had to start at 6.00 a.m. My new employer expected too much, and was often cross with me. The housework I could manage, but was expected to cook dishes I had never even heard of, like kedgeree, souflettes etc. She had four sons, who required clean shirts every day. She would throw them at me if they were not perfectly ironed.

It was a relief to shop for her, and in one of those food shops, the Maypole Dairy, I was attracted to a tall, fair young man. There were other male assistants and soon one of them started to chat me up. He was quite short, had spots and a round pink face. He asked me if I would go to the pictures with him that evening. I hesitated. He was nick-named Baby-face, and seemed very boyish, although he was probably older than myself. The tall young man that I liked now leaned over and spoke in a low voice. 'You don't want to go with him, why not come with me?' I was delighted but said 'You don't really mean it, do you?' He attended to a customer, and just as I was leaving the shop, he stepped over to the door, 'See you tonight at the Cross about 7 o'clock,' then disappeared inside.

I could scarcely get home quick enough to tell Gertie. This was my first real date and I hugged the fact to myself in joyful anticipation. Gertie told me not to get excited, 'maybe he was just having you on, he won't likely be there', a statement which certainly deflated me. However, I dressed carefully, and left the house early, so that I could watch the Cross from a distant door-way, feeling that if he did not come, no-one would see my disappointment. To my great relief he was there promptly at 7.00 p.m. He looked around, glanced at his watch then started to cross the road. I pretended to be hurrying and said 'Sorry I'm late.' His face brightened 'I thought you were not coming.' We both laughed when I said I thought exactly the same. That was the first of many outings and a few weeks later we decided to get married as I was keen to leave my unpleasant and demanding employer.

The young man's name was James Hardie. He lived alone with his elderly parents and he seemed to enjoy my company. We were married in April 1930, just two weeks before my eighteenth birthday.

I wore the blue satin dress that I had used at Violet's wedding. Little did she know that her parting words were to be realized so soon, when she threw her wedding posy to me and called, 'You're next, Mary.' What memories the dress brought back. What of little Edith? We lived with James' parents for a short time, but we wanted to have more time together. He worked very long hours in the shop. Saturdays especially were lost days. He had to leave home at 7.00 a.m. and did not return till 11.00 p.m., a sixteen hour day. The reason for this was that he and his staff had to take stock after the shop closed at 8.00 p.m. The stock-sheets were to be posted Saturday night to be in Head-Office first post Monday morning. Football interested him but he could not see the matches played on Saturdays.

We looked around for something more congenial, and he became an insurance agent in Larkhall. His company insisted we live in the agency. Try as we may, we could not get a rented house. We each had a little money, sufficient to place a deposit on a one-bedroom cottage with a large kitchen in Machan Road, right at the top of the hill. The house needed repainting outside and redecorating within. How lovingly I surveyed this, my very own house. I could have kissed every stone, every door, every window. To a homeless girl, dependant on domestic work, having a roof over her head was heaven.

We papered every wall, I sewed curtains, and searched shops for the cheapest and best furniture and carpets. James could now spend more time with me. He was pleased he could attend football matches held on Saturday afternoons. We were so happy, so much in love with each other, our wee house and large garden.

Soon a change took place within me. I had always eaten everything I was given, now I turned down some foods and craved for others. When I rose in the mornings I felt quite sick, not even enjoying my first cup of tea to start the day.

James' mother said I should see a doctor, but I put this off as long as I could, as I felt well during the day.

Eventually I did make an appointment, and the doctor astounded me by saying I was three months pregnant. I felt strange and confused, but James was calm, saying 'You will have to slow down, and take care of yourself.' He was very protective of me from then on, and would not let me ride pillion on his motor-cycle. I missed that very much, having to stay home while he went out with his pals. I felt cheated and frustrated, hoping the lump in my stomach would somehow go away. When we walked out together I thought everyone stared at my bulky figure. I visited Gertie and Granny. They would tell me what I wanted to know. They were pleased to see me and interested in my condition, but I wanted answers. What happened at birth? Was it very painful? What should I do to help myself and the baby? To all these questions they just smiled mysteriously, 'It's something you have to find out for yourself.'

I came home no wiser than when I started out, but did learn that Gina was now married and living in London, that father had bought a house in Edinburgh, and lived there with a lady friend. She was not much older than his daughters. They had visited Granny, only staying for a short time. Granny said 'She is a delicate-looking creature, I hope George looks after her.'

I still wanted to know more about having a baby and asked my mother-in-law where the baby would come from. She seemed quite embarrassed, but answered 'It will come out where it went in.' I blushed furiously, I had not really associated our tender love-making with the baby, except in a vague sort of way. Girls at school used to say if a boy kissed you in the dark, you would get a baby!

On my next visit to the doctor, when I was seven months pregnant, I was informed that a bed would be booked for me in Motherwell Maternity Hospital. I was given a list of things to have packed and ready to take when my time came.

Seven weeks later I wakened at about 4.00 a.m. Uncomfortable and restless I lay as long as I could, not wishing to get James up too early. Two hours later I had to rise quickly to be violently sick. My stomach was churning and heaving. James jumped out of bed. 'Is this it? I'll get a taxi.' He ran to the nearest phone box, and when he returned I was fully dressed, and shivering with apprehension, dreading the down-bearing pains that made me gasp, and stop whatever I was doing, even walking.

Arriving at the hospital James left me in the charge of an elderly tired-looking nurse who did not look too pleased to be interrupted in her work. Another nurse led me to a ward, where mothers were nursing very small babies. Stopping at an empty bed, she told me to undress and put on a coarse cotton gown, and put my things in the locker provided. The nurse then threw a bundle of sheets and pillowslips on the bed, and told me to make it up. All this time the back pains were getting stronger and more painful, and I sank to my knees with a deep groan. This went on for hours, I could not lie down, and was forced to walk between bathroom and ward, the nurses telling me not to make so much noise, it was disturbing the other patients. When I could no longer contain the cries of pain, I eventually sat in the cold bare bathroom. No one came near and I was very frightened. At last a young nurse entered the bathroom, and ran water into the bath, telling me to give myself a good scrub, using the red carbolic soap provided. A few minutes later she proceeded to shave me in a very private place. I felt so humiliated, I could not bear to watch. She washed me again and told me to get out of the bath. Her only comment was 'That was not so bad, was it?' She left me to dry myself, and put on the coarse nightgown. Now the pains grew stronger, one very severe pain sent me screaming to my knees, as much from fear as pain. I felt so utterly helpless and alone. My cries brought two nurses running. The older one said crossly 'Shut up, what is all the noise about?'

Doubled up with pain as I was, I could not speak. They each took one of my arms and propelled my unwilling body to a door marked "Labour Room." Here I had to climb onto a trestle-type bed, no sheet or pillow, just a square of waterproof over the canvas. This room was even colder than the bathroom, even more like a cell. Was it also the Mortuary? I was going to die in here! Women often died in childbirth, didn't they? Nurse said 'Hold on to the bar above your head, and push downwards.' The other nurse plunged something sharp between my open legs, and at once a torrent of water came rushing out of me. They were ready with bed-pans and towels. I said with great relief 'Is it all over?' 'Don't be stupid woman, that is only the water broken, you will really start having your child now' she replied coldly. I was more frightened than ever, and drew myself up to ease the pressure in my back. The pain came more often, forcing screams from me. The nurse said, 'You are only making it worse for yourself, push down and grip the bar.'

A searing spasm sent me yelling to the floor, someone smacked my face very hard, then I was lifted on to the trestle again. Strong hands began pushing at my stomach, hurting, hurting, while pain tore at my body. A voice said 'The head is showing, push harder.' I made a great effort, an explosion of pain seemed to tear my body apart, as the baby emerged.

They showed me the tiny body, streaked with blood and mucus. 'It's a boy, he weighs 8lbs 2oz.' Dazed with fright and the cessation of pain, I could not respond. Just as relief began to enfold me, the hands were probing and hurting, pushing at my stomach. I cried out 'Leave me alone, you have hurt me enough.' A voice said 'You know we must remove the afterbirth don't you?' I did not even know what after-birth was! Again the inside of my body seemed to be torn from me, although not quite as painfully. I was then washed with stinging disinfectant, padded and put into my own nightdress, laid on a stretcher and taken to the bed in the ward. I glanced at the ward clock, it was 6.30 p.m. Twelve hours of unbelievable indignities and excruciating pain. I lay back on my pillows, exhausted and sore, feeling the lower part of my body had been beaten mercilessly for hours. Within minutes a nurse brought me a cup of strong sweet tea which I drank gratefully, although my hands were shaking so much the nurse had to hold the cup to my lips. No sooner had I finished drinking than another nurse came to me, carrying a howling infant, now washed and dressed. She laid it on the bed, then, opening the buttons of my nightdress, proceeeded to wash the nipples of my breasts. She then lifted the child and guided the open mouth to the nipple. The tiny mouth clamped like a vice. A long shuddering gasp of pain broke from me, how much more pain could I take? The nurse said 'He is sucking well, put him to the other breast in ten minutes.'

'No, no,' I cried 'I can't, put it on a bottle.'

'Nonsense, you won't feel anything after a few feeds.' She clamped the child on to me again. I wanted to hit her. The pain made me feel sick and my head was aching. When she took the child away, I covered my face with the sheet, refusing to speak to anyone, hating everything connected with the baby.

A gentle hand touched my forehead. How cool it felt on my aching head! I looked up, a lady doctor was smiling at me, the only comforting smile I had seen all day. She tested my blood pressure, took my pulse, and said I would be put into a side room as my blood pressure was up and I needed to sleep quietly. She gave me something in a small glass and told me I would feel much better tomorrow. My head ached, my thoughts were in turmoil. I would demand answers! Why was I not warned about what would happen? Why was I kept in such ignorance? Why did no-one want to talk about having a baby? There and then I made up my mind, I would never have another child. How could a wonderful love like ours bring such pain and suffering? I drifted into sleep, remembering Violet's words. 'I don't want children.' How I wished I could be with her at this moment!

Next morning I was wakened by a nurse who handed me a cup of tea. She was young and cheerful, which made me feel better right away. Her next words dispelled that feeling. 'That son of yours has cried all night, he must be hungry.' I shouted 'No, I don't want to feed him, put him on the bottle.' The nurse stared at me 'I can't do that, orders are you have to feed him yourself.'

She brought the red-faced squealing child to me, and once again tried to put him to my breast. I pushed the child back into her arms 'I can't, I won't, it is too sore' and burst into tears. Someone sent for the doctor, who gently rubbed a little oil on the raw red nipples. She spoke for a few minutes telling me that feeding the child myself would be of great benefit to us both, that the baby would be immune from germs for as long as I fed him. She also talked about a name for him. I suddenly realised this was my baby, and I was to be responsible for him. After a short period, the doctor watched as I once again tried to feed that hungry mouth. To my amazement and relief the pain was much less severe and I relaxed. I had been so tensed up. Now the doctor's soothing words brought peace to my mind. When she left, I studied the little face, and opened the tiny clenched fist. His fingers gripped mine and a surge of pure joy rose in my heart. This wonderful little being was part of me, my very own! I would never have to part with him, as I had had to part with the children of my employers. He lay rosy and replete in my arms. He opened his eyes, they were very blue, and a fuzz of dark downy hair covered his head. How wonderful he was!

James came to visit that evening. He looked at the sleeping child lying in the cot beside my bed. 'So that is what all the fuss was about, what an ugly wee twister.' he said, but his eyes were merry and the gentle squeeze of his hand on mine filled me with happiness.

Talking to the other mothers I found it strange that none mentioned the birth of their babies, though most of them looked ill and tired. Not wishing to appear as ignorant as I felt I did not speak of my experience either.

A woman of about thirty lay in the bed next to mine. (I only spent one night in the side-room) She had just had her third child, and was pleased that it was a boy, as her first two children were girls. She told me if this baby had been another girl her husband would have been angry and disappointed. It made me think of my own father. Why did men always seem to want a son? I put this question to James on his next visit. He answered 'A boy will carry on the family name. My father is very pleased, and wants the baby to be named Andrew, after him.'

Eight days later I came out of hospital vowing in my heart I would never return! There would be no more children!

When Andrew was six weeks old, I decided to visit Granny and Gertie, to show them my lovely new baby. They were so pleased to see us, and Gertie's little daughter was quite enchanting, golden curls framing her happy little face. Granny was in bed, she only rose for an hour or two each day. I put my baby in her arms, she stroked his head and said 'God bless him.' Gertie made tea, and we chatted non-stop. We had so much to catch up on, of our new husbands, babies and a home of our own at last. Gertie and Willie (her husband) had bought new curtains and linoleum, Willie had papered over the varnished walls and Granny's house looked so fresh and much lighter. Will was employed in Dalziel Steel Works. He would not be home until 4.00 p.m., so we looked forward to a very pleasant afternoon. We gave Granny her lunch, and were sitting at the table when we heard heavy footsteps in the lobby. The kitchen door opened, Beatrice stood in the doorway. I stiffened with fear. Gertie lifted her wee girl onto her knee, as though to protect her, her face as white as the table-cloth. I had not seen Beatrice for five years, she looked so much older, and heavier, but well made up and well-dressed. Neither of us spoke, just stared at this woman we had hoped was out of our lives for ever. Beatrice looked at Granny. She was asleep. Beatrice pulled the curtain across, then sat down at the table. Taking off her gloves, she said quite pleasantly, 'Have you had your dinner? I could do with a cup of tea.' Gertie replied 'We do not have dinner till Willie gets home from work. He will be here soon.' Beatrice's mouth curled, 'I see you've both got kids, didn't take you long. How many men did you have till you got pregnant? Just like your rotten father running around with anyone you can get.' Beatrice was working herself up, Gertie sensed it too, 'If you only came here to insult us why don't you go? Father would be angry if he knew you were here, he told us he had stopped you from visiting his mother.'

Beatrice laughed, 'I'll go when it suits me, I'll just have another cup of tea,' and proceeded to butter a scone. She turned to me, 'Well, did you find your mother? I thought the two of you would be living with her, seems to me she had no use for any of you.' I was getting angry, 'Yes, I found my mother. She is married and does not beat her children.'

'So she has children? Your father's too mean to get married, not that he will get the chance, I will never agree to a divorce. I'll make him and his brats suffer, like this.' She stood up, smiling queerly, and poured the contents of the milk-jug over the little girl who had been staring up at her. The child screamed as the milk ran down her face, and she ran to her mother. I took the baby from my breast, laid him in the cot, so that I could be free to protect him. He howled, still hungry, the sound of both children crying made Beatrice angry. 'Shut them up, can't stand squalling brats.'

I shouted 'You don't need to hear them, just go away please.' Beatrice moved over to the cot, picking up a cushion on the way. I too moved over to the cot, not sure what she would do next. She lifted the cushion, and with both hands put it on Andrew's face. I screamed at her, and tugged at the cushion, trying to get it from her fat, heavy hand. For one fraction of a second I remembered Violet's hat-pin. Beatrice's hat was close to my face, with one hand I pulled out a long hat-pin and jabbed Beatrice's arm. She let go, and dropped the cushion at my feet, the baby yelling, very red in the face. Now we stood over the cot, eye to eye, the hat-pin inches from her face. She arched back, then turned, looking for a weapon. With a sick feeling I realized the hat-pin was no defence if she attacked me. Gertie's voice spoke at my shoulder. I dare not take my eye off Beatrice, but the sight of the long, razor-sharp bread-knife directed at Beatrice's heart made my heart leap.

Gertie said, 'GET OUT NOW, or I will kill you myself.' Beatrice's eyes widened, her mouth fell open. She turned and ran, we followed her, shoulder to shoulder, the point of the knife almost touching her back. We pushed her outside then heaved the heavy outer door shut, and turned the key.

'Quick Gertie, the back-door, I will get her bag.' Beatrice was banging on the door, shouting through the letter-box that she wanted her bag, and calling us every foul name she knew. I opened the front window only a few inches and pushed her bag through with her gloves. She used both hands to push up the window then spat at me in the face. I threw the hat pin out to fall on the pavement. When she bent down to retrieve it, I slammed down the window, snibbed it, and Gertie closed the heavy curtains to shut out the sight of that hideous face. We ran to the kitchen, both babies were crying loudly. I thought, 'Thank god, what if Beatrice has suffocated him? He would not now be crying.'

We were now laughing and crying hysterically and saying 'We've won, for the first time, and she hasn't left a mark on us.' For a few minutes we held on to each other, then picked up our crying children.

We decided not to tell our husbands. Willie had warned Gertie to keep the door locked when he was out. He would be angry and say it was her own fault.

I would not tell James either that my step-mother had tried and nearly succeeded in killing our baby, nor could I face the censure of James' parents, or their anger at my visitng Gertie without James.

An hour after Beatrice's departure I crept out, scanning the road but there was no sign of Beatrice. Telling Gertie to lock up behind me, I hurried to Motherwell Cross, where I boarded a tram to Hamilton, searching the faces of the passengers. From there I changed to get on a bus to Larkhall. Once on the bus I relaxed, knowing Beatrice would not be following me. Sinking into a seat, Andrew's weight numbed my arm, and I felt mounting nausea. Putting the baby into a woman's arms, I pulled a nappy out of my bag and vomited violently. I tried to control the retching, and took Andrew from the woman. 'Will you be alright?' she said and I nodded.

Arriving at my bus stop I got out to find my legs were like rubber, the pavement swayed and the street lights swirled. An elderly couple each took one of my elbows and crossed the road with me, helped me to open the door, then went away. I closed the door and managed to reach the baby's pram, where I laid my sleeping infant. Looking at his flushed face, the whole enormity of Beatrice's action overwhelmed me. What if he had now been still, white and dead? Again I retched, and was still retching when James came in. 'Good God, woman, you look like death.'

He glanced at the baby and said, 'He's alright anyway what has happened?'

I could scarcely speak but murmured 'I was sick on the bus.' I managed to feed and bathe Andrew then went to bed utterly shattered. During the night I had a nightmare, Beatrice was suffocating me and gouging out my eye with a hat-pin. James could not understand why I was so upset. He called the Doctor, who said I was overwrought. He could not give me medicine as it would affect the baby's milk. I was quite ill for a few days. James' parents came over, both chiding me for travelling so soon after the baby's birth.

I wrote to Gertie saying that I had been sick on the bus. She wrote by return that she could not keep food down even yet; and had asked a friend to stay with her when Willie was at work.

I had thought that my last battle with Beatrice had finished her visits, but she seemed determined to molest us. I hoped Gertie would tell Father to keep her away. When she did see him, he said we were old enough to defend ourelves. Beatrice was a coward who would run if we stood up to her.

Gertie immediately applied for a new Council house. She wanted to get away from the area, to where Beatrice would not find her. We discussed the events of Beatrice's last visit. I said 'Would you really have killed her?' She replied 'Would you have stuck the hat-pin in her eye?' We both agreed we would have attacked her, had she not turned and run or if she had hurt our babies.

About a year later Gertie's husband met Beatrice coming to their house as he walked to work. He stood in front of her and demanded to know where she was going. 'To visit my step-daughter.' she announced, 'Get out of my way.'

Willie answered 'Turn round and walk back to the station, or I will run you in to the police.' She went quietly enough. Willie told Gertie that she would not come back again, after what he had said to her. Alas, that prediction was to be proved wrong.

How Gertie's nerves stood up to the constant threat of Beatrice's visits I could only guess. Her hair turned prematurely white, and she was always thin and nervous. I was lucky in that Beatrice never found out where I lived.

The following year James changed his solo moto-cycle for a big B.S.A. motor-cycle with a very smart launch side-car. He could now take Andrew and myself out, and we were protected from the weather. How we enjoyed these runs, and picnics on the moors! The scenery, the tiny lambs, the rolling hills and moors of Lanarkshire. The streams where we paddled, and watched the little fish dart about in the clear water.

Time passed quickly, Andrew grew tall and fair. His grandparents adored him, buying him toys and sweets at every opportunity. I had been taught that sweets were bad for children's teeth, also that they should not eat between meals. I adhered rigidly to the routine I had been taught by Mrs Herbert, and would put Andrew to bed at exactly 7.00 p.m. every night. Mr & Mrs Hardie objected to this, saying I was too strict, but I felt it was best for my child. I would see children running about, while their mothers gossiped at the doors till 10.00 p.m. or even later on a summer evening. This seemd very slack and careless to me.

A year after Andrew was born, my Father's wife gave birth to a son. He was also named George after my father and was rather delicate, having a chest condition. Father was completely obsessed with him. We visited him in Edinburgh, I wanted to see his son, and to show him mine. Comparing him with my strong and sturdy boy I thought I had the most beautiful child in the world.

Grannie Hardie thought so too. She had entered him in a Bonny Baby Contest at the Church Fete. To our joy he won second prize, a little blue knitted jacket. Once home, Granny took baby and jacket in the pram to visit all our neighbours and friends, even the local shop-keepers. Full of pride as I was, I was quite taken aback when one lady said 'There is only one lovely child in the world, and every mother has it!'

About three years later Father's young wife died in child-birth, the baby dying with her. At the funeral Father seemed more annoyed than sad. As we stood by the coffin he said 'She's not much use to me now, I'll have to get someone to look after George.'

Andrew was now five years old and ready for school. He was a happy little lad, and loved nothing better than to help his Dad work on the motor-cycle, an interest that stayed with him all his life. When he did go to school, I would walk there every day to hand him a 'play-piece' (a Scottish tradition to give children a snack at the interval when they played outside in the playground) through the iron bars of the school-gates.

A year later he contracted Scarlet Fever and was taken to Roadmeetings Infectious Diseases Hospital, near Carluke. Never having been parted from him since birth, I cried a great deal. We visited hospital every Saturday, but we could not speak to the children, only seeing them through a glass panel. He recovered quite well from the fever, but after a few weeks he looked quite neglected. His hair was long and untidy, the old clothes he wore did not fit, but were ragged and washed out. He was very pale, and would just gaze at me through the window. That was a very severe winter. Snow was piled high at each side of the country road where the small bus lurched along. When the road became blocked, the passengers had to get out and walk nearly a mile in deep snow to reach the hospital. My feet were always wet and cold, and although I wore strong leather shoes, it was no surprise when I took a severe chill and had to stay in bed. I missed my visit to the hospital and felt quite guilty, although James went on Sunday.

About this time James exchanged the motor-cycle outfit for a small car, a Ford Austin Seven. I was sorry to see the motor-cycle go to its new owner. What wonderful holidays we had had. Trips to Scarborough, where James bought me a pretty necklace. At Stratford-on-Avon we lodged in a guesthouse where the bathroom was tiled sea-blue and the bath itself was sunk into the floor. Here we visited Ann Hathaway's cottage with its thatched roof. There were many houses with these roofs and all looked very pretty. We also visited Devon and Cornwall. On a very steep hill at Lymington James said, 'Hope that connection is all right, the one for the sidecar.' I had visions of hurtling down the hill we had just climbed, a gradient of 1 in 5, James told me later.

The car was very handy at this time. James' father was very ill, and spending a lot of time in hospital. Granny Hardie came to live with us, refusing to live alone. She slept with Andrew in the kitchen bed when he left hospital after nine weeks. He was now seven years old.

By November I knew I was pregnant again. The nightmare of Andrew's birth had faded from my mind, and I felt happier and confident, having read all the books on the subject I could find. I also attended a clinic regularly and had plenty of good advice from them.

When I was four months pregnant my father-in-law died. It happened on the 10th December 1937. That was a bad winter. Heavy snow and blizzards made the funeral journey to Kirkcaldy extremely hazardous. At one time the drivers thought they would be bogged down in wet snow. All the Hardie family had been buried in Kirkcaldy Cemetary and there was a vacant layer in the burial ground. Granny Hardie was determined her husband would be buried with his own folks, and did not flinch from the journey. The minister of Clason Church in Motherwell went with them. I stayed at home with Andrew. We were poor travellers in cars, and my being pregnant did not help.

In April, Gertie sent a note to say she was in the Maternity Hospital and had had another son, her third child. James took me in the car to see her, but he stayed outside. I laughed to myself as I entered the hospital, remembering the vow I had made all those years ago never to have another baby.

Gertie looked tired and thin. When she saw how stout I was she said, 'I'm keeping the bed warm for you.' Her words were prophetic. Ten days later she left hospital, and I entered to be given the bed she had just vacated. The nurses were quite amused. This birth did not frighten me, I knew what to expect and did all the right things to make the birth quicker and easier.

The actual moment of giving birth was the worst, as the baby weighed over 10lbs! The first glimpse I had of him, he looked so like James, with fair hair and blue eyes. When James visited me he looked quite disappointed. 'Another boy, I would have liked a wee lassie.' As he had no sisters I wondered if that was the reason. We named our new son James, but shortened it to Jim.

Right from the start he was different from Andrew. I could scarcely leave him for a few minutes, he was so restless and adventurous. Granny Hardie said 'He is a masterful little rascal!' He was also a beautiful child, with his crop of golden curls, pink and white skin and long lashes that curled over his cheeks when he was sleeping. A neighbour, looking down at him as he slept in his pram said, 'You will never rear him, he is too bonny for this world'. I laughed at this remark, but the thought lingered.

June, 1939, we went on holiday to Aberdeen. The landlady was the widow of a fisherman. Granny Hardie and she had much to talk about, both coming from fishing families. Granny hoped she would get some nice fish here. Imagine our surprise when at breakfast next morning, two dozen juicy kippers were placed on the table. We did our best to demolish the pile, but the children did not like the bones. At 'high tea' that evening a huge plateful of some thirty sweet herrings, fried in oatmeal were placed before us, accompanied by new potatoes and green peas, smothered in fresh butter. Granny was delighted, but again the children would not eat them because of the many small bones. On Sunday we had a whole salmon set in aspic jelly, and decorated with parsley. The boys were fascinated by its wide-open mouth, rows of sharp teeth and staring eyes. It seemed a pity to cut it up, but even the boys enjoyed it after I removed the bones. It was really delicious.

After a week of fish at nearly every meal, I asked the good lady for some meat courses. Always obliging, the dear soul served mince for the children, and beautifully cooked joints of meat for the adults. We left so much food on the table, I felt quite guilty, and asked what happened to the left-overs. Apparently her son had a pig farm, and nothing was wasted.

Andrew, like myself, could not travel in the car without being sick. It always took us two or three days to recover. How we missed the motor-cycle, where the fresh air kept travel sickness at bay.

In September of that year war was declared. James was called up to join the R.A.F. in December. At first he was sent to Blackpool, where with others, he was vaccinated for small-pox and tropical diseases. His arm was painful and swollen to twice its normal size. He lay in a tiny attic at the top of the hotel, which had been taken over by the Government to accomodate the troops. He and others stayed in bed for a few days, dependant on other airmen to bring them food and drink. It was the most miserable Christmas he would ever have!

From there he was sent into the country. He came home on every leave bringing food we could not buy on our ration books. Mostly farm produce, such as apples, vegetables, cheese and especially eggs. How eagerly we watched him unpack his kit-bag. Sometimes he had as many as two dozen eggs. We were overjoyed when we found that none were broken. Now we would have fresh eggs instead of powdered dried eggs.

To people who could afford them, new clothes were a problem, if they did not have enough clothing coupons. I made all my family's clothing so I was able to exchange my coupons for meat rations. As the war stretched into years, nourishing food became very scarce.

The Government decreed we should all "Make do and mend." Soon I was fully occupied making boys short trousers out of suits their fathers had left behind. Coats were made into skirts or jackets, curtains into dresses, bed-mats into dressing-gowns or chair-covers. One amusing request came from the Church Guild. Mens' drawers and vests were cut up to make frilly knickers, which would be sold like hot cakes at the Church stall.

One Sunday morning we sat down to breakfast, looking forward to our ration of one boiled egg each weekly. I carefully removed the tops, and we were about to eat them when part of our ceiling collapsed, showering the table with dust and plaster. That was one of the few occasions when I wept. The damage to the ceiling meant little at that moment, but the loss of our precious eggs seemed a tragedy at the time!

James thought we needed a holiday, and he arranged lodgings for us in a house near the airfield where he was stationed. I was to take a train from Glasgow to Crewe with the two boys, and he could meet us there. Little Jim wore a kilt in Royal Stuart tartan, with a badger-hair sporran. The train from Glasgow was filled with soldiers, airmen and sailors. They were quite attracted to Jim whose blond curls led one man to ask if he was a boy or girl. Although he was only 3 years old he stood red-faced and angry in front of the speaker 'AHM NO A LASSIE.' They filled his sporran with florins and half-crowns which mollified him.

At Swindon we stayed with Flossie Williams, whose husband Ernie, was a soldier, and quite the biggest man I have ever met. They were market-gardeners in peace-time, and Flossie still worked in the garden. She made the most wonderful salads and cooked on a wood-fired stove.

We stayed there for six happy weeks, James coming from the air-field at week-ends and time-off. It was 1941, many children were being evacuated to the area to escape the Blitz in London. We were sorry to come home. The name of the village was Wambourne, little Jim said "Warm Bum."

Once I asked the local butcher if he would sell me a marrow bone to make soup with. He produced a two foot long bone, and seemed quite puzzled when I said I only needed a piece about 5" long.

The pot of Scotch Broth was much appreciated by Mrs Williams' family, as much of its goodness came from the variety of fresh vegetables which she grew.

In 1942 the blitz on Clydeside escalated. The huge steel-works, shipyards and docks were the targets of the German Luftwaffe only a few miles away from our home in Larkhall. Almost every night the wailing sirens alerted us to seek safety in the shelters provided. We would listen to the heavy beat of the German bombers as they passed overhead. Our search-lights probed the night sky as the noise of gunfire mingled with the sickening crump of falling bombs. Only when the all-clear sounded could we breathe naturally – we were safe for another night! Our hearts were sad, knowing that only a few miles away firemen were fighting amid flames and falling buildings. Ambulances were rushing people to hospital, the dead, dying, injured and homeless all being taken care of by brave volunteers. On these nights we did not undress but lay down, with gas-masks and shoes at the ready to grab as we ran down to the shelters. I also had a 'tuck bag' which held a large flask and a box of jam 'pieces' (bread and jam.)

In June of that year I gave birth to my third child, a little girl. I named her May, after myself. James was allowed ten days compassionate leave to be with me. We were so thrilled with our beautiful little daughter, but I was angry when he left us. How I hated this war, why could it not end and let us all be together? James would not see the children growing up. I was forced to hide my feelings and get on with bringing them up myself.

American soldiers were now billeted in our local school halls, some of them waiting to be admitted to hospital in Stonehouse, just two miles away. They were suffering from chest complaints, but mostly T.B. (tuberculosis). Most of these soldiers were coloured, wore a very smart uniform and had more money than our own service men. Local girls and lonely wives were attracted to them. As time went on, a few girls married, but often the girls became pregnant, only to find out the men were married already. Rumours and jokes abounded about this state of affairs. One friend I knew personally had a coloured baby. She was married, but her husband had been abroad for two years. Having contracted malaria he was shipped home for treatment, arriving unexpectedly at his home. Hurriedly she put the child in a drawer, and pushed it underneath the bed. The husband heard the baby crying, pulled out the drawer and exclaimed, 'Jesus Christ! I thought I had left you in India.' His wife overheard him and they quarrelled bitterly. After a while they realised that the long separation was to blame, and they made it up. The sad part, to my mind, was that the husband would have none of it and the child was put into a home. The story brought back memories of the Sky-eye babies in New Zealand. The missions were full of abandoned babies. We were no better than these uneducated people, or the selfish white settlers.

Thinking of New Zealand, I wrote to Violet, but she did not reply immediately. A few years later, she sent me a package containing press cuttings and newspaper photographs of herself and Neil opening various buildings, hospitals, schools, etc. Neil had been knighted for his work with the Young Maori Party and was now a powerful figure in Politics. Luke Pearson had lived long enough to see his great-grandson being made Sir Neil Grant. When he died, Neil sold everything and moved to a mansion in Christchurch, now the seat of government. The cuttings described Violet as the beautiful Lady Violet Grant, she looked as slim and lovely as on her wedding day. Neil never celebrated his birthday (too great a tragedy had happened that day) but they had a wonderful celebration on each anniversary of their wedding, the cake having a candle for each year that passed. Dr Rewi (Neil's natural father) had died during a flu epidemic after working himself to exhaustion. He left all his money to fund a training college for all Maori students, regardless of their parentage. Named the Princess College, it was a memorial to his mother, the Princess Laella. Violet did not mention her sisters or family, so I presumed she had lost touch with them. Her postscript was pure Irish: 'Still need to use the hat pin, Mary, noble skins be no thicker than a travelling tink's.'

I was pleased to know that all was well, the ghosts of the past would now be laid to rest. Also it was comforting to think that Neil Grant's name was an honoured one in the country that had been so unkind to him and his brother.

When May was almost three-years-old, in 1945, James came home on embarkation leave, which meant he was sailing for an unknown destination. We had three weeks together, and he took us all to Fife for a holiday. The thought of this more permanent posting lay heavy on my spirits. Would he come back? I asked myself this question many times. Outwardly I appeared as cheerful as I could. Life had to go on, the family had to be looked after. James provided extra money from his pay as a Sergeant, and we had no money troubles, but the empty days, weeks and months seemed to drag wearily, the highlights being the letters we wrote constantly to each other.

On V.E. day the war in Europe ended with the German surrender. Many men returned home, with tales of unbelievable atrocities, suffering and deprivation. I was almost frantic with worry. To take my mind off the war, I tried to trace my sister Gina. Writing to Somerset House, I received news that she had married and was given an address in Portsmouth. I wrote to her immediately, but her response was disappointing. She said in her letter that she was not interested in me or my family, and I was not to write to her again. I sent a card at Christmas, but it was returned to me unopened. I had had the foresight to write my name and address on the outside of the envelope. A few years later we had a visit from two welfare officers, who had discovered my first letter to her. Gina was having treatment for "persecution mania". She imagined that everyone was her enemy, refused to open doors, to go outside. Her husband was a quiet man who cared for her, but her condition was deteriorating. They asked me many questions, and they thought her illness could be the result of her unhappy childhood. All this upset me very much and I offered to take her, even for a holiday, but they said she would disrupt my family, she hated children and might even attack them. They promised she would be looked after. I was not to hear of her for many years.

Gertie now had three children, two boys and a girl. Her husband was exempt from active Service, as he was employed in the steelworks. Gertie and I seemed to drift apart, too busy with young families. Granny died peacefully about this time, but I did not hear of her death till later, but her memory will always be with me, the one sure refuge in our troubled lives.

The Home-Coming

Although peace was declared in August, it was November before I received a letter from James. He had spent the last nine months in Bombay, and was about to be sent in to man air-fields in the jungle, which were swarming with enemy Japanese soldiers. However, the atomic bombs put a stop to that, and he was now waiting for a ship to take him home. We were overjoyed, he was well and coming home for good. Up to then I had not kept the house as it should be, taking the children out as much as possible to ease the fear in my mind.

We all set-to cleaning and polishing till the house shone. I found time to make myself a new dress, and bought our golden-haired daughter a lovely warm green pantaloon suit. The boys had hair cuts, and Granny, (James' mother) would wear her best dress. On the morning of the 15th December the longed-for telegram arrived 'Arriving 5.30 a.m. Motherwell station on 16th December.' There was little sleep that night. By 4.00 a.m. we were up and dressed, ready for the taxi which I had ordered for 5.00 a.m. Arriving at Motherwell Station we found a great mass of people on the platform, waiting for the troop train to arrive. We stood in a doorway, back from the excited crowd, our own excitement mounting. Suddenly a shout went up, 'The train is coming!' Everyone surged forward, trying to be the first to greet their menfolk, but we stayed in the doorway. I knew I would see his tall figure above the heads of the crowd. I had not realized that the service men had all been kitted out with civilian suits, trilby hat, raincoats and shoes. They all looked the same as they tumbled out of the carriages. Suddenly, there he was, his tall figure pushing through the crowd towards us. His mother greeted him first, wiping the tears from her eyes, then the boys. He lifted May up, put his hand on my shoulder, and propelled us towards the waiting taxi. The feel of his strong firm hand on my shoulder made me realize he was actually here, safe and sound. How we chattered in the taxi, I don't remember what about, but my hand was in his, and that was enough.

Arriving home, we gathered round as he emptied his kit-bag. A silk shawl for his mother, toys and sweets for the children. Brass ornaments, a silk kimono, perfume and chocolates for me, but the most wonderful and precious present of all that he had brought was himself.

It was late when the last of our visitors departed. All that day friends, neighbours and colleagues had dropped in to welcome James home. The children and Granny were asleep. It had been a long and exciting day for them.

At last we were alone, sitting together before the dying embers of the fire. James poked at the coals, and the cinders sent a shower of sparks up the chimney. As I gazed into the cinders, I thought with compassion of my father's home-coming. So different from this one, and now I realized how bitter the blow must have been. Now he had the son he had always longed for, which was a comforting thought. I had attended church regularly since the christening of my first child, then took the children to Sunday School as they grew older. It was very difficult for me to believe in a just God, even now, with so many broken homes, so much pain and suffering and my own unhappy childhood. At this moment I envied no one, Violet's wealth and position could never have brought me the wonderful happiness I was experiencing at this moment. My heart was full of gratitude as I turned to my husband. He would never know the depth of meaning when I murmured: 'Thank-you God.'